YEATS AND EUROPEAN DRAMA

Michael McAteer examines the plays of W. B. Yeats, considering their place in European theatre during the late nineteenth and early twentieth century. This original study considers the relationship Yeats's work bore with those of the foremost dramatists of the period, drawing comparisons with Henrik Ibsen, Maurice Maeterlinck, August Strindberg, Luigi Pirandello and Ernst Toller. It also shows how his plays addressed developments in theatre at the time, with regard to the Naturalist, Symbolist, Surrealist and Expressionist movements, and how Symbolism identified Yeats's ideas concerning labour, commerce and social alienation. This book is invaluable to graduates and academics studying Yeats but also provides a fascinating account for those in Irish studies and the wider field of drama.

MICHAEL MCATEER is a lecturer at the school of English, Queen's University Belfast.

YEATS AND EUROPEAN DRAMA

MICHAEL MCATEER

CAMBRIDGE
UNIVERSITY PRESS

CAMBRIDGE
UNIVERSITY PRESS

University Printing House, Cambridge CB2 8BS, United Kingdom

One Liberty Plaza, 20th Floor, New York, NY 10006, USA

477 Williamstown Road, Port Melbourne, VIC 3207, Australia

314-321, 3rd Floor, Plot 3, Splendor Forum, Jasola District Centre, New Delhi - 110025, India

79 Anson Road, #06-04/06, Singapore 079906

Cambridge University Press is part of the University of Cambridge.

It furthers the University's mission by disseminating knowledge in the pursuit of education, learning and research at the highest international levels of excellence.

www.cambridge.org
Information on this title: www.cambridge.org/9781108798488

© Michael McAteer 2010

This publication is in copyright. Subject to statutory exception and to the provisions of relevant collective licensing agreements, no reproduction of any part may take place without the written permission of Cambridge University Press.

First published 2010
First paperback edition 2020

A catalogue record for this publication is available from the British Library

ISBN 978-0-521-76911-2 Hardback
ISBN 978-1-108-79848-8 Paperback

Cambridge University Press has no responsibility for the persistence or accuracy of URLs for external or third-party internet websites referred to in this publication, and does not guarantee that any content on such websites is, or will remain, accurate or appropriate.

For My Mother
In Loving Memory

Contents

List of illustrations	*page* ix
Acknowledgements	x
List of abbreviations	xii
Introduction	1

PART I   EARLY PLAYS

1   Revolutionary revelation: *The Land of Heart's Desire, The Countess Cathleen, Cathleen ni Houlihan* — 13

2   Space, power, protest: *The King's Threshold* and *Deirdre* — 41

PART 2   THE CUCHULAIN CYCLE

3   'I'll not be bound': *On Baile's Strand* and *The Green Helmet* — 65

4   The turn to Noh: *At the Hawk's Well* and *The Only Jealousy of Emer* — 87

5   'When everything sublunary must change': *The Death of Cuchulain* — 110

PART 3   LATER PLAYS

6   'The heart of a phantom is beating': *The Dreaming of the Bones* and *Calvary* — 131

7 'O self-born mockers': *The Player Queen, The Words upon the Window-pane, The Herne's Egg* 152

8 History inside out: *Purgatory* 176

Conclusion 193

Bibliography 200
Index 219

List of illustrations

Figure 1 Sketch for lighting plan for the steps in *The King's Threshold*. W. B. Yeats Collection, Stony Brook.   *page* 55

Figure 2 Edward Gordon Craig, 'The Steps' (1905), *Towards a New Theatre: Forty Designs for Stage Scenes with Critical Notes* (London: J. M. Dent & Sons, 1913).   56

Figure 3 Edward Gordon Craig, 'The Masque of London', *Towards a New Theatre: Forty Designs for Stage Scenes with Critical Notes* (London: J. M. Dent & Sons, 1913).   154

Acknowledgements

This study was carried out with the support of the Arts and Humanities Research Council, which funded a semester leave to carry out research on this project under their Research Leave scheme in autumn 2006. I am also grateful to the British Academy for funding a research visit to the United States in March 2006. Queen's University Belfast was supportive in funding my visit to the W. B. Yeats Collection at Stony Brook and granted me a semester leave to work on the project.

My thanks to A. P. Watt on behalf of Gráinne Yeats for permission to cite extracts from *Pages Written in a Diary of Nineteen Hundred and Thirty* and from the Cornell Series Manuscript Materials. Quotations taken from the manuscript and newspaper holdings of the National Library of Ireland are included here with the kind permission of the Board of the National Library of Ireland, and I am indebted to the staff for their assistance during the course of my research. My thanks also to Marie J. Taylor on behalf of the Edward Gordon Craig Estate for permission to publish two of Craig's drawings from *A Living Theatre*.

Quotations from the following publications are reprinted with the permission of Scribner, a Division of Simon & Schuster, Inc. All rights reserved in each case: 'The Man and the Echo', *The Collected Works of W. B. Yeats, The Poems, Revised*, vol. 1, edited by Richard J. Finneran. Copyright © 1940 by Georgie Yeats; copyright renewed © 1968 by Bertha Georgie Yeats, Michael Butler Yeats & Ann Yeats. 'The Double Vision of Michael Robartes', *The Collected Works of W. B. Yeats: The Poems, Revised*, vol. 1, edited by Richard J. Finneran. New York: Scribner, 1997. W. B. Yeats, *A Vision*. Copyright © 1937 by W. B. Yeats; copyright renewed © 1965 by Bertha Georgie Yeats and Anne Butler Yeats. W. B. Yeats, *Autobiography*. Copyright © 1916, 1936 by Macmillan Publishing Company; copyright renewed © 1944, 1964 by Bertha Georgie Yeats. *The Collected Works of W. B. Yeats*, vol. x, edited by Colton Johnson. New York: Scribner 2000. Writings by W. B. Yeats copyright © 2000 by Anne Butler Yeats and Michael Yeats. W. B. Yeats, *Essays and Introductions*.

Copyright © 1961 by Mrs W. B. Yeats. W. B. Yeats, *Explorations*. Copyright © 1962 by Mrs W. B. Yeats. W. B. Yeats, *On the Boiler*. Copyright © 1939 by Macmillan Publishing Company. W. B. Yeats, *Plays and Controversies*. Copyright © 1924 by Macmillan Publishing Company; copyright renewed © 1952 by Bertha Georgie Yeats. W. B. Yeats and Shree Purhoit Swami, *The Ten Principal Upanishads*. Copyright © by Shree Purhoit Swami and W. B. Yeats; copyright renewed © 1965 by Bertha Georgie Yeats and Ann Butler Yeats. W. B. Yeats, *Collected Works of W. B. Yeats*, vol. v. New York: Charles Scribner's Sons, 1994. W. B. Yeats, *Wheels and Butterflies*. Copyright © 1934 by Macmillan Publishing Company; copyright renewed © 1965 by Bertha Georgie Yeats.

I am most grateful to staff of various libraries for their assistance during the course of my research. These include the Special Collections and University Archives, Frank Melville Jr Memorial Library, Stony Brook, State University of New York; the Harry Ransom Center, the University of Texas at Austin; the Henry W. and Albert A. Berg Collection of English and American Literature, the New York Public Library; the Manuscripts, Archives, and Rare Book Library, Robert R. Woodruff Library, Emory University, Atlanta; the Special Collections, Queen's University Belfast. Enjoying Martha Campbell's hospitality and meeting with Elizabeth Cullingford made my visit to Austin all the more memorable. P. J. Dolan was very welcoming during my stay at Stony Brook.

Ray Ryan was steadfast in his support of this project over the past few years at Cambridge University Press. The encouragement of Richard Cave and Christopher Morash is also much appreciated, while Terence Brown's prompting on historical contexts for Yeats's drama was an important catalyst to my embarking on the project. Edward Larrissy generously took the time to read and comment upon an early draft of this work. I have learnt much through discussions on Yeats at Queen's with Eamonn Hughes, Emilie Morin, David Dwan, Fran Brearton and Aisling Mullan. Queen's lost a great scholar with the passing of Siobhán Kilfeather in 2007; I was fortunate to have known her for a brief period as a colleague. Conversations with Edith Shillue, Nicholas Allen, Colin Graham, Joe Cleary, Cyril McDonnell and Des O'Rawe have always been lively and enriching. Participating in workshops on Yeats's drama run by Sam MacCready and Carol Moore at the Yeats International Summer School in Sligo lent new insights into the performance aspects of Yeats's plays. Eglantina Remport has deepened my perspectives on European cultural experience; I am indebted to her friendship. I thank dad, my sisters and brothers for the support shown over the years. I dedicate the book to my dear mother Bridget, who sadly passed away in 2009.

List of abbreviations

Berg	The Henry W. and Albert A. Berg Collection of English and American Literature, the New York Public Library.
Emory	William Butler Yeats Collection, Manuscripts, Archives, & Rare Book Library, The Robert W. Woodruff Library, Emory University, Atlanta GA.
HRHRC	Harry Ransom Humanities Research Center, University of Texas at Austin.
NLI	The National Library of Ireland, Dublin.
Stony Brook	William Butler Yeats Collection, Special Collections & University Archives, Frank Melville Jr Memorial Library, Stony Brook, State University of New York.
VP	*The Variorum Edition of the Poems of W. B. Yeats*, Peter Allt and Russell K. Alspach, ed. (London: Macmillan, 1957).
VPl	*The Variorum Edition of the Plays of W. B. Yeats*, Russell K. Alspach ed. (London: Macmillan Press, 1966).

Introduction

Was W. B. Yeats awarded the Nobel Prize in 1923 as much for his achievements in the theatre as for his poetry? Yeats himself thought so, a belief that R. F. Foster thinks 'laughable'.[1] The claim in 'The Bounty of Sweden' should not be dismissed so lightly. The reception speech delivered by Per Hallström, then chairman of the Nobel Foundation, did indeed suggest that the prize was being awarded as much for Yeats's accomplishments in poetic drama as in lyric poetry, making no specific mention of his poetry volumes yet lavishing praise on *The Land of Heart's Desire* and *The King's Threshold* as well as Yeats's attempts to reform the modern stage.[2] This may have been due to the fact that the figure of Yeats the dramatist was more readily identifiable as European than that of Yeats the lyric poet. Through the identifications he made with August Strindberg in 'The Bounty of Sweden', Yeats was making a connection between the achievement of Scandinavian theatre and that of the Irish dramatic movement, one made on several occasions as the movement was getting underway in the early 1900s. Sweden's most famous contemporary dramatist shared with Yeats a lifelong interest in esoteric mysticism and the possibilities of thought-transference.[3] In 'The Bounty of Sweden', Yeats recollected first encountering in Strindberg's Paris circle the idea of stage scenery suggesting a scene without attempting anything that a painting could do just as well.[4] Strindberg's *There are Crimes and there are Crimes* was staged at the Abbey Theatre in March 1913 under the direction of Lennox Robinson

---

[1] R. F. Foster, *W. B. Yeats: A Life: The Arch-Poet*, vol. II (Oxford University Press, 2003), p. 250.
[2] Per Hallström, Presentation Speech, 10 December 1923, *Nobel Lectures, Literature, 1901–1967*, ed. Horst Frenz (Amsterdam: Elsevier, 1969), pp. 194–8. On this point, see Carle Bonafous-Murat, 'The Reception of W. B. Yeats in France', *The Reception of W. B. Yeats in Europe*, ed. Klaus Peter Jochum (London: Continuum Press, 2006), p. 39.
[3] In an early draft of 'Ireland after Parnell', Yeats wrote that 'a friend of Strindberg's, in *delirium tremens*, was haunted by mice, and a friend in the next room heard the squealing of mice'. W. B. Yeats Collection, ms. 600, Emory.
[4] W. B. Yeats, *Autobiographies* (London: Macmillan Press, 1955), p. 358.

I

and several of his works were performed by the Dublin Drama League during the course of the 1920s.[5] Making his own relation to Synge a central component of the Stockholm address, Yeats was implicitly comparing it to that vibrant rivalry between Strindberg and Ibsen as the international profile of Scandinavian drama reached new heights towards the end of the nineteenth century, Yeats claimed to have met Strindberg in Paris in his 1917 essay 'Per Amica Silentia Lunae' and his autobiographical volume, 'The Trembling of the Veil'.[6] In so doing, Yeats was presenting himself as the Symbolist complement to the Naturalist genius of Synge, creating a context through which his achievement would resonate strongly for a Scandinavian cultural community shaped deeply by the legacies of Ibsen and Strindberg.

Helen Vendler has recently demonstrated the astonishingly rich variety of poetic forms Yeats engaged throughout his life.[7] In no poem, however, do we encounter experiments in form and subject quite so anarchic as *The Player Queen* and *The Herne's Egg*, dramas influenced by French Surrealism, German Expressionism and the Absurdist mode of Pirandello. Vendler took this experimentation to task in her 1963 study of the later plays, writing of *The Player Queen* as not really fit for performance.[8] Given the extent to which Yeats's reputation as poet has overshadowed his writing for the stage, this is not unexpected, but it characterises a long-standing disagreement in the critical reception of the drama, as Bernard O'Donoghue notes.[9] Vendler's disapprobation shows up a pervasive anomaly in this reception dating back to reviews of the earliest performances. From the outset, the forms of poetic speech Yeats wrote for the stage received a mixed reception, largely on the suspicion that the medium of poetic drama had become obsolete. At the same time, critics have felt that Yeats's plays were too ambitious in the degree of experiment envisaged. Reviewing the first run of *The Land of Heart's Desire* in April 1894, the *Daily Chronicle* praised its 'simplicity and freshness' for separating the play from 'the dismal category of pseudo-Elizabethan blank-verse dramas'. By contrast *The Bookman Review*, while admiring

---

[5] See, Robert Welch, *The Abbey Theatre, 1899–1999: Form and Pressure* (Oxford University Press, 1999), p. 61; Hugh Hunt, *The Abbey: Ireland's National Theatre, 1904–1978* (Dublin: Gill and Macmillan, 1979), p. 101; Brenna Katz Clarke and Harold Ferrar, *The Dublin Drama League, 1919–1941* (Dublin: The Dolmen Press, 1979).
[6] Yeats, *Autobiographies*, pp. 32, 347–8.
[7] Helen Vendler, *Our Secret Discipline: Yeats and Lyric Form* (Oxford University Press, 2007).
[8] Vendler, *Yeats's Vision and the Later Plays* (Oxford University Press, 1963), p. 124.
[9] Bernard O'Donoghue, 'Yeats and the Drama', *The Cambridge Companion to W.B. Yeats*, ed. Marjorie Howes and John Kelly (Cambridge University Press, 2006), pp. 101–14.

Introduction 3

the play, worried that the contemporary theatre was not yet ready to accommodate the kind of experiment it involved.[10] So the first public performance of a Yeats play was praised for its success in staging a form that was in decline, and criticised for attempting an experiment too far ahead of its time.

This dichotomy endured through the course of the twentieth century. In his highly influential 1947 essay on Yeats's drama, Eric Bentley decried Yeats for becoming mired in late nineteenth-century poetic drama, a style, he worried, that might lead an audience to quickly lose interest in life itself. He went on to contrast the weakness of literary language in Yeats's plays to the vibrancy of Eliot, yet proceeded to argue that Yeats was 'perhaps the only considerable verse playwright in English for several hundred years'.[11] In his impressive 1976 study of Yeats's Noh plays, Richard Taylor objected that because he worked with 'outmoded material', the plays bore no relevance to 'modern outlook'. At the same time, he believed audiences of Yeats's day just were not ready for the level of experimentation he brought to the theatre; his drama was anachronistic yet ahead of its time.[12] Taylor's criticism touched upon a problem with which Yeats struggled, the harmonisation of form and theme – the many years spent reworking plays such as *The Countess Cathleen*, *The Shadowy Waters* and *The Player Queen* bore testament. Nonetheless, it illustrates an uncertainty that has remained in critical reception of Yeats's drama – that he was somehow too antiquated yet too experimental. Katharine Worth's 1978 study of the plays in *The Irish Drama of Europe* is a singular exception, a work that has largely fallen into obscurity as attention moved to post-colonial and later biographical rereadings of Yeats in the 1980s and 1990s.[13] Despite her efforts and those of other scholars such as James Flannery and Karen Dorn during the 1980s, the enduring impression of Yeats's drama to present times is that of a corpus valuable in understanding the development of the poet and anticipating the more assured achievement of Beckett, but of limited significance in itself.[14]

---

[10] *Daily Chronicle*, 24 April 1894; *The Bookman Review*, June 1894, NLI ms. 12145.
[11] Eric Bentley, *In Search of Theater* (New York: Vintage, 1947), pp. 296–7.
[12] Richard Taylor, *The Drama of W. B. Yeats: Irish Myth and the Japanese No* (London: Yale University Press, 1976).
[13] Katharine Worth, *The Irish Drama of Europe* (London: The Athlone Press, 1978).
[14] In recent assessments, Joep Leerrsen judges the drama an 'idiosyncratic side-product of Symbolism' and Bernard O'Donoghue sees its lasting value confined to the manner in which it anticipated Beckett. Joep Leerrsen, 'The Theatre of William Butler Yeats', *The Cambridge Companion to W. B. Yeats* (Cambridge University Press, 2004), pp. 47–61; O'Donoghue, 'Yeats', pp. 101–14.

This study examines the development of Yeats's drama as the evolution of a vision of estrangement directed against the values of middle-class culture as industrial and commercial activity accelerated at the end of the nineteenth century. In so doing, it makes the case for Yeats as a major figure in early twentieth-century European avant-garde theatre in ways that call for a reassessment of his political thought. Yeats saw in the theatre a space for artistic experiment that might impact on society at large. One of his most famous lines has been read universally as a bitter reflection on his earlier part in the creation of a movement out of which the political turmoil of Ireland since 1916 emerged: 'Did that play of mine send out / Certain men the English shot?' (*VP*, 632). Beneath its note of despondency lay a certain fascination at the possibility that artistic experiment might have had such a revolutionary impact in the Ireland of his day. So much of Yeats's later writing appears a lament for the decline in status of the arts as scientific orthodoxy and commerce deepened their influence in Europe. Yet 'The Man and the Echo' is troubled by the opposite anxiety – the possibility that the theatre lay at the heart of political revolution in Ireland, releasing forces it could not control. Yeats saw in the theatre a laboratory in which the kinds of experiments practised in Scandinavia, France and Germany could be undertaken in shaping the direction of Irish social development from the 1890s.

Those conflicting criticisms that Yeats's drama was anachronistic yet too experimental derive in part from a misreading of his interests in folklore, mythology and magic. Through the long course of his career, Yeats saw the potential in these elements to disturb not only audience expectations of the theatre but also trends in wider society. He looked to these ancient forms of belief in representing what he sensed were processes hidden beneath the shift towards secular rationalism and a consumer culture. Bernard O'Donoghue argues that Yeats's plays were bedeviled by uncertainty as to precisely the kind of theatre he envisaged.[15] The judgement underplays the fact that Yeats was continually experimenting throughout his career in the theatre, responding to debates and new developments as they arose, beginning with the arrival of Ibsen's Naturalism and Maeterlinck's Symbolism in 1890s Paris. Furthermore, it is symptomatic of a contemporary presumption deeply contested in the European culture of Yeats's age; the idea of myth, magic and folklore as resources invoked in conservative resistance to liberalism, democracy and science. Coming under the influence of William Morris in his twenties, Yeats's early

[15] O'Donoghue, 'Yeats', pp. 111–12.

political attitudes were formed by a sense that the destitution of working-class life in contemporary industrial England was as much spiritual as material. In the combination of Morris's literature of medieval fantasy, his arts and crafts movement, and the socialism he preached through his pamphlets and Sunday evening gatherings, Yeats encountered a figure who pursued artistic refinement, cultural experiment and imaginative enrichment in the hope of creating a more just social order. Morris's revival of English folk traditions looked back to earlier times as a means of resisting the brutal exercise of power in defence of commercial interests. Through Morris, Yeats came into contact with the socialism of Shaw and Annie Besant, and also the anarchism of Prince Kropotkin. Within this milieu, different ideas on social experiment provided a political frame for Yeats's immersion in Blake during the 1890s. Drawn to the visionary power of Blake's mysticism, Yeats had also imbibed Blake's social radicalism, seeing in Blake's idea of magic a release of revolutionary energies in the modern world.

The Symbolist form of theatre that Yeats began in the 1890s with the first performance of *The Land of Heart's Desire* developed in this context. Part 1 of this study examines the early plays as contributions to the Symbolist movement in Paris and indebted in particular to the dramas of Maurice Maeterlinck. Challenging the widespread view of Symbolism as a hostile reaction to Naturalism, the ways in which Symbolist theatre conjured a mood of estrangement is examined as a response to changes in the system of economic value in modern Europe, their impact on family life and the social roles of men and women. Yeats's response to Villiers de l'Isle Adam's *Axël* indicates that he came under the influence of Symbolism not in outright rejection of Ibsen, but through a desire to extend the revolutionary impact of Naturalism beyond the model of the social criticism play. In their treatment of money and work, Yeats's early plays bore a significant relation to Marx's *Capital*, mediated through the influence of Morris. Drawing upon his knowledge of customs, beliefs and rituals, his presentation of Irish rural life in these plays combined Naturalist and Symbolist tendencies, in which the theme of social alienation in Ibsen's *A Doll's House* was transformed by the larger vision of spiritual loss in Maeterlinck's *The Blind*. Yeats engaged situations at once familiar and strange; familiar to Irish audiences at least, but estranged in the unsettling presences of the otherworld in performances – the Fairy Child, the Demon Merchants, the Old Woman Cathleen ni Houlihan. Maeterlinck's influence on Yeats's representation of fetishism and taboo was important here, and the relation it bore both to Marx's idea of the commodity fetish and to Freud's reading of childhood and primitive civilisation in *Totem and Taboo*. The incendiary impact of the co-authored *Cathleen ni Houlihan* in Dublin in 1902 derived from a coalescence of competing forces – Symbolism, Naturalism and Primitivism conceived as the estrangement of contemporary social experience. The opening chapter looks at how these elements shaped Yeats's first contributions to the Irish Dramatic Movement.

The experiments Yeats employed for the performances of his plays were far-ranging. His use of space, shadow and light to the end of static theatre, the vocal delivery demanded by the psaltery experiment, and the later use of dance and mask, together contributed to the creation of a theatre of art. This study challenges the presumption that this carried with it an elitist anti-democratic set of political values that Yeats would make explicit in his final years. The experiments Yeats undertook in the 1900s arose from his renewed interest in Ibsen and a desire to represent Ibsen's treatment of social alienation through the theatre of estrangement Maeterlinck had developed in the 1890s. This was particularly striking in his use of stage space in representing power relations and issuing forms of protest through Symbolist methods. Seanchan's hunger-strike in his 1903 play *The King's Threshold* is considered in this regard, as is the influence of the socialism Wilde espoused in his 1891 essay 'The Soul of Man under Socialism' on the 1906 version of *Deirdre*. Considered in the light of two plays significant to Yeats in the 1900s, Ibsen's *An Enemy of the People* and Wilde's *Salomé*, the radical nature of the political ideas attaching to those experiments Yeats undertook in the 1900s comes into view, against the background of heated debates on cultural reform in Ireland.

Following the performances of Shakespeare's history cycle at Stratford-upon-Avon that he attended in the spring of 1901, Yeats began composing the first play in his own Cuchulain cycle, perhaps his defining achievement in the theatre.[16] The following study contests the view that Yeats engaged the Cuchulain myth to champion aristocratic ideals of heroism and nobility in a conservative denunciation of modern society as cheap and vulgar. This opinion ignores two important features of the Cuchulain plays – the internal subversion of heroism and the revolutionary power of the myth presented. The occult forms Yeats employed in the first two plays of the cycle, *On Baile's Strand* and *The Green Helmet*, hover uneasily between tragedy and farce, particularly the latter, Yeats's response to the

---

[16] See Terence Brown, *The Life of W.B. Yeats: A Critical Biography* (Dublin: Gill & Macmillan, 1999), p. 133.

Playboy riots marked here by his memory of Alfred Jarry's Surrealist farce of 1896, *Ubu Roi*. Responding to crowd energy in an age of expanding mass culture, this tension illustrated the influence of Nietzsche and Le Bon on Yeats's sense of revolutionary energy as the expression of collective will. The impact of the psaltery experiment on the 1904 production of *On Baile's Strand* and the recourse Yeats makes to medieval carnival and the grotesque in *The Green Helmet* were important dimensions to Yeats's sense of the historical forces shaping his age. Aspiring to create a radical popular movement in Ireland led by an artistic vanguard, Yeats was trying to harness the solemnity of Wagner and the ribaldry of Jarry.

Generally regarded as Yeats's retreat to an elite theatre of art, the Noh experiment in the later plays of the Cuchulain cycle, *At the Hawk's Well* and *The Only Jealousy of Emer*, are explored here as forms of anti-theatre through which he responded to the crisis in European culture made manifest in the First World War. While considerable attention has been given to the occult symbolism of these plays, little interest has been shown in their relation to Expressionism and Surrealism, artistic movements developed largely out of the trauma of the war in Europe. Yeats's work with Edward Gordon Craig in creating a new vision of the theatre lay within this context, explored here through the parallels between *At the Hawk's Well* and Oskar Kokoschka's *Murderer, Hope of Woman*, and the relation the Automatic Writing experiment behind *The Only Jealousy of Emer* bore to the practices of Surrealism. Since Theodor Adorno's damning judgement on the complicity of occultism with totalitarian ideology, the place of the occult within the European avant-garde has been the subject of critical disapproval. Drawing on Walter Benjamin's reading of Surrealism, I contend that the occult basis of these plays was more than simple mystification. An important development in Yeats's sense of the historical processes shaping his age became evident in the concept of race deriving from the Automatic Writing experiment that informs the Noh plays. Whatever the reactionary and eugenicist aspects of Yeats's later ideas on race, they served the purpose of expressing his sense of the machine age as a re-emergence of totem power in contemporary European society. Themes present since the 1890s in Yeats's critical response to modern industrial advance took on a new urgency in the aftermath of the First World War.

Yeats's last Cuchulain play, *The Death of Cuchulain*, was the outcome of a long process of reflection and experiment in the theatre extending over five decades. The influence of Luigi Pirandello is evident in the way Yeats structured the play, a dramatist whose plays shared more with the later work of Yeats than is acknowledged. Evidence of the complex nature of Yeats's perspective on politics and culture in his last years, *The Death of Cuchulain* was significant in refusing to dramatise Cuchulain's death through a heroic struggle with his enemies, instead presenting it as ignominious and inseparable from the form of theatre itself. Considering the Old Man's prologue to the play and the Harlot's ballad with which it concludes, it is evident that the alienating effects Yeats sought in his final play testified not only the power of that struggle between heroism and farce but equally his very contemporary sense of myth. In its interruption of the ancient with the contemporary in conditions of pronounced artifice, *The Death of Cuchulain* involved a complex temporality within which the contingent and situational became the site from which a destiny might be realised, refusing the totalising authority of the traditional idea of myth. Alluding to Pearse, Connolly and Oliver Sheppard's statue of Cuchulain in the GPO commemorating the 1916 Rising, the Harlot's song suggested that this was the frame Yeats offered for understanding the Rising and its legacy.

The place of the Cuchulain cycle within the European avant-garde provides a framework for evaluating the range of theatrical experiments Yeats engaged from 1920. Yeats's response to the Easter Rising in the context of the First World War is explored here through a comparison of two dance plays published in 1921, *The Dreaming of the Bones* and *Calvary*. Deriving from his collaborations with Edmund Dulac and the Automatic Script begun after Yeats's marriage to George Hyde-Lees in 1917, both plays presented a situationalist treatment of myth later dramatised in *The Death of Cuchulain*. As a response to the 1916 Rising, *The Dreaming of the Bones* was part of a wider critique of modern culture evident in *Calvary*, a play instructive on the nature of Yeats's response to socialism in the aftermath of the Bolshevik Revolution. The influence of critical writing associated with *The New Age* on Yeats is important here, in particular the anonymously published *Cosmic Anatomy* of 1921, authored by Richard Wallace. The dance plays demonstrated the extent to which Yeats saw the degeneracy of modern political culture encapsulated in the First World War, and the Irish Rebellion an act of resistance, however ill-judged, to that trend.

Yeats's perspectives on contemporary history are explored further through a consideration of will and passivity in the later plays as responses to mass culture and totalitarian politics, addressing in particular the problem of agency in the modern world. The influence of Expressionism is considered here through the interest Yeats shared with the German dramatist Ernst Toller in Schopenhauer's philosophy of will when responding to the current of contemporary European politics. Yeats's reservations about Expressionism was evident in his criticism of O'Casey's *The Silver Tassie*, yet its influence was discernible in the techniques employed for some of his own plays, developed under Craig's direction. In Toller he encountered a dramatist who engaged Expressionist techniques to address the dehumanising aspects of mass politics. In *The Player Queen*, Yeats developed through allegory, mask and apocalyptic symbol that idea of a blind, impersonal will so important to Toller, creating a work sharply consonant not only with Toller's *Masses and Man* but also Pirandello's *Six Characters in Search of an Author*. In London, the Stage Society were first to produce the 1915 version of *The Player Queen* in 1919, a version first published in 1922 (*VPl*, xxii). The first major production of Toller's play had taken place at Berlin's Volksbühne Theatre the previous year in 1921, the same year as the first performance of Pirandello's work in Rome.[17] Looking at Yeats's play on Jonathan Swift, *The Words upon the Window-pane*, I consider the influence of Pirandello's notions of performativity and the absurd on the Expressionist themes of will and passivity Yeats shared with Toller. To dismiss as obscurantist Yeats's representation of history through esoteric mysticism overlooks the incisive manner through which *The Player Queen*, *The Words upon the Window-pane* and *The Herne's Egg* captured the profundity of spiritual disturbance and revolutionary change Europe was undergoing in the 1920s and 1930s. In their meta-theatrical aspects and the subversive representation of transcendence through violation and bestiality, these plays brought the perspective of farce to their treatment of will and passivity in presenting a vision of contemporary history through the medium of esoteric mysticism. In so doing, they occupy an important place within the European avant-garde between the wars.

The final chapter assesses *Purgatory* in terms of the criticism of contemporary European culture Yeats had developed since his engagement with Morris at the end of the 1880s. Here the influence of Expressionism is addressed through the significance of Strindberg's 1907 play, *The Ghost Sonata*, to the treatment of perception in *Purgatory*, a defining aspect of Yeats's penultimate play. Strindberg's work became significant to Yeats in the 1920s, a number of his plays performed at the Abbey Theatre by the Dublin Drama League. The influence of *The Ghost Sonata* on *Purgatory* also marks an important connection to Beckett, who had attended the opening performance of Yeats's play in 1938 and who was inspired by a Paris production of Strindberg's play to offer the first production of

---

[17] Ernst Toller, *Plays One*, ed. and trans. Alan Raphael Pearlman (London: Oberon Books, 2000), p. 15.

Waiting For Godot to Roger Blin. The preoccupation with perception that *Purgatory* inherited from *The Ghost Sonata* is traced here to Yeats's extended debate with Thomas Sturge Moore in the 1920s following his introduction to the new physics via Bertrand Russell's *ABC of Relativity*. The political perspectives informing the exchanges with Moore are evident in the references made to John Ruskin during its course. Yeats's rejection of theories of common sense and probability here had its origin in the attack on contemporary middle-class values he encountered in Morris and Ruskin in the 1880s. The treatment of perception in *Purgatory*, linked to Expressionism through the influence of Strindberg, was part of a larger critique of the commercialisation of European society Yeats had undertaken through his Symbolist plays since the 1890s. Both reactionary and radical elements in *On the Boiler*, the pamphlet with which *Purgatory* was first published, are traceable to Ruskin in particular. The ideas of race informing the play are best understood in relation to the ambivalence between totemism and commodity fetishism that inflected Yeats's attacks on contemporary middle-class pecuniary values throughout his life as poet and dramatist, shaped deeply by the intellectual culture Ruskin and Morris had developed in England.

Above all, this study aims to convey the range, sophistication and intellectual seriousness of Yeats's body of plays as responses to dramatic changes in the cultural landscape of Ireland and Europe from the 1890s to the 1930s. From his first publicly performed play at the Avenue Theatre in April 1894 to the double-bill of *On Baile's Strand* and *Purgatory* at the Abbey Theatre in August 1938 just months before his death, his sense remained undiminished of powerful historical forces working to diminish or destroy the most precious elements of human intellect and feeling. If his experiments with voice, movement and staging appeared at times overambitious, it was testament in part to the scale of what he sought to achieve. In seeking to cultivate a theatre that might awaken audiences to processes of commodification while holding out for a new sense of spiritual consciousness strong enough to address the social and intellectual transformations of the era, Yeats pursued an ideal that would inevitably meet with criticism and hostility. Dismissing his entire theatrical achievement as anachronistically idealist, however, represents in some measure a failure of criticism to grasp the visionary power of that ideal so pertinent to an age of secular and religious fanaticism, and all-encompassing consumerism.

PART I

Early plays

CHAPTER 1

Revolutionary revelation: The Land of Heart's Desire, The Countess Cathleen, Cathleen ni Houlihan

Yeats's earliest contributions to the Irish Theatre movement have been received as forms of spiritual drama deliberately set against the commercialist and realist trends within British theatre of the time. While the precise nature of the nationalism evident in these plays has been the subject of considerable critical disagreement, there has been virtual unanimity in the view that Irish nationhood was their central concern. This image of Yeats as a spiritual dramatist seeking adequate representations of Irish national identity informed the controversy that followed the 1899 performance of *The Countess Cathleen* at Dublin's Antient Concert Rooms, the inaugural performance, along with Edward Martyn's *The Heather Field*, of the new Irish theatre movement envisaged by Augusta Gregory, Martyn and Yeats in 1897. Frank Hugh O'Donnell's attack on the play, circulated in May 1899 as the pamphlet *Souls for Gold*, did not dispute the fact that spirituality, nationhood and their interrelationship were the central concern of Yeats's play; he simply denounced the form of spirituality it offered as bogus and the presumption that the kind of nationality it evinced might be suitable for a cultural nationalist movement in Ireland.[1] As for its value as a play to modern audiences, Adrian Frazier judges it to be about 'as insignificant a piece of drama as a press keeps in print'.[2] Likewise, contemporary critical interest in *Cathleen ni Houlihan* concentrates predominantly on its place in the development of cultural nationalism in the Ireland of the 1900s, and Augusta Gregory's role in its composition; the notion that it might be of significance in understanding larger processes of social change in European society of the time has not been seriously considered.[3] Lionel Pilkington instructively draws

---

[1] Frank Hugh O'Donnell, *Souls for Gold: A Pseudo-Celtic Drama in Dublin* (London: Nassau Press, 1899).
[2] Adrian Frazier, *Behind the Scenes: Yeats, Horniman, and the Struggle for the Abbey Theatre* (Berkeley, CA: University of California Press, 1990), p. 3.
[3] Maria Tymoczko has described it as a piece of amateur political theatre, while Ben Levitas suggests its achievement was to align spiritual and prosaic political dimensions of nationalism

attention to the fact that the 1902 Dublin production of the play took place under the banner of Inghinidhe na hÉireann at St Teresa's Hall. Rightly asserting that the audience would not have been able to separate its action from the work of that organisation, his stress on performance history in this instance suggests that this was the play's primary – even exclusive – significance.[4]

This chapter considers three plays from the earliest period of Yeats's work for the theatre – *The Land of Heart's Desire*, *The Countess Cathleen* and *Cathleen ni Houlihan* – in exploring the European theatrical context from which they emerged. My intention in so doing is to address the political nature of these plays and the critique of the forces shaping contemporary European civilisation they offered. In their nationalist and mystical aspects, each of these plays sought to express estrangement as experience and idea. In so doing, they engaged the theatrical revolution visited upon French, German and Scandinavian drama during the course of the 1880s and 1890s, a revolution felt most palpably in the alliances and conflicts between Naturalist and Symbolist movements. The political nature of the representations of Irish culture in Yeats's early plays derived in the first instance from their place in this revolution, a revolution most evident in the crisis of value they expressed through the mood of estrangement and sense of dislocation they conjured. Drawing on images from Irish history, folklore and mythology, they involved more than Romantic ideas of nationhood guided by belief in the reality of supernatural existence. Colouring these images in a pronounced mood of anxiety, these plays bore sharp affinity with those of the Symbolist dramatists Maurice Maeterlinck and Philippe-Auguste Villiers de l'Isle Adam. In so doing, they offered a telling commentary on processes of modernisation, articulating a sense of alienation bearing a significant relation to Marx's critique of value, modified in the socialism of William Morris with which Yeats was directly familiar. Furthermore, in addressing a crisis of value through their treatment of family and the power of the fetish, these plays not only testified the general influence of Marx's accounts of family as an economic structure and of the fetishism of the commodity, but also anticipated the ways in which Freud's notion of *unheimlich* would come to characterise a growing sense of dislocation in the society of modern industrial Europe.

on stage. 'Amateur Political Theatricals, *Tableaux Vivants*, and *Cathleen ni Houlihan*', *Yeats Annual*, vol. x, ed. Warwick Gould (London: Macmillan Press, 1993), pp. 33–64. *The Theatre of Nation: Irish Drama and Cultural Nationalism 1890–1910* (Oxford University Press, 2002), p. 68.

[4] Lionel Pilkington, *Theatre and State in Twentieth-Century Ireland: Cultivating the People* (London: Routledge Press, 2001), p. 34.

On the surface, the representation of supernatural presences in Yeats's early dramas was squarely at variance with the materialist emphasis in Marx and Freud. The Symbolist movement to emerge in Paris during the 1890s was in significant measure a reaction not only against the commercialisation of the theatre, but also the growing influence of Naturalism reflected in the critical enthusiasm for the plays of Henrik Ibsen in Copenhagen, Stockholm, Berlin, Paris and, to a lesser degree, London. Greeting Symbolism with enthusiasm and remembering Ibsen with a certain disdain in later years, Yeats appeared to set himself against the materialist undercurrent in Naturalist theatre.[5] In the emphasis placed upon the struggle of the individual against repressive social convention and the apparatuses of social power in nineteenth-century Europe – church, state and press – Ibsen's later work bears a strong relation both to Marx's analysis of ideology and to the theory of the human psyche later undertaken by Freud. The Naturalist movement for which Ibsen was exemplar shared profoundly that scientific spirit informing the intellectual revolutions enacted by Marx and Freud: a determination to confront the facts of the human situation no matter what the impact upon the systems of values – religious, political and cultural – predominating European society of the late nineteenth century.

Yeats's attitude to Ibsen and his influence during the 1890s went beyond anti-materialist antipathy, however. This was first evident in his review of Villiers de l'Isle Adam's *Axël*, the performance of which he attended in Paris with Maud Gonne at Aurélien Lugné-Poe's *Théâtre de l'Œuvre* in February 1894. The occasion was to have a profound effect on Yeats, prompting a hugely enthusiastic review in which he proclaimed *Axël* as heralding a new revolution in the theatre. In the process, the complex nature of Yeats's attitude to Ibsen first became apparent. Critical of 'realism and Ibsenism' for what he felt to be its exclusively destructive impulse and a confidence in its own permanence, he nonetheless admired the way in which the 'scientific movement has swept away so many religious and philosophical understandings of ancient truth'. *Axël* may have represented the death of 'the merely analytic and rationalistic critics' in Yeats's eyes, yet it was these same Ibsenites who had made Symbolism possible 'by clearing away the rubbish and wreckage of the past', Villiers de l'Isle Adam's play exemplifying how 'Revolutions have notoriously eaten their own children.'[6] The seductive mysticism, medieval imagery

---

[5] In 'The Tragic Generation', Yeats recalled Ibsen as the favourite of 'clever young journalists', and of his *Rosmersholm* remarked, 'a stale odour of spilt poetry'. *Autobiographies*, p. 280.
[6] W. B. Yeats, 'A Symbolical Drama in Paris', *The Bookman* (1894), *Uncollected Prose by W. B. Yeats*, vol. I, ed. John P. Frayne (London: Macmillan Press, 1970), pp. 322–3.

and portentous tone of *Axël* stood in marked contrast to the realist, modern, scientific spirit informing works such as *A Doll's House*, challenging the certitude of Ibsen's moral critique at the level of theatrical style. Yet what is striking about Yeats's response is that he saw this as an extension of the original Naturalist revolution, albeit subsuming Naturalism in the process. His sense of Symbolism as revolution was reiterated in his 1897 review of Maeterlinck's essays on mysticism, *The Treasure of the Humble*, Yeats writing that '[w]e are in the midst of a great revolution of thought, which is touching literature and speculation alike; an insurrection against everything which assumes that the external and the material are the only fixed things, the only standards of reality'.[7]

Yeats's early drama did not reject the social criticism of Ibsen but subsumed it under a larger Symbolist transformation of the terms through which human experience was represented. This first becomes evident in *The Land of Heart's Desire* performed at London's Avenue Theatre in April 1894. In 'The Tragic Generation', Yeats claimed that the idea for this play first came to him upon the prompting of Florence Farr that he write something for the stage in which her nine-year-old niece, Dorothy Paget, would play her first theatrical role as the Fairy Child.[8] Her dance and song lent the play a magical quality that endured over time. Along with *Cathleen ni Houlihan*, it was the only early Yeats play to be revived by the Abbey Theatre in later years, and Joseph Hone has noted that a separate edition of *The Land of Heart's Desire* in 1925 sold ten thousand copies.[9] Its influence was remarkably diffuse, evident in pieces published in *The Yellow Book*, *The New Age* and *To-Day*.[10]

The rural Sligo setting and the fairy theme of this play suggest that it was simply a contribution to Yeats's marketing of Irish folklore within London literary circles of the early 1890s through his essays 'Irish Fairies, Ghosts, Witches', published in *Lucifer* in 1889 and 'Irish Fairies', published in *The Leisure Hour* in 1890.[11] This aspect is undeniable but, in an interview for *The Freeman's Journal* to coincide with the 1899 performance of

[7] W. B. Yeats, 'The Treasure of the Humble', *The Bookman* (1897), *Uncollected Prose by W. B. Yeats*, vol. II, ed. John P. Frayne (London: Macmillan Press, 1975), p. 45.
[8] Yeats, *Autobiographies*, p. 280.
[9] Joseph Hone, *W. B. Yeats, 1865–1939*, 2nd edn (London: Pelican Press, 1971), p. 391.
[10] Netta Syrett, 'Thy Heart's Desire', *The Yellow Book* (July) 1894 (London: Elkin Mathews & John Lane), p. 255; Beatrice Hastings, 'The Image, Heart's Desire', *The New Age*, 7:22 (1910), 519. In 1923, Holbrook Jackson wrote of the perpetual war between individuals and groups 'for a claim or a concession in the Land of Heart's Desire – the realm of reality'. 'The War for Reality', *To-Day*, ed. Holbrook Jackson, 9:54 (1923), 127.
[11] W. B. Yeats, *Writings on Irish Folklore, Legend and Myth*, ed. Robert Welch (London: Penguin, 1993), pp. 19–25, 60–4.

The Countess Cathleen, Florence Farr revealed that the desire to cultivate a European sensibility in London theatre audiences lay behind the staging of Yeats's fairy play. Here she expressed the desire to create in London a taste for the kind of serious drama to which German and Scandinavian audiences were accustomed.

> One of the few countries where there is a living and intellectual drama is Scandinavia, and that drama had its beginning in an even less ambitious experiment than the Irish Literary Theatre … It is perfectly useless to expect the general great bulk of the public outside Scandinavia and Germany to like serious literature on the stage, unless it is old enough to have become a superstition. When I was manager of the Avenue in 1894 I produced Mr Yeats' little play, 'The Land of Heart's Desire.' It succeeded very well at first, but it ceased to be understood as soon as Mr. Bernard Shaw's extravaganza, 'Arms and the Man,' which filled up the rest of the bill, began to draw the ordinary kind of fashionable audience.[12]

Striking here is the fact that Farr saw in Yeats's play the kind of seriousness characteristic of Ibsen concealed within the frivolity of its fairy motif.

The Land of Heart's Desire was originally a contribution to the repertoire of the Independent Theatre, a company founded in response to the performance of *A Doll's House* in 1888 with the intention of promoting the kind of serious progressive theatre Ibsen embodied. Winifred Fraser played the role of Mary Bruin in the 1894 production of Yeats's play, the recently married young woman in a rural Irish household who falls under the spell of the Fairy Child. Fraser had already made her name as an actress in London productions of Ibsen's work; she played the role of the innocent young girl Hedvig in a single subscription performance of *The Wild Duck* at the Royalty Theatre on 4 May 1894 while *The Land of Heart's Desire* was still running at the Avenue Theatre with Shaw's *Arms and the Man*. This performance won the admiration of London critics otherwise contemptuous of the play, suggesting that Fraser brought to the role that quality of foreboding innocence haunting Yeats's piece.[13]

The significance of this context for *The Land of Heart's Desire* is magnified by the impetus of the play's notable success to the creation of *Cathleen ni Houlihan*, the incendiary performance of which was to elevate Yeats's

---

[12] *The Freeman's Journal*, Wed. 4 April 1899, p. 5.
[13] For discussion of J.T. Grein's production of *The Wild Duck* at the Royalty Theatre, see Frederick J. Marker and Lise-Lone Marker, *Ibsen's Lively Art: A Performance Study of the Major Plays* (Cambridge University Press, 2005), p. 128. Frank Fay remembered the founding of the Independent Theatre as the backdrop to the 1894 performance in a piece for *The United Irishman*, 27 July 1901. *Towards a National Theatre: The Dramatic Criticism of Frank J. Fay*, ed. Robert Hogan (Dublin: Dolmen Press, 1970), p. 70.

centrality in Irish public life to a new level in 1902. In May 1901, Frank Fay published an important review of *The Land of Heart's Desire* and *The Countess Cathleen* following a successful American tour of the plays earlier that year; Adrian Frazier observes how this piece prompted Yeats to set aside other projects and begin working with Gregory towards the text that would eventually become *Cathleen ni Houlihan*.[14] Fay followed this up in July 1901 with a further piece on *The Land of Heart's Desire*, in which the achievement of the Norwegian National Theatre founded in Bergen by Ole Bull was offered to Yeats as a model for what an Irish National Theatre might become, Bull's theatre being the launching pad for Ibsen's stunning international success.[15] Fay was simply responding to the high esteem in which Yeats held the achievement of Scandinavian theatre. In 1900, Yeats wrote of Scandinavia 'passing from its moments of miracle' and Ireland 'passing into hers', anticipating the analogy that Fay was to employ in a more ardently nationalist tone.[16] Responding to Yeats in 1900, Albert Kinross hoped that the 'awakening' which had given Norway its Ibsen, Germany its Sudermann, the French-speaking countries their Brieux and Maeterlinck, was beginning to take form in Dublin and London with the 1899 performance of *The Countess Cathleen*.[17]

Ibsen's influence on the composition of *The Land of Heart's Desire* is most evident in the theme of the young woman who rebels against the restrictions imposed on her through marriage. The acrimony in the play between Mary Bruin and her new mother-in-law, Bridget, derives from Mary's refusal to perform the duties of housewife, preferring instead to lose herself in wistful imagining stimulated by her discovery of an old book of Irish folk tales. The obvious precedent here was *A Doll's House*, Yeats having attended a performance of the play at the Royalty Theatre in 1893; there had been thirty performances of Ibsen's play at the Avenue Theatre in 1892, where Yeats's play would be staged two years later.[18] *The Land of Heart's Desire* adapted the social criticism of Ibsen's play to social life in rural Ireland, investing Mary Bruin's desire to rebel from the façade of marital stability with the power of magic imagined in Irish folk

---

[14] Frazier, *Behind the Scenes*, p. 58.
[15] Fay, *Towards a National Theatre*, p. 103.
[16] W. B. Yeats, 'The Irish Literary Theatre, 1900', *The Dome*, 5 (1899–1900), 235. Ben Levitas observes that even in the pages of Pearse's *An Claidheamh Soluis*, Ibsen was admired as 'a role model who had succeeded in making obscure Norwegian a linguistic force in Europe'. *The Theatre of Nation*, pp. 50–1.
[17] Albert Kinross, 'The German Theatre', *The Dome*, 6 (1900), 8.
[18] John Kelly and Eric Domville, eds., *The Collected Letters of W. B. Yeats*, vol. 1, *1865–1895* (Oxford: Clarendon Press, 1986), p. 350.

culture. In so doing, magic became, in Yeats's play, the expression of Nora Helmer's revolt against bourgeois values in *A Doll's House*. Marriages are destroyed in both plays and, with this, the financial security of the families involved. If this points up the depth of social criticism implicit in Yeats's play, it does not deny the great stylistic differences between the two works. Though he could not escape Ibsen and his admirers, they having 'the same enemies' as he, though 'not the same friends', Yeats nonetheless hated *A Doll's House*. He felt it embodied the scientific empiricism of Huxley and Tyndall, and its dialogue was that of 'modern educated speech'.[19] Criticism of the values shaping modern middle-class society implicit in *The Land of Heart's Desire* required expression in a form more capable of artistic vitality than the Naturalism of *A Doll's House*.

It was for this reason that Maurice Maeterlinck proved such a crucial influence on Yeats in the 1890s, an influence that would endure through his later years. The remoteness and concentration of his plays presented alternative, and potentially more unsettling, challenges to middle-class values than those offered in plays such as *A Doll's House*. Maeterlinck's *The Blind*, *The Intruder* and *Pelléas and Mélisande* denied audiences the security of familiar scenery, dialogue and action. Instead, they carried a claustrophobic and menacing atmosphere in settings that were deliberately remote. These plays succeeded brilliantly in conjuring a sense of alienation given mystical significance through religious imagery, a sense that subsumed the social criticism of Ibsen into a larger vision of the human subject in a state of spiritual crisis. In April 1895, Yeats wrote to Olivia Shakespear of his delight upon reading *The Blind* and while he believed that Maeterlinck lacked 'that ceaseless reverie about life we call wisdom', he nonetheless felt he was of immense value in bringing people to the kind of drama Yeats envisaged.[20] Maeterlinck's influence was evident in 'The Theatre', Yeats's important essay published in the April 1899 issue of *The Dome* to coincide with the first Dublin run of *The Countess Cathleen* and reprinted the following month in *Beltaine*. As John Kelly and Eric Domville have shown, a number of phrases used in this essay, an elaboration of the idea of theatre embodied in *The Countess Cathleen*, were taken from Maeterlinck. Emphasising the priority of poetic voice, Yeats wanted no scenery that would not be immediately forgotten the moment an actor had said 'The dew is falling', or 'I can hear the wind among the

---

[19] Yeats, *Autobiographies*, p. 279.
[20] Yeats to Olivia Shakespear, 7 April [1895]. Kelly and Domville, *Collected Letters*, vol. 1, pp. 459–60.

leaves.'[21] These phrases had their origin in *The Intruder*, translated in 1892, and *The Blind*, translated in 1895. In the former, the eldest daughter tells her blind grandfather that there is 'un peu de vent dans le jardin ... et les roses s'effeuillent' [a little wind in the garden ... and the roses shed their petals]. The first character born blind in *The Blind* thinks he hears 'le vent dans les feuilles mortes' [the wind in the dead leaves].[22]

The strongest instance of Maeterlinck's influence on Yeats's drama in the 1890s is *The Intruder*, first staged at Lugné-Poe's *Théâtre d'Art* in April 1891. Its premise is sufficiently close to that of *The Land of Heart's Desire* to suggest that Yeats may have had it in mind when composing his play at the end of 1893; it is significant that he went to Paris for rest after rehearsals for his play had got under way.[23] *The Intruder* was the first Maeterlinck play to be performed in London, an English translation staged under the direction of Beerbohm Tree at the Haymarket Theatre in January 1892.[24] This tense introverted work depicts a room occupied by a blind grandfather, a father, an uncle and three daughters. There are two doors upstage left and right leading to two rooms offstage, the mother in one room and a recently born child in another, neither of whom appear at any point. The mother has been ill through the weeks since giving birth, and the child has been completely silent since her delivery. This short play concludes with the first cry of the child rising quickly to a high-pitched scream of terror as the light of the moon floods the onstage room through both doors. At this moment, a nun appears on the threshold of the mother's sick-room, signifying that she has died.[25] All points to the child as the intruder, a creature who may not be human. Remarking on her complete silence since her birth, the uncle says, '[o]n dirait un enfant de cire' [it's called a wax child].[26] The comparisons with *The Land of Heart's Desire* are striking; the presence of a Catholic priest seeking to ward off an unhuman power recalls the appearance of the nun at the end of *The Intruder*. This priest's words echo those of the uncle in Maeterlinck's play

---

[21] To the Editor of *The Daily Chronicle*, 27 Jan. 1899, Warwick Gould, John Kelly and Deirdre Twoomey, eds., *The Collected Letters of W. B. Yeats*, vol. II, *1896–1900*, (Oxford: Clarendon Press, 1997), p. 348. Yeats changed the phrases to make them sound more direct in the version of the essay published in *Beltaine*, disguising Maeterlinck's influence to suggest instead the Irish weather, giving the piece a slightly more Gaelic feeling: 'I can hear the wind among the leaves', becomes '[t]he wind is shaking in the trees'. W. B. Yeats, 'The Theatre', *Beltaine*, 1 (1899), 23.

[22] Maurice Maeterlinck, *Pelléas et Mélisande, Les Aveugles, L'Intruse, Intérieur*, ed. Leighton Hodson (London: Bristol Classical Press, 1999), pp. 46, 71.

[23] On 9 February 1894, Yeats wrote to John Quinn from Paris that his play had 'turned out one of my best things'. Kelly and Domville, *Collected Letters*, vol. I, p. 379.

[24] Maeterlinck, *Pelléas*, p. xxiii.

[25] Ibid., pp. 42–57.   [26] Ibid., p. 43.

when he describes the Fairy Child as 'the child that may be no child at all (*VPl*, 188)'. The uncanny takes the form of a child in both plays; whether in the form of the unseen baby uttering its first sound in *The Intruder* or the Fairy Child appearing in *The Land of Heart's Desire*, it brings about the death of women in both instances. As with the mother in *The Intruder*, Mary Bruin dies at the end of *The Land of Heart's Desire*. Both deaths occur at night under the light of a full moon.

The intimacy of these comparisons, Yeats's reservations about Ibsen's drama of social criticism, and the promotion of Maeterlinck's plays at the Théâtre d'Art through several performances in 1893 just as Yeats was composing *The Land of Heart's Desire*, each point strongly to *The Intruder* as an important source for Yeats's original conception of his fairy play. He had made a point of defending *The Intruder* against accusations of immorality some years later in his 1904 essay 'The Dramatic Movement'.[27] As Jared Curtis shows, the subject of Yeats's own play was similar to a number of folk stories from the Sligo locality that Yeats had gathered in *The Celtic Twilight* (1893); however, Maeterlinck's play offered a distinctive theatrical framework within which the fairy theme could carry contemporary relevance.[28] The significance of his influence lay in the nature of the social vision attaching to the cultural reform Yeats sought through the medium of theatre in the 1890s. Declan Kiberd's thoughtful reading of childhood in *The Land of Heart's Desire* nonetheless points up the need to reconsider the nature of Yeats's social critique in the light of his work for the theatre. Observing how the Fairy Child leaves the stage when the young Mary Bruin dies at the end of the play, Kiberd provocatively identifies in this Yeats's endorsement of 'an unreal state of changelessness' having its ideological origin in 'the Imperial strategy of infantilizing the native culture'.[29] This is misleading to the degree to which the precedent of Maeterlinck, a Jesuit-educated Belgian mystic, is ignored. Furthermore, it underestimates the strength of nationalist sentiment shaping Yeats's outlook in his twenties, most clearly evident in his 1886 essay on Samuel Ferguson, published in *The Dublin University Review*. Contrasting Ferguson favourably against Tennyson, Yeats ended this essay with an appeal to young Irishmen 'whom the emotion of

---

[27] W. B. Yeats, 'The Dramatic Movement', *Plays and Controversies* (London: Macmillan Press, 1923), p. 75.
[28] W. B. Yeats, *The Land of Heart's Desire: Manuscript Materials*, ed. Jared Curtis (New York: Cornell University Press, 2002), pp. xxiii–xxv.
[29] Declan Kiberd, *Inventing Ireland: The Literature of the Modern Irish Nation* (London: Vintage, 1996), p. 103.

Patriotism has lifted into that world of selfless passion in which heroic deeds are possible and heroic poetry credible'. In contrast, he referred disparagingly to the professional classes, who 'appear at no time to have thought of the affairs of their country til they first feared for their emoluments', and 'the shoddy society of "West Britonism" '.[30] The conclusion is striking, exploding the myth that the phrase 'West Briton' entered modern Irish critical discourse in the series of essays D. P. Moran published in *The Leader* at the end of the 1890s, gathered in 1905 into the single volume, *The Philosophy of Irish Ireland*.[31]

Significant to understanding the social vision implicit in Yeats's early drama is the centrality of estrangement to the Symbolist plays that most influenced him. Yeats was absorbed by the sense of mystery and pathos generated from the plays of Maeterlinck and Villiers de l'Isle Adam. What emerges in his own work is awareness of the social, historical and psychic aspects to the sense of human alienation their plays evinced. For all the quality of timelessness conjured in the works of both dramatists, there are important economic and familial dimensions to the dislocations their plays effect. In transposing their distinctive theatrical style to the politically loaded and historically recognisable Irish settings, these dimensions became more pronounced in Yeats's plays, leading to some hostility in the reception of *The Countess Cathleen* and volatile excitement in that of *Cathleen ni Houlihan*. In so doing, the mood of estrangement in French Symbolist theatre was shaped into a social vision Yeats had encountered in William Morris. Through the medium of Irish folk life and mythology, Yeats followed Morris in relating that spiritual anxiety characteristic of Symbolism to the alienating effects of modern industrial capitalism on human consciousness.

Although Yeats had strong reservations about the degree of political commitment Morris demanded, his early plays were markedly influenced by Morris's utopianism, in which the enhancement of social life through artistic creation was conceived in relation to the transformation of production practices and social relations along the lines of a collectivism positively regarded as medieval. Reviewing Morris's 'The Well at the World's End' for *The Bookman* in November 1896, Yeats wrote that more than anyone in modern days, he had sought to 'change the life of his time into the life of his dream', aiming to bring a sense of beauty and an ideal of perfection into practical affairs.[32] Yeats first came into contact

[30] W. B. Yeats, 'The Poetry of Samuel Ferguson', *The Dublin University Review* (April 1886), p. 941.
[31] D. P. Moran, *The Philosophy of Irish Ireland* (Dublin: Gill & Murphy, 1905).
[32] W. B. Yeats, 'The Well at the World's End' (review), *Uncollected Prose*, vol. I, p. 419.

with Morris in June 1887 when he began attending the 'Sunday Nights' at Morris's home in Hammersmith.[33] At that time Morris was a leading figure in the Socialist League and his stature in the Labour movement was to grow enormously following events at Trafalgar Square on 13 November 1887, that came to be known as 'Bloody Sunday'. On this day a large demonstration of over ten thousand people was violently broken up by the police, leading to hundreds of arrests and injuries, and the deaths of three people. Specifically a protest against the imprisonment of the Irish MP William O'Brien, it was the culmination of almost weekly public gatherings that year involving socialists, anarchists and Irish nationalists, but cemented by the ranks of the East End unemployed, predominantly migrants of Irish and Jewish extraction. Among the protesters that day were Morris, Shaw and Annie Besant, and the behaviour of the police confirmed in Morris the necessity for a revolutionary transformation in the social order if his utopian aspirations were to be effected.[34]

Yeats thus encountered Morris at a period when Morris's hopes for imminent social revolution were confronted with the brutality with which the ruling classes secured their interests and, in Thompson's words, 'the complicity of almost the entire capitalist Press, the treachery of professed fighters for freedom in Parliament and public life'.[35] This was important in shaping Yeats's later attitudes to the press in Ireland as elsewhere, and, more generally, to political liberalism. Bloody Sunday had brought home to Morris the enormous power of the industrial middle classes, extended through the instruments of state and media, shaping Britain in his day. If it led him to an evolutionary model for socialism, it equally testified the degree to which the utopian sentiment of *News from Nowhere* (1890) had its seeds in direct experience of state brutality. It was through Morris that Yeats came into contact with Shaw and other socialists and anarchists, including W. T. Stead, Annie Besant and Prince Kropotkin.[36] While Yeats worried deeply at the religious scepticism pervasive within these circles, he was hugely influenced by Morris's ideas at this time, seeing in his arts and crafts work of the 1890s all that was 'best and most thoughtful in London Society – above all whatever is "advanced" in any direction – literature,

---

[33] John Kelly, *A W. B. Yeats Chronology* (London: Palgrave Macmillan, 2003), p. 10.
[34] For a full account of the backdrop to Bloody Sunday, Morris's role in events on the day and the long-term impact it had on him, see E. P. Thompson, *William Morris: Romantic to Revolutionary* (London: Lawrence & Wishart, 1955), pp. 568–89.
[35] Thompson, *Morris*, p. 587.
[36] Yeats met Shaw at Morris's house in February 1888 and again in April that year at a lecture Morris delivered on anarchism. Kelly, *Chronology*, p. 12.

politics, art'.[37] He took seriously Morris's belief in the necessity of social transformation to the realisation of the highest artistic achievements. Proposing Morris and Swinburne for the position of poet laureate in November 1892 – just five years after Bloody Sunday – Yeats was discreetly seditious in his remarks: 'When the conditions attaching to a post intended for the chief poet of an age are such as to render it impossible to the only two men fitted for it alike by genius and the acclaim of the best public of their day, surely the time has come when these conditions should be mended.'[38]

It was from this context that the Symbolist mood of estrangement acquired its social pertinence in Yeats's plays. Conscious of Morris's arguments that the contemporary class system lay at the root of modern vulgarity and the spiritual destitution it generated, Yeats adapted the motifs of Maeterlinck and Villiers de l'Isle Adam to Irish settings, accentuating the challenges they posed to priorities of financial stability and public reputation pervasive in an expanded middle-class culture. Through this experiment coursed the influence of Morris's belief that the impoverished state of the arts in modern England was directly consequent upon the enslavement of labour by commerce, exalted 'into a sacred religion'.[39] In any case, the relation of spiritual alienation and economic disequilibrium was already intimated in French Symbolist theatre. Maeterlinck's *Pelléas et Mélisande* was a case in point. This was first performed as a play with incidental music by Gabriel Fauré in London in 1898 and later produced as an opera by Claude Debussy in Paris in 1902. It tells the story of a mysterious young woman, Mélisande, discovered by a nobleman, Golaud, deep in a forest beside a well; he immediately falls in love and takes her to his castle. As time passes, Golaud grows suspicious with jealousy that Mélisande and his brother Pelléas have fallen in love. The play ends with Golaud killing his brother before attempting suicide out of remorse, and Mélisande giving birth to a son as her death approaches. Yeats was familiar with Erving Winslow's 1894 translation of the play, and Mrs Patrick Campbell's performance of Mélisande in the 1898 version in London may have been a significant influence on the May 1899 Dublin performance of *The*

---

[37] W. B. Yeats, 'An Exhibition at William Morris's', *Providence Sunday Journal* (1890), *Uncollected Prose*, vol. 1, p. 183.
[38] To the Editor of *The Bookman* (November 1892). Kelly and Domville, *Collected Letters*, vol. 1, p. 325.
[39] William Morris, 'Art and Socialism', *Political Writings of William Morris*, ed. A. L. Morton (London: Lawrence and Wishart, 1973), p. 111.

Countess Cathleen.⁴⁰ Joseph Holloway was convinced that Maeterlinck had seen the Dublin performance, so close were the similarities he observed between it and Campbell's production of *Pelléas et Mélisande* at Dublin's Theatre Royal the following year.⁴¹ It was, in fact, the other way round, *The Countess Cathleen* offering Maeterlinck's theatrical style as the medium through which theatrical revival in Ireland might contribute most effectively to a larger cultural revolution.

The parallels between both plays are most striking in their leading female protagonists. Like Mélisande, we first encounter Cathleen lost in a forest, and throughout Yeats's play she carries those dispositions of wistful longing, forgetfulness and foreboding redolent of Mélisande. Yeats would develop some of the motifs and imagery of Maeterlinck's play subsequent to *The Countess Cathleen*. The theme of blindness and the image of the well would receive its most concentrated treatment decades later in *At the Hawk's Well*, a play that owes much to Maeterlinck's influence. However, what is most noticeable in comparing the two plays is that both are set in a time of famine. The references to famine in Maeterlinck's play are scant, but there nonetheless, and of sufficient importance to suggest something more than coincidence in the fact that the first versions of both plays appeared in the same year, 1892. Imploring Pelléas not to go to the bedside of his dying father, Arkël the king of Allemonde warns of the imminent threats to his kingdom, their enemies 'wakeful', and the people 'dying of hunger about us'. Later, as Golaud's mood changes under suspicion of Mélisande and Pelléas, he reveals that another peasant who had starved to death had been found, commenting that 'it would seem as if they all chose to die here under our eyes'.⁴² This situation of social crisis shapes the landscape in which the tensions within the household of King Arkël finally implode.

Yeats made the subject of famine central to *The Countess Cathleen*; in so doing, he lent a strong historical and political resonance to the Symbolist vision he encountered in *Pelléas et Mélisande*, given how fresh the trauma of the Great Famine was in the memories of Irish people. This was accentuated in the manner through which he incorporated into his 1895 version

---

⁴⁰ For consideration of Campbell's 1898 production in relation to the composition history of Debussy's 1902 operatic version of *Pelléas et Mélisande*, see Roger Nichols and Richard Langham Smith, *Claude Debussy: Pelléas et Mélisande* (Cambridge University Press, 1989), pp. 140–6.
⁴¹ See Christopher Morash, *A History of Irish Theatre, 1601–2000* (Cambridge University Press, 2002), p. 119. Yeats threatened to write a letter of protest at the scathing reviews Campbell's August 1900 performances of Maeterlinck's play received. Gould, Kelly and Twoomey, *Collected Letters*, vol. II, p. 615.
⁴² Maurice Maeterlinck, *Pelléas and Mélisande* (1894), trans. Erving Winslow (Amsterdam: Fredonia Books, 2001), pp. 55, 96.

of the play that other major French Symbolist work of the 1890s, *Axël*. In the second part of Villiers de l'Isle Adam's play, the audience learns that during the Napoleonic Wars in Germany, great amounts of gold were deposited from the various kingdoms to the National Bank in Frankfurt to avoid its being pillaged. As the Treasury could not cope with the sum, a huge reserve of gold was entrusted to the safekeeping of the Count of Auersberg, father of Axël, who kept it hidden in the forest surrounding his castle. The military commander, Kaspar of Auersberg, learns this from one of Axël's servants and insists that, following the death of the Count, the gold belonged to the new German state, calling Axël a state subject who was bound to notify its representatives of its existence. Axël rejects this entirely, blaming the state for a betrayal that led to his father's death in the war with the French, and subsequently kills Kaspar in a duel. Axël's resistance to state authority would exert a more direct influence on *The King's Threshold* than *The Countess Cathleen*, but these competing claims to the ownership of gold go to the heart of the latter. Behind the story lay a conflict between gold as an occult power, symbol of regal mystique in feudal Europe, and gold as the modern standard of economic equivalence in a system of universal exchange that would accelerate in the aftermath of the French Revolution.[43]

Like *Axël*, *The Countess Cathleen* addressed, through the medium of esoteric symbolism, a crisis in the structure of value generated by commodification in contemporary European culture. This was most visible in the role of the Demon Merchants in the play, simultaneously supernatural presences and manifestations of a historical situation in which materialism was destroying faith in supernatural reality. The gold they offer the starving peasantry in exchange for their immortal souls embodied that crisis in value within the mysticism of *Axël*. The exchange proposed represented the equalisation of value, in which everything became susceptible to the power of commerce, yet the gold offered also had specific occult provenance in Yeats's esoteric studies. Just after the Countess Cathleen departs the cottage of Shemus Rua, the merchants make their first appearance in the play. Rejecting his wife's entreaties to maintain his Christian faith against them, Shemus speaks of the Mother of God who 'cannot hear the poor', of Satan pouring 'famine from his bag', and has in mind to pray to him 'to cover all this table with red gold' (*VPl*, 29). In the ritual of the wayfarer's entrance recorded in notes

---

[43] Philippe-Auguste Villiers de l'Isle Adam, *Axël*, trans. Marilyn Gaddis Rose (Dublin: Dolmen Press, 1970), pp. 94–8.

for a Celtic Order of Mysteries that Yeats was formulating with Maud Gonne, George Russell, William Sharp and Annie Horniman from 1898, gold was taken to represent the sun on the Philosopher's stone. Red was the colour symbol on the western axis of the circular colour spectrum devised for the ritual entrance of the wayfarer in the third part of this proposed rite of initiation for the Celtic Order.[44] These symbolic allusions were hidden in 'the red gold' to which Shemus refers in the 1899 performance of the play. The gold the Demon Merchants offer is thus riven by contradiction, a magic substance of absolute value that was yet pivotal to a system of exchange in which everything was reduced to commercial measurement.[45]

This contradiction derived in the first instance from Yeats's knowledge of the idea of esoteric correspondences elaborated in Immanuel Swedenborg's *Secrets of Heaven* (1749–56) and *Heaven and Hell* (1758) in conjunction with his close study of William Blake during the 1890s and the social theories of Morris. These interacting influences on Yeats's treatment of commerce in *The Countess Cathleen* gave expression to the same crisis in the structure of value evident in Marx's theory of the commodity. Like the merchants' gold in the play, Marx saw in gold and silver the embodiment of pure value, 'by their nature' suited to act as the universal equivalent form of all commodities. Yet in so doing, they became emblematic of a modern economic system in which everything, gold and silver included, was interchangeable, reducible to market value.[46] In gold and silver, Marx saw 'the magic' of money even as commerce threatened belief in non-material value.[47] This paradox in Marx's theory is present in *Cathleen ni Houlihan*, where a bag of gold stands in for one of the characters, Delia. Michael Gillane, who follows Cathleen ni Houlihan off the stage in a trance, is betrothed to Delia. She only appears on stage at the end, appealing to Michael to waken from this trance. The bag of gold

---

[44] NLI ms. 13568, part 3.
[45] Notwithstanding the specific esoteric context of the proposed rituals of the Celtic Order of Mysteries, it is significant that in the Rite of the Cauldron, the wayfarer takes an oath in which he promises to bow his head 'before no God nor Spirit except such as sacrifice daily to Eternal Man, for Man only is the eternal labourer', NLI ms. 13568, part 1. This informed the understanding of labour that shaped much of Yeats's later poetry and drama, and indicates the esoteric ideas that influenced his reception of Morris's ideas on labour.
[46] Karl Marx, *Capital*, vol. 1, trans. Ben Fowkes (London: Penguin Press, 1990), p. 183. For a complete formulation of the role of money in Marx's theory of value, see *Grundrisse*, trans. Martin Nicolaus (London: Penguin Press, 1973), pp. 115–238.
[47] Marx, *Capital*, vol. 1, p. 187. Baudrillard sees in this evidence of the fascination with magic and fetishism in nineteenth-century anthropology at the root of Marx's theory of commodity fetishism. *For a Critique of the Political Economy of the Sign*, trans. Charles Levin (St Louis: Telos Press, 1981), p. 88.

through which her presence in the play is represented makes her condition of servitude palpable, a commodity with measurable commercial value. By contrast, Cathleen sets herself apart from commerce, refusing the offer of a shilling from Michael Gillane's father (*VPl*, 226). The play makes clear that the intervention of this supernatural presence was to be understood in relation to the governing force of commerce in the Gillane household, particularly as manifested in the dowry. The influence of *The Land of Heart's Desire* on the composition of *Cathleen ni Houlihan* is evident here. Michael tells his new bride Mary to 'put away your dreams of discontent' in the earlier play because he has 'a stocking full of silver and gold'. This immediately follows the moment in which Mary gives an old beggar woman some milk, the exchange that enables the Fairy Child to appear in the household.[48]

Appearing in circumstances in which the scarcity of resources induced families to accommodate religious belief to economic needs, the supernatural beings in Yeats's early drama manifested the distorting effect of this compromise on the quality of human experience. Whether in the form of the Fairy Child of *The Land of Heart's Desire*, the Demon Merchants of *The Countess Cathleen*, or the vampiric Old Woman of *Cathleen ni Houlihan*, the idea of the unhuman is obsessively recurrent in these early plays.[49] Arising in situations marked by destitution or the discreet threat of poverty, the theme of the alienating effect of commerce that Yeats learned from Morris received its most concentrated expression through these personifications of the unhuman and the impact of their interventions. From the outset of *The Countess Cathleen*, the supernatural takes sinister form, and derives directly from the collapse of the community into famine. Speaking of a land that was 'famine-struck', Teigue tells of a herdsman who had 'met a man who had no mouth, / Nor eyes, nor ears; his face a wall of flesh' (*VPl*, 7). The image is redolent of those characters Yeats encountered in Maeterlinck's *The Blind*, devoid of sight and hearing.

This theme is developed further in *The Land of Heart's Desire* and *Cathleen ni Houlihan*. Like the Demon Merchants of *The Countess Cathleen*, these plays bear out Sartre's account of evil, an existentialist development of Marx's theory of alienation. Sartre argued that the tendency to see other people as less than human arose from a historical situation in which the terrain of human history itself derived from conditions

---

[48] W. B. Yeats, *The Land of Heart's Desire: Manuscript Materials*, p. 25.
[49] Foster Hirsch has noted how this obsession would persist. 'The Hearth of the Journey: The Mingling of Orders in the Drama of Yeats and Eliot', *Arizona Quarterly*, 27 (1971), 297.

of scarcity.[50] This is exemplified in *The Land of Heart's Desire* in the appearance of the Fairy Child as the unhuman Other at a moment when a family's economic stability is under threat, manifesting the danger posed by Mary. Refusing the role of housewife following her recent marriage, she jeopardises the moderate security her husband's family has achieved. The inability of her mother-in-law to understand why she chooses to spend time over old legends rather than household tasks magnifies into a fear of the Other as evil, evident in her response to the appearance of the Fairy Child. Significantly, a reviewer for *The Chicago Herald* in 1901 found the play 'a depressing thing, for its implication is that all our impulses are snares of the devil'.[51] Likewise the commodification of Delia in *Cathleen ni Houlihan* is projected on to Cathleen in her form as a vampire.[52] One of Cathleen's most zealously nationalist lines, '[m]any that are red-cheeked will now be pale-cheeked' (*VPl*, 229) was a political inversion of the vampiric quality Marx saw in Lord Dufferin's blood-letting panacea for Ireland's economic woes in the post-Famine era.[53] The material circumstances in which the supernatural powers present themselves in these plays are intrinsic to the sense of the uncanny they generate.

Yeats represents the unhuman as the form of supernatural power in conditions of material scarcity most effectively through fetishes and the fetish structure of human relations in these plays. In both *The Land of Heart's Desire* and *The Countess Cathleen*, the statue of the Virgin Mary is presented as a fetish. When the Demon Merchants enter the cottage for the first time in the latter, the statue falls to the floor. In *The Land of Heart's Desire*, Mary grows afraid in the presence of the Fairy Child, calling on the Virgin Mary in fear that '[s]ome dreadful thing will happen' (*VPl*, 202). At the request of the Fairy Child, Father Hart removes the crucifix hanging on the wall, enabling her to exercise magical power over Mary.

---

[50] Jean-Paul Sartre, *Critique of Dialectical Reason*, trans. Alan Sheridan-Smith (London: New Left Books, 1976), pp. 125, 130. See also, Fredric Jameson, *Marxism and Form: Twentieth Century Dialectical Theories of Literature* (Princeton University Press, 1971).

[51] *Chicago Chronicle*, Sept. 1901. NLI ms. 12145.

[52] Complaining to Yeats of his subservience to Gregory and Synge in a letter of 7 August 1907, Horniman did not mince her words: 'Lady Gregory and Mr. Synge grovel at Fay's feet. They sacrifice your work and keep you a bound-slave to them because you are "touched" by that vampire *Cathleen ni Houlihan*.' NLI ms. 13068. For the critical view of Cathleen as a vampire see Henry Merritt, 'Dead Many Times: *Cathleen ni Houlihan*, Yeats, Two Old Women and a Vampire', *Modern Language Review*, 96:3 (2001), 650.

[53] Of Dufferin's proposal that further depopulation was required, Marx commented that here we had 'a physician of the school of Sangrado, who, if he failed to find an improvement in the condition of his patient, ordered blood-letting after blood-letting, until the patient lost his sickness when he had lost his blood'. *Capital*, vol. I, p. 868.

He is then powerless, observing that 'because I put away the crucifix, / That I am nothing, and my power is nothing' (*VPl*, 207). As an externalisation of psychic energy in the form of a material object, this crucifix is a talisman, an example of James Frazer's notion of the totem – the externalisation of the soul in primitive religion.[54] In breaking the Virgin statue or removing the crucifix, the taboos governing intra-family relations in both plays are disturbed. Illicit power enters the household as a consequence, a power imagined malign in *The Countess Cathleen*, though less emphatically so in *The Land of Heart's Desire*.

The symbolic power of the Virgin statue and the crucifix in these plays exemplifies the pervasiveness of totemism in the rural Irish settings presented. A further instance is the bunch of primroses hung upon the door to ward off evil in *The Land of Heart's Desire* (*VPl*, 226).[55] In scene one of the 1892 version of *The Countess Cathleen*, Mary speaks to Shemus of her fear of the 'wood things' (*VPl*, 22). In versions between 1895 and 1908, she observes that the merchants pour out wine 'as the wood sidheogs do' (*VPl*, 41). These merchants are 'not human' – Mary's fear of totemic power consistent with those features Freud described in *Totem and Taboo*.[56] The origins of such beliefs were considered extensively within the emerging discipline of anthropology in the late nineteenth century.[57] Yeats's representation of beliefs and practices in rural Ireland in these plays showed his awareness of the role accorded totemism in the work of ethnologists such as James Frazer and Andrew Lang. Sinéad Garrigan Mattar points out that Yeats often contorted their writings to suit his own argument. Most of all, he sought to direct their findings towards a belief in the reality of supernatural revelation. Although *The Land of Heart's Desire* was written before Yeats's reading of works such as Lang's *The Making of Religion*

---

[54] James Frazer, *Totemism and Exogamy*, vol. IV (London: Macmillan Press, 1910), p. 5. Andrew Lang and Max Müller were the leading authorities on totemism in the late nineteenth century. For disagreement on the nature of fetish origin, see Lang, *Custom and Myth*, 2nd edn (London: Longmans, Green & Co., 1893), pp. 212–42. Whereas Müller saw fetishism as a debased form of an earlier religious sense of the infinite in nature, Lang saw it as the earliest projection of power from which religion subsequently grew.

[55] This meets the definition of a totem offered by Frazer in 1887 as a class of material objects that primitive people treated with respect on the basis of their belief that it protected them. James Frazer, *Totemism and Exogamy*, vol. I, 2nd edn (London: Macmillan Press, 1910), p. 3. Cited in Freud, *Totem and Taboo*, trans. James Strachey (London: Norton, 1950), p. 103.

[56] Significant here are Deleuze and Guattari's objections to the lack of historical perspective in Freud's Oedipal theory. See *Anti-Oedipus: Capitalism and Schizophrenia*, trans. Robert Hurley, Mark Seem and Helen R. Lane (London: the Athlone Press, 1984), pp. 51–67.

[57] Freud gives a schematic outline of the debate around this question in *Totem and Taboo*, pp. 100–26.

or Frazer's *The Golden Bough*, its preponderance for totemism anticipated the concerns of these works, if not the conclusions.[58]

This suggests that Yeats promoted a primitivist view of rural Ireland consistent with the ideology of Empire and, more locally, the conventional attitudes of Unionism to native Irish culture. This was certainly how Frank Hugh O'Donnell regarded *The Countess Cathleen*. In his attack on the play, O'Donnell clearly took offence at the suggestion that native Irish customs and beliefs might be indistinguishable from those of African tribes studied by comparative ethnologists during the nineteenth century. Most objectionable, in his view, was the idea that the native Irish of earlier centuries might be 'just like a sordid tribe of black devil-worshippers and fetish-worshippers on the Congo or the Niger'.[59] As a leading member of the Irish Parliamentary Party, O'Donnell was inevitably going to object to an influential piece of drama in which this association was drawn, insofar as it would strengthen further the Tory prejudice that the Irish were unfit for self-government, thus deepening resistance to Home Rule. O'Donnell's insistence that artistic representations of Ireland should infer no association with African tribal society was a measure of how pervasive the influence of comparative ethnology had become, particularly in its attention to totemism and fetishism. It also anticipated nationalist support for the Boer cause when Maud Gonne, Arthur Griffith and James Connolly founded the Transvaal Committee in 1899.[60] If identification with the Boers lent nationalism in Ireland an anti-Imperial flavour at this time, it also heightened sensitivities to any associations drawn with native African civilisations regarded as primitive, unworthy of self-governance.

While understandable in the context of the political situation in Ireland in 1899, O'Donnell's attack on *The Countess Cathleen* was ill-judged in ignoring the European literary sources for those aspects of the play that aroused his ire. As Sinéad Garrigan Mattar demonstrates, Yeats was indeed influenced by the work of ethnologists such as Lang, Frazer and Müller on the subject of fetishism and totem worship. By engaging some

---

[58] Sinéad Garrigan Mattar, *Primitivism, Science and the Irish Revival* (Oxford: Clarendon Press, 2004), pp. 63–76. See also, 'Frazer, Yeats and the Reconsecration of Folklore', *Sir James Frazer and the Literary Imagination*, ed. Robert Fraser (London: Palgrave-Macmillan, 1991), pp. 121–53.
[59] Frank Hugh O'Donnell, 'Celtic Drama in Dublin', *Freeman's Journal*, 1 (1899), 6.
[60] For discussion of the significance of the Boer War to the Irish Revival in the 1900s, see P.J. Mathews, *Revival: The Abbey Theatre, Sinn Féin, the Gaelic League and the Co-operative Movement* (Cork University Press in association with Field Day, 2003), pp. 66–75, and 'Stirring up Disloyalty: The Boer War, the Irish Literary Theatre and the Emergence of a New Separatism', *The Irish University Review*, 33:1 (2003).

of their ideas in his early plays, however, he produced dramas expressing the same forms of estrangement we encounter in Maeterlinck and Villiers de l'Isle Adam. This was important in that the quality of estrangement their plays evoked was taking the social criticism of Ibsen in a new direction and preparing the way for the theatre of the avant-garde that emerged in the new century.

This is evident, for example, in Maeterlinck's treatment of the subject of inbreeding. The topic enfolds *The Intruder*, his first play to receive a performance, and first produced in London under the direction of Beerbohm Tree at the Haymarket Theatre in January 1892. The deeply interiorised form of this play, its atmosphere of claustrophobia and intense concentration upon a family closed off from the external world, heighten anxieties around the nature of family relations. The opening of *The Countess Cathleen* adapts this form to a historical situation: an Irish family closed in upon itself as the land outside presents nothing but death. Considering Freud's later writings on totemism and the role of the totem as an incest taboo in tribal culture that Frazer and Lang observed, Mary's devotion to the Virgin statue appears a displacement of forbidden desire within family relations. Likewise, the father of the three young girls in *The Intruder* trusts nobody outside the family circle. Intimating an incestual undertone here, the blind grandfather believes that the child to which his daughter-in-law has given birth will be deaf and dumb because she is the offspring of a marriage between blood relations.[61] From this introversion emerges the paranoid fear of a presence lurking in the household, a fear that paralyses the actors and is finally expressed in the awakening scream of the baby. The parallel with *The Land of Heart's Desire* is striking, but mediated through the frame of Irish folk customs, the effect of which is to lighten the tone. The family of Maurteen and Bridget are closed off from outside influence under the authority of Father Hart; the eve of May is considered threatening, no night being '[s]o wicked as to-night' (*VPl*, 188).

The Fairy Child only appears onstage in *The Land of Heart's Desire* after the new bride Mary has given the Old Woman milk. As Edward Hagan notes, milk drinking had a specific esoteric meaning, representing the third epoch of Rosicrucian history.[62] Like Mary, the young novice Sarah is absorbed in reading ancient writings in Villiers de l'Isle Adam's

---

[61] Maeterlinck, *Pelléas*, p. 43.
[62] Edward Hagan, 'The Aryan Myth: A Nineteenth-Century Anglo-Irish Will to Power', *Ideology and Ireland in the Nineteenth Century*, ed. Tadhg Foley and Sean Ryder (Dublin: Four Courts Press, 1998), p. 205.

Axël, books of Rosicrucian arcana stored in the Abbey from a war three centuries previously.[63] The exchange of milk as pretext for the appearance of the supernatural stranger in *The Land of Heart's Desire* is reversed in *Cathleen ni Houlihan*. In the earlier play, the old beggar woman is transformed into a fairy child after receiving the gift of milk; in the latter, the mother recognises Cathleen as a supernatural presence only after she refuses an offer of milk (*VPl*, 226). Reversing the transformation in the earlier play, the old woman becomes 'a young girl' with 'the walk of a queen' at the end of *Cathleen ni Houlihan* (*VPl*, 231). Using childhood in this way, Yeats was exploring the ambivalence of innocence and forbidden desire within the family circle that was also the subject of Maeterlinck's *Pelléas and Mélisande*. As this play advances Golaud's jealousy and suspicion grows, feeling that the love between his brother Pelléas and his wife Mélisande is not innocent. In the pivotal final scene of the third act, he prompts his little boy Yniold to spy on Pelléas and Mélisande who are together in the room of Mélisande, pressurising Yniold to report all he sees. The boy grows frightened, not daring to look further at his uncle and mother staring at each other in the bedroom.[64] Significantly, Yeats was very much taken by a performance of this play in French at the Vaudeville Theatre in July 1904, in which Sarah Bernhardt played Pelléas and Mrs Patrick Campbell played Mélisande. Joseph Holloway recalled the effect this performance had on Yeats, deriving from the fact that they played the role of lovers 'as if they were a pair of little children'.[65]

On this subject of inbreeding and taboo, Maeterlinck's plays were distinguished from Yeats's in the 1890s in the absence of any specific ethnographic references. Rather than dramas representing customs, beliefs and taboos of so-called primitive cultures, *The Intruder* and *Pelléas and Mélisande* engaged these issues, preoccupations of comparative ethnologists, to articulate the psychic trauma of a modern world in a state of spiritual crisis. In this sense, Maeterlinck was mapping out in the theatre a field similar in kind to that which Freud was in the process of developing in psychology, his subscription to spiritualism notwithstanding.[66] To the extent to which it shared Maeterlinck's treatment of the incest taboo in relation to the supernatural,

---

[63] Villiers de l'Isle Adam, *Axël*, p. 3.   [64] Maeterlinck, *Pelléas*, pp. 22–6.
[65] Robert Hogan and Michael J. O'Neill, eds., *Joseph Holloway's Abbey Theatre: A Selection from His Unpublished Journal 'Impressions of a Dublin Playgoer'* (Dixon, CA: Proscenium Press, 1967), p. 59. John Kelly and Ronald Schuchard, eds., *The Collected Letters of W. B. Yeats*, vol. III, *1901–1904* (Oxford: Clarendon Press, 1994), p. 312.
[66] On the spiritualist and Egyptological aspects of Maeterlinck's mysticism, see 'The Awakening of the Soul', *The Treasure of the Humble*, trans. Alfred B. Sutro (1897) (Amsterdam: Fredonia Books, 2001), pp. 25–42.

Yeats's representation of Irish folk customs likewise evoked a mood of estrangement mediating psychic dislocations effected through the development of technologies of mass production in Europe during the latter half of the nineteenth century.

This avant-garde nature of Yeats's early folk plays shows through in their anticipation of August Strindberg's *The Ghost Sonata* (1907), one of the first Expressionist plays in Europe. Like *The Land of Heart's Desire*, this play adopts the structure of the fairy tale and, like *The Countess Cathleen*, it is heavily influenced by the writing of Immanuel Swedenborg.[67] Indeed, it employs the same idea we encounter in *The Land of Heart's Desire* and *Cathleen ni Houlihan*: the exchange of milk as catalyst for a supernatural intervention that is, in its turn, sign of an epochal change. The play begins with an old man confined to a wheelchair reading while a milkmaid gives a student before him some milk; he recalls the blind grandfather of *The Intruder* and anticipates the wheelchair-bound Hamm of Beckett's *Endgame* decades later. The student's destiny is somehow under the control of this old man who cannot see the milkmaid, indicating that she is a supernatural vision. When he realises the student is in conversation with her, he is overcome with terror.[68] Here we encounter the same fear that seizes Bridget when she discovers that Mary has given milk to the old beggar woman in *The Land of Heart's Desire*, or the fear that comes over Bridget when the Old Woman refuses milk in *Cathleen ni Houlihan*. Significantly, Yeats was very much taken with this play in later years, citing it alongside *Ulysses* in a 1926 essay published in *The Dial* defending artistic experiment, Yeats regarding the 'Spook Sonata' as 'mad and profound as King Lear'.[69] The Dublin Drama League presented two performances of the play at the Abbey Theatre in April 1925, Lennox Robinson playing the role of the Student under the pseudonym Paul Ruttledge, the protagonist of Yeats's 1902 play *Where There Is Nothing*.[70]

---

[67] See Milton A. Mays, 'Strindberg's *The Ghost Sonata*: Parodied Fairy Tale on Original Sin', reprinted in *Eight Modern Plays*, 2nd edn, ed. Anthony Caputi (London: Norton, 1991), pp. 508–19.

[68] August Strindberg, *The Ghost Sonata*, *Strindberg: Plays One*, 2nd edn, trans. Michael Meyer, (London: Methuen, 1976), pp. 157–91.

[69] W. B. Yeats, 'The Need for Audacity of Thought', *The Dial* (February 1926) in *The Collected Works of W. B. Yeats*, vol. x, ed. Colton Johnson (New York: Scribner, 2000), p. 201. It is possible that Yeats intended the Old Woman in *The Land of Heart's Desire* to be a witch; in *The Golden Bough*, Frazer describes a belief among Scottish highland clans that witches were abroad on May eve attempting to steal cows' milk. *The Golden Bough* (London: Wordsworth Editions, 1993), p. 620.

[70] Clarke and Ferrar, *The Dublin Drama League, 1919–1941*, p. 29.

Like *Cathleen ni Houlihan*, *The Ghost Sonata* also deals with the subject of vampirism. The Old Man Hummel exercises the same power over the student Arkenholz as that exercised by Cathleen over Michael Gillane in Yeats's play. The main difference lies in the fact that the student is conscious that he has been chosen as a 'medium' in *The Ghost Sonata* and that he tries to resist the Old Man's control. The vampiric undertone of Cathleen's line, 'many that are red-cheeked will now be pale-cheeked', finds a sharp echo in the student's response to the old man's declaration that their destinies were wedded: 'Let go of my hand, you're draining my strength, you're freezing me.'[71] Like *Cathleen ni Houlihan*, a discreet connection is drawn between vampiric power and the power of commerce in *The Ghost Sonata*; the Old Man exercises his influence over the student because Arkenholz's father was financially indebted to Hummel. The pattern of Yeats's early plays is repeated but in a more intentionally disorientating theatrical form. Drawing on Scandinavian folk customs and Swedenborg's mysticism, the supernatural elements in *The Ghost Sonata* are invested with a fetishistic quality reflecting the stagnation into which the household depicted has sunk.

This relationship between the fetishistic aspect of supernatural power and the material circumstances into which it enters is most concentrated in the figure of the Colonel's wife, described by the footman as a mummy. She certainly appears a vampire, locking herself in a cupboard because she cannot endure daylight. The complex relation of Strindberg to Ibsen is evident in the influence of *A Doll's House* on Strindberg's invention of this character. In one sense she is an extreme outcome of that social subordination of women within marriage that Ibsen attacked. She speaks like a baby and a parrot, responding in parrot-like fashion to the footman's command to whistle, calling her 'Pretty Poll'.[72] The echo of Helmer at the opening of *A Doll's House* is palpable here, repeatedly calling Nora his 'pretty little pet' and 'pretty little song-bird'.[73] In its treatment of this character, *The Ghost Sonata* develops further that pattern in 1890s Symbolism of subsuming the social criticism of Ibsen into a vision of human beings in a state of spiritual crisis. Engaging Ibsen's concern at the infantilisation of women within marriage as instruments of property, a criticism bearing the influence of Marx's attack on marriage in *The Communist Manifesto*, *The Ghost Sonata* incorporates this into a drama of estrangement through its preoccupation with the supernatural.[74]

[71] Strindberg, *The Ghost Sonata*, p. 165.   [72] *Ibid.*, p. 172.
[73] Henrik Ibsen, *A Doll's House, Four Major Plays*, trans. James McFarlane and Jens Arup (Oxford University Press, 1981), pp. 4–5.
[74] See Marx and Engels, *The Communist Manifesto* (London: George Allen & Unwin, 1948), p. 141.

Yeats's treatment of Mary Bruin in *The Land of Heart's Desire* is significant here in mediating the social criticism of Ibsen and the Expressionism of Strindberg. Setting her desire for spiritual and imaginative vitality against the responsibilities of her new role as wife, the play takes up Ibsen's criticism of marriage. Daring to behave as she does, Mary is denounced by her mother-in-law as a 'good-for-nothing wife'. Significantly, Shaw would take up this phrase in Larry Doyle's denunciation of the Irish temperament at the start of *John Bull's Other Island*, no doubt remembering the performance of Yeats's play in 1894 along with his own *Arms and the Man*.[75] However, by expressing this vitality through the dance of the Fairy Child, Yeats reverses the argument of *A Doll's House*; Mary realises her freedom from marital constraint not through breaking out of childhood but in returning to it. Ibsen himself moved in a similar direction in *The Wild Duck*, a play in which the death of the young girl Hedvig parallels that of Mary at the end of Yeats's play, Winifred Fraser having played both roles in 1894. Furthermore, Mary achieves her freedom through learning, but not of a modern kind. Like Sarah in *Axël*, her vague longings find their expression through her discovery of ancient books of legend and magic. In so doing, Yeats and Villiers de l'Isle Adam engaged the debate on educational reform Ibsen's plays had encouraged, but challenged the belief that such reform should be exclusively scientific in nature. The same idea was taken up in Frank Wedekind's hugely controversial play of 1891, *Spring Awakening*, an attack on the prevailing educational norms in the Germany of his day. Like Mary Bruin, the adolescent Melchior takes to reading an ancient tale, in his case the legend of Faust, leading eventually to his derangement and the suicide of his friend Moritz.[76]

Mary's submission to the lure of the Fairy Child, then, did not simply infantilise native Irish culture as Kiberd suggests, but challenged the terms upon which any project of social reform might be founded. Crucial here is the fact that Mary's refusal of household duties is the pretext to her becoming a medium through which the Fairy Child appears on stage, for this points to the crisis in the structure of value informing the play. A strong echo of Ibsen's Nora, this not only testifies the lure of folk legend, but engages it in protest against what Baudrillard describes in more recent times as the moral fanaticism of housework.[77] Likewise, Cathleen enters as Bridget is preparing the house for the arrival of bride-to-be Delia in

---

[75] Yeats, *The Land of Heart's Desire: Manuscript Materials*, p. 29; George Bernard Shaw, *John Bull's Other Island*, 2nd edn (London: Penguin, 1984), p. 81.
[76] Frank Wedekind, *Spring Awakening*, trans. Edward Bond (London: Methuen, 1980), pp. 19–20.
[77] Baudrillard, *For a Critique*, p. 45.

Cathleen ni Houlihan, her intervention rendering Bridget's labour redundant (*VPl*, 218). In later versions of *The Countess Cathleen*, the opening scene has Mary, the mother in the starving household, grinding a quern (*VPl*, 5). The tapestries that adorn the hall in the house of the Countess allude to a contrasting form of labour, the arts and crafts movement that Morris inaugurated at the end of the 1880s. Yeats's sister Lily began studying embroidery under Morris's sister May soon after Yeats himself began attending Morris's Sunday nights in 1887.[78] In their treatment of work, the influence of Morris is most clear in these early plays, in particular the argument put forward in one of Morris's most popular essays, 'Useful Work versus Useless Toil', first published as a Socialist League pamphlet in 1885. Condemning the appalling conditions of factory production in England at this time, Morris declared that, rather than work relentlessly like slaves, it would be better if labourers simply refused to continue, lie down and die, or be packed off to a workhouse. He contrasted this with an alternative vision of labour that inspired his vision of an arts and crafts industry: work that would be productive but also provide space for rest and pleasure in labour itself.[79]

The opposition between household work and the imaginative, supernatural elements in Yeats's early plays bears the distinction Morris drew between 'useful work' and 'useless toil'. It is not true to say that Mary is idle at the start of *The Land Heart's Desire*; rather, her labour has no object, it is its own desire. This contrasts with her mother-in-law Bridget, enslaved by economic necessity. Mary reading folk tales may sit at odds with Morris's utopian idea of pleasurable labour in producing nothing practical, but this is more a comment upon the servitude of the labour-form presented to her rather than a judgement on indolence. Rejecting the demeaning banality of scraping and saving, she indulges instead her heart's desire and, in consequence, prepares her own death. Thus she quite literally follows Morris's advice on choosing death over slavery, a decision that would have more dramatic consequences when the argument of *The Land of Heart's Desire* was directed towards Irish political history in *Cathleen ni Houlihan*. Yeats saw the first as 'the call of the heart', the second 'the call of country'.[80]

Morris's theory of labour was indebted to Marx's belief that human freedom was dependent on the conditions under which human beings

---

[78] See W. B. Yeats, 'An Exhibition at William Morris's', *Providence Sunday Journal* (1890), *Uncollected Prose by W. B. Yeats*, vol. I, p. 182, and John Kelly, *Chronology*, p. 10.
[79] Morris, 'Useful Work versus Useless Toil', *Political Writings*, p. 87.
[80] W. B. Yeats, 'Interview', *The United Irishman*, 7:162 (1902), 5.

sustained themselves through material production. Morag Shiach argues that Morris departed from Marx in denying any potential for the abject working conditions of industrial England to have a positive effect in generating a radical proletarian consciousness; instead, Morris saw freedom only 'in the renunciation of the material conditions and social relations that sustained modern labour'.[81] This seems borne out in the medieval quality of Morris's utopian and imaginative writings, suggesting escape rather than transformation of prevailing social conditions. However, Morris's treatment of time in *The Well at the World's End* and *News from Nowhere* develops an important aspect of Marx's own theory of labour, and shows its influence on Yeats's early drama. This concerns the relation of work to time in Marx's theory of value. Believing that all forms of economics were ultimately 'an economics of time', he argued that the exchange-value of commodities was simply a measure of the units of labour-time required to produce them. Marx described these units as 'congealed quantities of homogeneous human labour' that carried a 'phantom-like objectivity' in the form of material goods with measurable commercial value.[82]

Considered against this theory of labour, mediated through the influence of Morris, the supernatural presences in *The Land of Heart's Desire*, *The Countess Cathleen* and *Cathleen ni Houlihan* display the illusionary nature of the commodity's material objectivity in circumstances where the forms of labour are demeaning and dehumanising. This is most obvious in the Demon Merchants of *The Countess Cathleen*, embodiments of a distortion of human relations effected through the money they dispense, 'phantom-like' figures who yet seek to reduce the spiritual to the material. But we can also regard the Fairy Child of *The Land of Heart's Desire* and the Old Woman of *Cathleen ni Houlihan* in this way, their sinister undercurrent providing a discreet signal of the dehumanising nature of material production in the situations into which they enter. The uncanny effect they were intended to create derived in large measure from their disturbance of a contemporary sense of time as dull repetition. Confounding a linear temporality in different ways, the Fairy Child, Demon Merchants and Old Woman prepare the way for the radical experiments with temporal consciousness Yeats would develop in his later drama. This was intimately connected to the challenge they posed to the continuation of

---

[81] Morag Shiach, *Modernism, Labour and Selfhood in British Literature and Culture, 1890–1930* (Cambridge University Press, 2004), pp. 43–4.

[82] Karl Marx, *Selected Writings*, ed. David McLellan (Oxford University Press, 1977), p. 362. Marx *Capital*, vol. 1, p. 128. See also *Theories of Surplus Value* in *Selected Writings*, pp. 399–409.

servile labour, making present a pre-industrial sense of time against the dullness of life as experienced by what Barbara Suess terms 'the bourgeois peasant' in Yeats's early drama.[83] The effect was to register the distortions of temporal consciousness consequent upon the emergence of labour-time as the measure of economic value in modern industrial society.

Observing the function of time within the process of commodification that Marx described, György Lukács recognised a process in which, through its abstraction as the form 'labour-time', time itself had become commodified, reduced to the category of space, losing its 'qualitative, variable, flowing nature' and frozen 'into an exactly delimited, quantifiable continuum filled with quantifiable "things"'.[84] Choosing to indulge her imagination rather than fulfil her role as housewife, Mary allows a new temporal dynamism embodied in the dance of the Fairy Child. Presenting her in this way, Yeats drew on Celtic ideas of festive *ecstasis* as a mode of representing and resisting the quantification of time that Lukács describes. *The Land of Heart's Desire* is set on the eve of May, the occasion of the Celtic festival of Bealtaine. The cheering crowds at the start of *Cathleen ni Houlihan* also suggest a festive occasion, but here it acquires a very specific political resonance, the period of rebellion in the west of Ireland occasioned by the arrival of French troops at Killala Bay in support of the United Irishmen in 1798. Both the Fairy Child and the figure of Ireland as the Old Woman suggest a temporality of eternal recurrence through which they connect to the occasion of festival, but an eternal recurrence that ruptures the continuity of daily life. Both households in *The Land of Heart's Desire* and *Cathleen ni Houlihan* are left ruined at the end. This temporal paradox of repetition-in-rupture illustrates the way these plays conformed to Yeats's view of Symbolist drama; a move beyond the revolution of Naturalism through a recuperation of pre-scientific custom in preparation of a new social consciousness.

Yeats's early drama conjured a quality of estrangement that was unsettling in its time, fully engaged with the radical changes visited upon European theatre with the advent of Naturalism and Symbolism. Concentrating on the destruction visited upon individual families in *The Land of Heart's Desire*, *The Countess Cathleen* and *Cathleen ni Houlihan*, he transposed a modern nuclear family structure to rural Irish settings. In so doing, he was not only proposing Irish society as a fitting subject

---

[83] Barbara A. Suess, *Progress and Identity in the Plays of W. B. Yeats, 1892–1907* (London: Routledge Press, 2003), pp. 57–63.

[84] György Lukács, *History and Class Consciousness*, trans. Rodney Livingstone (London: Merlin Press, 1971), p. 90.

for 'serious' theatre, but also directing Ibsen's criticism of bourgeois culture away from urban locations. The purpose here was to draw on folk custom and belief as a way of articulating the alienating effect of those social conditions of urban society Morris criticised in his various essays and pamphlets of the 1880s. In the process, Yeats engaged the discourse of primitivism in a manner that disturbed some in Ireland with connotations of racial backwardness. As the intimacy between *The Land of Heart's Desire* and Maeterlinck's *The Intruder* shows, however, primitivist motifs proved effective in delineating the psychic pressures engendered through the historical process of modernisation in European culture. In this way, the themes of these early plays participated in a larger response to this process in the work of Marx and Freud, particularly in relation to their ideas of fetishism, exchange, alienation and *unheimlich*. The following chapter considers the ways in which Yeats's vision of the stage developed during the 1900s in probing further the experience of modern society and culture as alienating. It addresses the manner in which *The King's Threshold* and *Deirdre* inscribed and critiqued forms of power through experiments with theatrical space, considering what kind of political perspective informed these experiments.

CHAPTER 2

Space, power, protest: The King's Threshold *and* Deirdre

On the same date as Yeats's forty-first birthday, 13 June 1906, an incident took place in the Egyptian village of Denshawai that led to the hanging of several natives following the death of a soldier in the local British Army garrison. In September 1907, following the publication of an official government report on the incident, Yeats, upon George Bernard Shaw's prompting, co-signed a letter with Lady Gregory to the Secretary of State for Foreign Affairs in protest at the British military response. The report revealed that the initial impression of a politically motivated assault on the garrison had no foundation. The letter warned of the unfavourable impression of the British Administration in Egypt that the event and its aftermath was creating not only in England but also in Ireland, no doubt a discreet allusion to the effect the Boer War had in winning many over to the cause of Irish nationalism, George Moore included.[1] Shaw denounced the hypocrisy of the British government in its handling of the affair in his 'Preface for Politicians' included in the 1906 edition of *John Bull's Other Island*.[2] Ancient Egyptian civilisation was immensely important to the circles in which Yeats had been moving since the 1880s, particularly that of the Egyptological mage MacGregor Mathers in Paris. Yeats attended *The Beloved of Hathor* with Shaw at Victoria Hall, London in November 1901, a performance inaugurating the Egypt Society and revived in January 1902 with *The Shrine of the Golden Hawk*, in which Florence Farr played.[3] With the publication of T. W. Rolleston's *Myths and Legends of the Celtic Races* in 1911, the case for the shared origins of Gaelic and Egyptian civilisation came into the public domain.

Yeats's contribution to formal protests at the Denshawai affair challenges Spurgeon Thompson's argument that his nationalism in the 1900s was

---

[1] John Kelly and Ronald Schuchard, eds., *The Collected Letters of W. B. Yeats*, vol. IV, 1905–07 (Oxford University Press, 2005), pp. 722–5.
[2] Shaw, *John Bull's Other Island*, pp. 39–50.
[3] Kelly and Schuchard, *Collected Letters*, vol. III, p. 121.

'quite plainly the nationalism of a plantation class that lost its power to be colonial and wants it back', strengthening the case Edward Said has made for Yeats as a pioneer anti-colonial author.[4] This chapter examines the politics of Yeats's drama in the 1900s in relation to the continuing influence of Ibsen and Maeterlinck, and the new impact of Nietzsche's writing on his work in the theatre. The influence of these figures on Yeats's experiments with stage space, undertaken in collaboration with Edward Gordon Craig, is examined here in terms of Yeats's developing sense of modern social and spiritual alienation. *The King's Threshold* and *Deirdre* are considered in this regard as treatments of the relation of the artist to society at a moment in which the regulative authority of the state was become all-encompassing.[5]

Maeterlinck's plays shaped profoundly the experiments with space that Yeats undertook in the 1900s and developed in a radical fashion from 1910, when he began using Craig's screens in performance. His influence marks a point of contact between these experiments and Yeats's protest over the Denshawai affair, for Maeterlinck's own experiments derived in part from his admiration of Egyptian mysticism. At the outset of *The Treasure of the Humble*, he envisages a future in which souls might communicate with one another without the intermediary of the senses. Contemporary knowledge of ancient Egypt led him to suggest that the country had passed through an epoch when this had become reality.[6] Many years later, in a book taking its title from Yeats's play *The Hour-Glass*, he wrote of space and time as unique abstractions, describing them as 'not lifeless abstractions from their birth, but rather living and moving abstractions, or abstractions within which everything is in motion, and which represent the beginning of something that we are capable of beginning to understand'.[7] The influence of Maeterlinck's treatment of

---

[4] Spurgeon Thompson, 'Yeats and Eugenicism: The Garrison Mentality in a Decolonizing Ireland', *W. B. Yeats and Postcolonialism*, ed. Deborah Fleming (West Cornwall, CT: Locust Hill Press, 2001), p 41. Edward Said, 'Yeats and Decolonization', *Culture and Imperialism* (London: Vintage, 1994), pp. 265–87.

[5] Maneck Daruwala argues that both plays can be read as companion pieces, *The King's Threshold* showing the material defeat of poetry and *Deirdre*, the defeat of love. 'Yeats and the Mask of *Deirdre*: "That love is all we need" ', *Colby Quarterly*, 37:3 (2001), 247. Richard Ellmann has traced both plays back to Gonne's marriage to McBride in 1903, Yeats's guilt at having separated himself from the 'normal, active man'. *Yeats: The Man and the Masks* (London: Faber, 1961), p. 169.

[6] Maeterlinck, *The Treasure*, p. 27.

[7] Maeterlinck, *The Hour-Glass*, trans. Bernard Miall (New York: Frederick A. Stokes, 1936), p. 54. The influence of Kant's thought also comes through here, wherein space and time were identified uniquely as synthetic a priori propositions, the formal conditions for the intuition of internal (time) and external (space) appearances. *Critique of Pure Reason*, 2nd edn, ed. Vasilis Politis (London: Everyman, 1993), p. 50. Yeats praised Kant in later years, distinguishing him from British empiricism. See *Pages from a Diary in Nineteen Hundred and Thirty* (Dublin: Cuala Press, 1944), pp. 49–50.

theatrical space on Yeats's experiments in the 1900s is indicated by the fact that a revival of *Deirdre* and *The King's Threshold* in April 1907 was immediately preceded by a production of *The Interior*, the first foreign play to be staged at the Abbey, on 16 March 1907.[8]

Yeats's desire to extricate art from political rancour in Ireland suggests a conservative and aristocratic bent to this fascination with Egypt and the theatrical experiments with space it motivated. This has to be evaluated in its historical context, however, and the kinds of pressure he faced in Dublin and London. Attacking the opening night's performances of *The King's Threshold* and Synge's *In the Shadow of the Glen* at Dublin's Molesworth Hall in December 1903, Maud Gonne decried the play's 'private' non-political nature, representing a foreign English influence.[9] Yeats's response was biting in the last of three articles published in *The United Irishman* in October 1903, 'The Irish National Theatre and Three Sorts of Ignorance', in which he singled out for criticism 'the more ignorant sort of Gaelic propagandist', along with 'the more ignorant sort of priest', in addition to 'the obscurantism of the politician and not always of the more ignorant sort'.[10] Whatever the private feelings motivating this riposte, it encouraged the view of *The King's Threshold* as a claim for the priority of poetry over politics. Max Beerbohm felt that the play's chief protagonist, the poet Seanchan, was the figure of Yeats himself demanding to be taken seriously in circumstances of political rancour.[11]

Yeats's response to the criticism of the opening night's performance, predominantly aimed at Synge's *In the Shadow of the Glen*, derived in significant measure from his new admiration of Ibsen, the Norwegian theatre movement from which he emerged, and Ibsen's courage in

---

[8] Hunt, *The Abbey*, p. 71.
[9] Gonne criticised the creeping influences of 'foreign thoughts and philosophies' distorting Gaelic heroes and heroines to a point where Irish people no longer recognise them. She objected that the distinction Yeats drew between private and public life in *The King's Threshold* did not obtain in Ireland as it did in England 'where factories have eaten up the intellects of the people'. Maud Gonne McBride, 'A National Theatre', *The United Irishman*, 10:243 (1903), 5.
[10] W. B. Yeats, 'The Irish National Theatre and Three Sorts of Ignorance', *Uncollected Prose by W. B. Yeats*, vol. II ed. John P. Frayne (London: Macmillan, 1975) p. 307.
[11] Max Beerbohm, 'The Irish Players', *W. B. Yeats: The Critical Heritage*, ed. Norman Jeffares (London: Routledge, 1977), pp. 144–5. See also Foster, *W. B. Yeats, A Life: Apprentice Mage*, vol. I (Oxford University Press, 1998), p. 295. Suheil Bushrui describes how the play embodied Yeats's belief in the heroism of poetry, the hero requiring the stuff of poetry. 'Yeats: The Poet as Hero', *Essays & Studies: The Poet's Power* (London: Murray, 1982), p. 105. Phillip Edwards sees in the play a warning of how poetry can be destroyed by politics, while Miki Iwata suggests that Seanchan seems to take poetry for an ideal form of politics. See *Threshold of a Nation* (Cambridge University Press, 1979), pp. 5–7, and 'Between Art and Life: W. B. Yeats's Cultural Dilemma in *The King's Threshold*', *Shiron*, 37:6 (1998), 57.

confronting a growing consensus of middle-class interests shaping public opinion through the press, acting in a fluctuating but crucial relation with the Lutheran Church and the Norwegian state. Yeats's willingness to champion Synge as the Irish Ibsen, while presenting his own drama of estrangement in the 1900s as consonant with Ibsen's later drama of protest, testifies the fruition of that conviction evident in his drama of the 1890s; Symbolism not as the neutralisation but the extension of the revolutionary element in Naturalist drama. Addressing in August 1900 D. P. Moran's contention that political nationalism in Ireland was destitute in its lack of a distinctive cultural foundation, Yeats looked to Norway as a model of 'intellectual and cultural nationalism' for an alternative way forward.[12] Responding in the pages of Arthur Griffith's *The United Irishman* to the enthusiasm with which *Cathleen ni Houlihan* was greeted in 1902, he again drew comparison with the movement that had produced Ibsen:

> The Norwegian drama, the most important in modern Europe, began at a semi amateur theatre in Bergen, and I cannot see any reason in the nature of things why Mr Fay's company should not do for Ireland what the little theatre of Bergen did for Europe.[13]

Presenting the success of *Cathleen ni Houlihan* in this way, Yeats was not only setting Irish cultural nationalism in a European context, but was also laying down a mode of interpretation by which audiences could read modern experimental literature as a decisive contribution to an awakened national consciousness.

The 1903 performances of *The King's Threshold* and *In the Shadow of Glen* were to test the fault lines of this endeavour. In undertaking it, Yeats was drawn to one Ibsen play in particular, *An Enemy of the People* (1882). Presenting the story of Dr Stockmann, how he and his family are driven from their community upon his disclosure that local health spa waters were being polluted, Ibsen wrote this play in furious anger at the widespread denunciation of *Ghosts* in the Norwegian liberal press in 1881. In a letter to *The United Irishman* of December 1901, Yeats cited *An Enemy of the People* in support of literature as 'the principal voice of conscience'.[14]

---

[12] To the editor of *The Leader*, 26 August [1900]. Frayne and Johnson, *Collected Letters*, vol. II, p. 562.
[13] W. B. Yeats, 'Interview', *The United Irishman*, 7:163 (1902), 5. Yeats wrote excitedly to Henry Newbolt some days earlier of a man who came to him with a play written in the manner of Ibsen after having witnessed the performance of *Cathleen ni Houlihan*: 'Something I think must come out [of] all this energy & delight in high things.' To Henry Newbolt, 5 April [1902], Kelly and Schuchard, *Collected Letters*, vol. III, p. 648.
[14] *The United Irishman*, 7 December 1901. Kelly and Schuchard, *Collected Letters*, vol. III, p. 132.

Florence Farr would play the role of Mrs Stockmann in Herbet Tree's production of the play at His Majesty's Theatre in January 1906 before joining Yeats on his lecture tour on 'Literature and the Living Voice'.[15] *An Enemy of the People* would have carried strong resonance for several reasons, but perhaps most of all for its representation of the power of the press in modern society as a spiritual sickness, manifested in the pollution of the springs. Addressing an assembly of the townspeople, Stockmann's words articulate the anger that Yeats himself would vent against different interest groups in Irish public life in later years:

> I have said I would speak of the great discovery I have made with the last few days – the discovery that all our sources of spiritual life are poisoned, and that our whole society rests upon a pestilential basis of falsehood.[16]

In September 1904, William Archer, who, along with Edmund Gosse, was chiefly responsible in bringing Ibsen to the notice of English theatre-goers, sent Yeats a copy of *An Enemy of the People*. Yeats was particularly taken by a letter reprinted in the preface to Archer's edition of the play, a 1901 translation by Eleanor Marx Aveling.[17] Writing to his friend George Brandes, Ibsen bemoaned the poor quality of public debate in Norway, expressing views remarkably prescient of Yeats after 1900. He denounced the attitude of the 'so-called Liberal press' to *Ghosts*, holding that 'that man is in the right who is most closely in league with the future'. He complained of the 'slow and heavy and dull' nature of the general intelligence in Norway, the dominance of the press and the crudity of public debate: 'The very praiseworthy attempt to make of our people a democratic community has inadvertently gone a good way towards making us a plebeian community.'[18] Yeats's spirited defence of *The King's Threshold* and *The Shadow of the Glen* in 'The Theatre, the Pulpit and the Newspapers' – against the objections of Arthur Griffith, Maud Gonne and James Connolly – was at one with Ibsen's sentiments here.[19]

This change in attitude to Ibsen derived in large measure from an essay on Scandinavian drama by C. H. Herford, professor of English Literature

---

[15] See Ronald Schuchard, *The Last Minstrels: Yeats and the Revival of the Bardic Arts* (Oxford University Press, 2008), p. 203.
[16] Henrik Ibsen, *An Enemy of the People*, *The Collected Works of Henrik Ibsen*, vol. VIII, ed. William Archer (London: William Heinemann, 1907), p. 129.
[17] Yeats to William Archer, 25 September 1904. Kelly and Schuchard, *Collected Letters*, vol. III, p. 648.
[18] Henrik Ibsen to Georg Brandes, 3 January 1882. *Letters of Henrik Ibsen*, trans. John Nilsen Laurvik and Mary Morison, 1908 (Honolulu: University Press of the Pacific, 2002), p. 351.
[19] W. B. Yeats, 'The Theatre, the Pulpit, and the Newspapers', *The United Irishman*, 10:242 (1903), 2.

at Manchester University, published in the first issue of *Beltaine*, journal of the new Irish National Theatre Society, in May 1899. Coinciding with the first Dublin performance of *The Countess Cathleen*, the essay was compelling for Yeats in comparing the mythological inheritance of the modern Scandinavian to that of the Celt, and in placing Ibsen firmly within a movement for Norwegian national revival. But Herford also illustrated the path through which a movement for political freedom developed into a quest for artistic freedom, a quest that necessitated Ibsen's break from the certitudes of the Norwegian cultural revival before 1860, at which point the Norwegian theatre had achieved its complete independence from the Danish theatre.[20] By this account, Ibsen's later career was an extension of an original radical energy driving Norway's quest for cultural independence, demanding a new public consciousness receptive to the artistic transformation of prevailing values. Herford's essay thus presented Yeats with a model for the development of his own career in the theatre subsequently; absorbing the energies of a movement for national revival into a new vision of theatre that drew upon the residues of myth and folklore fuelling the original project. Just as Shakespeare had passed, as Herford observed, from the history plays of *Richard II* and *Henry V*, so Ibsen moved from the *Warriors of Helgeland* to *An Enemy of the People*. Likewise, Yeats would move from folk naturalism of his early plays to the iconoclastic forms of *The Herne's Egg* and *Purgatory*.[21]

Yeats's renewed interest in Ibsen's social criticism is the point of departure for understanding the political attitudes behind the 1903 performance of *The King's Threshold*. Most critics agree that the play's structure and theme demanded a tragic ending in which the hunger-striking poet dies; most believe that Yeats was influenced by Gregory in deciding not to conclude the play in this manner in versions written and performed during the 1900s.[22] Free for over twelve years from the pressures of Annie Horniman's patronage of the Abbey Theatre and long past all collaborative theatrical enterprises with Gregory, Yeats's

---

[20] C. H. Herford, 'The Scandinavian Dramatists', *Beltaine*, 1 (1899), 13–18.
[21] *Ibid.*, p. 18.
[22] Brown, *The Life of W. B. Yeats*, p. 138. James Flannery, *W. B. Yeats and the Idea of a Theatre* (London: Macmillan Press, 1976), pp. 307–8. Richard Allen Cave, 'Staging *The King's Threshold*', *Yeats Annual*, 13, ed. Warwick Gould (London: Macmillan, 1998), pp. 161–2. Declan Kiely's brilliant scholarly edition of the manuscript drafts of the play confirms Gregory's influence. *The King's Threshold: Manuscript Materials* (New York: Cornell University Press, 2003). Ure observes that nothing in early versions of the play suggested a happy ending. *Yeats the Playwright: A Commentary on Character and Design in the Major Plays* (London: Routledge and Kegan Paul, 1963), p. 37.

1921 version of *The King's Threshold* realised the play's full dramatic vision in a way not possible in the context of the 1900s. This raises the difficult question of the nature of collaboration and reciprocal influence between Yeats and Gregory, suggesting that this was not always as fruitful as the success of *Cathleen ni Houlihan* attested.[23] But if the 1921 version was a greater artistic achievement, it also made the play explicitly political. Motivated by a desire to sustain communication lines between Protestant Ascendancy culture and Catholic nationalism, Gregory was clearly aware of the dangers in the image of Seanchan starving to death on stage in 1903 before an indifferent king.[24] Subsequent history would prove her right, as shown by the impossibility of Yeats retaining the original ending in the aftermath of Terence MacSwiney's hunger-strike in 1920. It is one of the small ironies of modern Irish cultural history that in 1903 Arthur Griffith, founder of *Sinn Féin* two years later, thought the hunger-striking Seanchan was lazy in *The King's Threshold* and ought to have been executed.[25] In the circumstances of 1921, Irish Republicans would have regarded this as treachery.

Phillip Marcus observes that the 1921 ending of *The King's Threshold* – like *Cathleen ni Houlihan* decades earlier – threatened to blur into a political allegory of diehard Republicans resisting moderate nationalism and the 'British presence' following the death of MacSwiney. Over sixty years later, Provisional IRA hunger-striker Bobby Sands would draw on Yeats's play as a source of inspiration.[26] R. F. Foster observes that the deteriorating military conflict in the country – MacSwiney's death, daily Black-and-Tan atrocities, IRA ambushes – motivated him to 'take a Sinn Féin line about events in Ireland', revising the ending of *The King's Threshold* and finally publishing 'Easter 1916', which appeared on

---

[23] In a letter to W.J. Lawrence written sometime in 1912, William Fay claimed that Synge had once written to him that a Yeats–Gregory theatre would be of use to nobody. Fay's claim that he burnt this letter on Synge's instruction and a further letter to Lawrence that year in which Fay complained bitterly of the 'Gregoryization of the theatre' indicate the bitter resentment Yeats's relation to Gregory generated. NLI ms. 10952(2).
[24] On Gregory's conciliatory aspirations see Robert Welch, 'Lady Gregory: A Language for Healing', *Lady Gregory, Fifty Years After*, ed. Ann Saddlemyer and Colin Smythe (Gerrards Cross: Colin Smythe, 1987), pp. 258–73.
[25] Arthur Griffith, 'Review', *The United Irishman*, 10: 242 (1903), p. 1.
[26] The figure of Seanchan comes through in the voice of the ballad, 'The Crime of Castlereagh', performed in the Maze prison by Republican prisoners in the late 1970s, a work that also bears striking similarity to Wilde's 'The Ballad of Reading Gaol'. Introducing a selection of Sands's writing, Ulick O'Connor draws direct connection between *The King's Threshold*, Terence McSwiney's death by hunger-strike in 1921, and Sands's death in 1981. 'The Crime of Castlereagh', *Skylark Sing Your Lonely Song: An Anthology of the Writings of Bobby Sands* (Dublin: Mercier Press, 1982), pp. 38–58.

23 October 1920.²⁷ However, Marcus's claim that the new version introduced a sombre quality out of keeping with Yeats's 'optimistic' mood at the time of its composition in 1903 is unsustainable when we think of other plays from that decade, *Where There Is Nothing*, *Cathleen ni Houlihan*, *On Baile's Strand* and *Deirdre*, all of which end in death.²⁸

Yeats was no doubt impressed by the excessive character of MacSwiney's protest in 1920: excess was a quality he admired, embodied in characters such as Seanchan, Paul Ruttledge from *Where There is Nothing* and Cuchulain in *On Baile's Strand*. Citing Yeats's calls for excess in his 1897 essay 'The Celtic Element in Literature', Michael Mays notes how this was 'incommensurable with the cash-nexus of modern life'.²⁹ In the extremity of its privation and the very public nature of its insular form, the hunger-strike became one of those 'befitting emblems of adversity' encapsulating the self-absorption of the modernist work of art that represented the alienating condition of modern society in literally eating itself away. This is precisely why Beckett would later include reference to MacSwiney's hunger-strike in *Malone Dies*, the protagonist speculating the length his body might hold up without food.³⁰ By offering *The King's Threshold* as commentary upon the distraught circumstances in the Ireland of 1921, Yeats lent this modernist image of the artwork a specific political edge. Looking ahead to the radical experiments of Beckett's theatre, *The King's Threshold* also carried with it the memory of Ibsen's *An Enemy of the People*, in which society stands on the threshold of revolution.³¹

The provocative nature of *The King's Threshold* in its 1921 context brought to the surface the revolutionary import of the play in its original 1903 version. Developing the preoccupations of Yeats's theatre in the 1890s, the estrangement consequent upon the reduction of people to commercial measurement was addressed in the 1900s through a mythological structure and experiments with theatrical space. Mocking the God of the monk in *The King's Threshold*, Seanchan compares him to a tamed

---

²⁷ Foster, *W. B. Yeats*, vol. II, p. 182. For a severe critical judgement on the timing of Yeats's publication of 'Easter 1916', see Tom Paulin, 'Yeats's Hunger-Strike Poem', *Minotaur: Poetry and the Nation State* (London: Faber, 1992), pp. 133–50.

²⁸ Phillip Marcus, *Yeats and Artistic Power* (London: Macmillan, 1992), p. 97. Peter Ure rightly observes that nothing in the various episodes of the play suggests a happy ending. *Yeats the Playwright*, p. 37.

²⁹ Michael Mays, 'Yeats and the Economics of "Excess"', *Colby Quarterly*, 33:4 (1997), 302.

³⁰ 'That reminds me, how long can one fast with impunity? The Lord Mayor of Cork lasted for ages, but he was young, and then he had political convictions, human ones too probably, just plain human convictions.' Samuel Beckett, *Malone Dies* in *Molloy, Malone Dies, The Unnamable*, 2nd edn (London: Calder Publications, 1994), p. 275.

³¹ Ibsen, *An Enemy*, p. 78.

bird, trained not to disturb the king (*VPl*, 292).³² Tugging derisorily at the monk's habit and pretending to stroke an imagined bird perched upon his hand, Seanchan's gestures carry overtones of marionette theatre and its ritual scolding of authority figures that Alfred Jarry employed in *Ubu Roi* in 1896, a performance Yeats attended with Arthur Symons.³³ In his 1906 play *Deirdre*, the heroine refuses to become as a caged bird, rejecting Naoise's entreaty that she remain silent in the presence of the King's messenger (*VPl*, 364). Like the Demon Merchants of *The Countess Cathleen*, the 'dark-faced' Libyans in this play come from the East. Conjuring an exotic sense of Arabian mysticism, their unsettling presence is likewise intended to suggest the estranging power of commerce. On the periphery of the action, they are almost entirely voiceless; in 1911, Yeats had played with the idea of having them appear only as shadows in front of a blood-red sunset.³⁴ King Conchubar reveals that he had spent seven years in pursuit of Deirdre, 'trafficking with merchants for the stones / That make all sure' (*VPl*, 380).³⁵ Like King Guaire in *The King's Threshold*, Conchubar is caught between feudal and modern value systems. In medieval fashion, he has sought the power of prophecy through these stones. Trading with merchants, however, he symbolises the modern era of commerce and, through the duplicity by which he traps the lovers, the coercive force of the modern state.

The stylised form and poignant tone of the 1906 Abbey Theatre production of *Deirdre* suggests that all questions of politics or ideology, no matter how discreetly hinted, were furthest from Yeats's mind. The arguments over who was to perform the lead role, however, or whether it was even to be staged at the Abbey, illustrated the contest over what this 'high-art' performance might signify. Frank Fay insisted the role should go to Sarah Allgood, strengthening its credentials as a specifically Irish

---

[32] Daniel Albright identifies a forerunner of the golden bird in 'Sailing to Byzantium' here who is 'even more rigid, servile, an objective puppet'. *Myth Against Myth: A Study of Yeats's Imagination in Old Age* (Oxford University Press, 1972), p. 56.

[33] Yeats, 'The Tragic Generation', *Autobiographies*, pp. 203–04. On the marionette form of *Ubu Roi*, see Harold B. Segel, *Pinocchio's Progeny: Puppets, Marionettes, Automatons and Robots in Modernist Avant-garde Drama* (Baltimore, MD: The Johns Hopkins University Press, 1995), pp. 87–92.

[34] W. B. Yeats, 'Note to "Deirdre" ', *Plays for an Irish Theatre* (London: A. H. Bullen, 1911), p. 215. See also, James Flannery 'W. B. Yeats, Gordon Craig and the Visual Arts of the Theatre', *Yeats and the Theatre*, ed. Robert O'Driscoll and Lorna Reynolds (London: Macmillan, 1975), p. 91.

[35] Maneck Daruwala plays down the racial element in the play, including Naoise's reference to 'a dark skin and a Libyan axe', arguing that the 'color contrasts that to Yeats may have been symbols (including alchemical symbols) are to us perhaps too close to the realities of racial and ethnic stereotyping'.'Yeats and the Mask', p. 252.

play and helping to develop acting standards at the Abbey. Yeats rejected this, however, distinguishing *Deirdre* from the 'peasant work' of Gregory and Synge.³⁶ In marked contrast, Annie Horniman, patron of the Abbey, begged him to grant Mrs Patrick Campbell the role and have the play toured in England.³⁷ She regarded his decision to stage *Deirdre* at the Abbey as betrayal, 'a sacrifice on the altar of Fay'.³⁸

Yeats finally chose Florence Darragh for the role, a decision motivated in large measure by Darragh's performance of the lead role in Wilde's *Salomé* in May 1905, as Noreen Doody has noted.³⁹ Yeats was highly critical of the play, however, feeling that Wilde's sense of the stage 'deserted him' when he moved away from comedy.⁴⁰ Nonetheless, his decision to choose Darragh for the role of Deirdre suggests that he saw in her performance of Salomé some of those qualities he was trying to express. The luxuriance of Wilde's oriental exoticism was grossly overstated to Yeats's ears, if we contrast the turgid passages of ornate rhetoric in *Salomé* to the sharp poetic diction of Yeats's play. The tone of both plays is decidedly at odds; *Salomé* is lascivious and decadent, *Deirdre* spartan and poignant. Like Salomé, however, Deirdre is ultimately defiant, choosing death rather than marriage to King Conchubar. Both women have a more developed intuition of destiny than those round them, Wilde and Yeats sharing Maeterlinck's belief that women were more directly swayed by destiny than men.⁴¹ Choosing the head of Iokaanan, Salomé brazenly transgresses religious and sexual taboos in defiance of King Herod.⁴² Indifferent to Fergus's sense of honour and Naoise's concern that she respect their hosts, Deirdre openly declares her belief that King Conchubar's pardon was deception (*VPl*, 358–61).

The 1905 performance of *Salomé* influenced Yeats's *Deirdre* in suggesting an oriental texture for an idea Yeats developed on stage through the course of the 1900s; the estranging power of becoming one's own destiny. One of the finest moments in Yeats's drama from the 1900s is Deirdre's change following the execution of Naoise. A cold solemnity comes over

---

[36] Yeats to Frank Fay, 13 August 1906, Kelly and Schuchard, *Collected Letters*, vol. IV, p. 472.
[37] Richard J. Finneran, George Mills Harper and William M. Murphy, eds., *Letters to W. B. Yeats*, 2 vols. (London: Macmillan Press, 1977), p. 168.
[38] Horniman to Yeats, 26 Sept. 1906. NLI ms. 13068.
[39] Noreen Doody, 'An Echo of Some One Else's Music: The Influence of Oscar Wilde on W. B. Yeats', *The Importance of Reinventing Oscar: Versions of Wilde during the Last 100 Years*, ed. Uive Böker, Richard Corballis and Julie A. Hibbard (Amsterdam: Rodopi, 2002), p. 177.
[40] Yeats to John Quinn, [29] May 1905. Kelly and Schuchard, *Collected Letters*, vol. IV, p. 103.
[41] Maeterlinck, *The Treasure*, pp. 83–4.
[42] Oscar Wilde, *Salomé*, *The Complete Plays* (London: Methuen, 1988), pp. 379–414.

her, in which she is most fully herself. To the king's surprise that she has not become hysterical, she responds that 'being myself / It is enough that you were master here' (*VPl*, 384). While this composure allows her access to Naoise's dead body that she would have been denied otherwise, it is more than mere pretence. In the statuesque mode, Deirdre becomes her own performance, ultimate synthesis of the performative elements unifying the play. This recurrent theme of becoming oneself in Yeats's drama of the 1900s is usually attributed to the influence of Friederich Nietzsche after John Quinn had presented Yeats with three volumes of his work in early 1903. Arthur Symons's essay on Nietzsche in *The Academy and Literature* the previous year prepared Yeats for the reception of Quinn's gift.[43] The influence of *The Birth of Tragedy out of the Spirit of Music* is particularly marked in Yeats's inclusion of the musicians in *Deirdre*. Nietzsche's enthusiasm for Schiller's idea of the Greek chorus as the expression of primordial suffering is given sharp expression through the musicians in *Deirdre*, whose chanting intensifies the poignancy of the lovers destined to consummate their passion in death.[44]

Becoming one's destiny was a notion Yeats encountered much earlier than his reading of Nietzsche however. Furthermore, it was an idea put forward in the context of a general argument for the kind of socialism Yeats encountered in Morris (Yeats first regarded Nietzsche himself as a Morrisite socialist).[45] This was Wilde's essay 'The Soul of Man under Socialism', published in February 1891 in Frank Harris's *Fortnightly Review*. Yeats would certainly have read the essay, given that he was still attending Morris's socialist meetings in 1891. It appears hugely influenced by Morris and, in rejecting authoritarian state socialism, anticipates Yeats's opposition to doctrinaire Marxism following the Russian Revolution decades

---

[43] Symons, 'Nietzsche on Tragedy', *The Academy and Literature*, London, 30 August 1902. Symons's essay on Wagner that year was another important motive in Yeats's turn to Nietzsche. See 'The New Bayreuth', *The Academy and Literature*, London, 27 September 1902, pp. 311–12. For further discussion of Nietzsche's influence, see Malcolm Humble, 'German Contacts in the Lives and Works of W. B. Yeats and D. H. Lawrence, with special reference to Friedrich Nietzsche', unpublished PhD thesis, Cambridge University (1969); Karen Dorn, *Players and Painted Stage: The Theatre of W. B. Yeats* (Brighton: Harvester, 1984), p. 15; Foster, *W. B. Yeats*, vol. I, pp. 159, 213; Brown, *The Life of W. B. Yeats*, p. 150.

[44] Friedrich Nietzsche, *The Birth of Tragedy out of the Spirit of Music*, ed. Michael Tanner, trans. Shaun Whiteside (London: Penguin Press, 2003), pp. 29–30, 38. Yeats drew attention to these ideas in letters to George Russell and John Quinn in May 1903. Kelly and Schuchard, *Collected Letters*, vol. III, pp. 369–70, 372–5. They inspired him to reformulate earlier themes in his publication *Ideas of Good and Evil*.

[45] Yeats wrote to Quinn of Nietzsche as a moderniser of Blake; apart from odd comments, he found nothing 'incompatible with the kind of socialism I learned from William Morris'. Yeats to John Quinn, 6 February 1903. Kelly and Schuchard, *Collected Letters* vol. III, p. 313.

later, considered in Chapter 6 of this volume.[46] Wilde argued that the central value of socialism lay in creating conditions through which individuals would achieve their perfection in becoming themselves. He saw Jesus as the ultimate historical example of this individualism, replacing Socrates's dictum, 'Know Thyself' with 'Be Thyself'.[47] Wilde proposed that because he made no attempt to overturn the prevailing social order, Jesus could only realise himself in pain and solitude.[48] In light of the essay, Yeats's interest in *Salomé* when composing the 1906 version of *Deirdre* appears more than aesthetic. Representing *Deirdre* as a woman who fully realises her perfection in becoming her performance, she is the type of Wilde's artist, the figure closest to the fully realised individual.[49] She stands as an image of human society free from what Morris saw as the essential ugliness of commerce, the coercive restraints of middle-class proprieties, and the slavery of the working classes in factory production.

This social vision lay behind the experiments with theatrical space that Yeats began to develop in *The King's Threshold* and *Deirdre*. Positioning Seanchan on the steps between the entrance to the court and the space in which his students are gathered, Yeats intended the meaning of *The King's Threshold* to be entirely spatial – would King Guaire descend to the level of Seanchan, would the poet ascend to the level of the king? In this way, the play is not so much a representation as an enactment of power, realising its meaning only in performance. Likewise, by suspending the climactic moment of the lovers' deaths through a game of chess, *Deirdre* itself is shown as a game.[50] The notes for a Celtic Order of Mysteries that Yeats drew up in 1899 show how he saw in the origins of chess a set of mystical beliefs expressed through spatial form. One of the proposed rites, 'The Evocation of the Cromlecs', was preceded by the following reflection on the embodiment of the four primary elements – earth, air, fire, water – in the quadratic structure of the chessboard:

The chess board was undoubtedly of quite mystical importance in ancient times in attribution to certain cromlecs ... Each square on the chessboard represents a cromlec seen as from above and all the uppermost stones of the cromlec, or the chessboard, when it is attributed to the city of fire are red or red yellow, when the city of air a blue green, when of water, violet or saffron, and when of the

---

[46] Oscar Wilde, 'The Soul of Man under Socialism', *The Complete Works of Oscar Wilde*, vol. IV, ed. Josephine M. Guy (Oxford University Press, 2007), p. 233.
[47] *Ibid.*, p. 240.   [48] *Ibid.*, p. 265.   [49] *Ibid.*, pp. 248–9.
[50] Jacqueline Genet observes this relation between game and play. See 'Yeats's Deirdre as a Chess-game and a Poet's Game', *Multiple Worlds, Multiple Words: Essays in Honour of Irene Simon*, ed. Helena Maes-Jelinek, Pierre Michel, Paulette Michel-Michot (University of Liège, 1988), p. 125. See also Marcus, *Yeats and Artistic Power*, p. 82.

earth yellow. Each uppermost stone is supported of four supports corresponding to the four elements, and then support is allotted to the elements.

Each other quarter is again divided into four quarters which is again divided into four quarters containing a single square each.[51]

In *Gods and Fighting Men*, Lady Gregory brought into the public domain tales from Irish mythology in which warriors and noblemen played chess, most notably the game Finn and Oisin play in the story of Diarmuid and Grania.[52] Yeats heightened the mystical significance of these references here, in the process moving from an antiquarian to a spatial perspective. Anticipating the experiments with Gordon Craig's screens from 1910, the spatial treatment of myth through the chess-game in *Deirdre* placed it within the avant-garde of the 1900s, anticipating what Henri Lefebvre has described as a break-down in the common-sense idea of space within Western culture around 1910.[53] Like Yeats's description of the chess-game, *Deirdre* is synaesthetic; music, voice and movement harmonise in the synchronicity of a suspended moment.[54]

The influence of 1890s Symbolist theatre shows through in the pronounced emphasis upon space in *The King's Threshold* and *Deirdre* and the power struggles represented through it. Part three of *Axël*, 'The Occult World', is set entirely on the threshold. Here, the adept Janus implores Axël to renounce himself completely, and so achieve spiritual immortality.[55] The literal space of the threshold acts as a metaphor for the limit-experience Janus compels Axël to undergo. The struggle between Janus and Axël is an important precedent for that between King Guaire and Seanchan in *The King's Threshold*. Yeats reverses the terms of the struggle; the king seeks to entice Seanchan away from self-immolation on the threshold of the palace. In Villiers de l'Isle Adam's play, Axël eventually renounces himself, but only through consummation of his love for Sarah in suicide, a conclusion anticipating that of Yeats's *Deirdre*. The threshold space in the opening scene of Maeterlinck's *Pelléas and Mélisande* symbolises the birth of a new epoch. Servants arrive to open an ancient door

---

[51] NLI ms. 13568.
[52] Lady Augusta Gregory, *Gods and Fighting Men* (London: John Murray, 1904), pp. 374–5.
[53] Henri Lefebvre, *The Production of Space*, trans. Donald Nicholson-Smith (Oxford: Blackwell, 1991), p. 25. See Flannery's discussion of Craig's screens in productions of Yeats's plays from 1910. 'W. B. Yeats', p. 94. Karen Dorn observes how language and imagery in Yeats's plays became spatial under Craig's influence, an effect strongly resonant with the Cubist aesthetic. *Players*, pp. 17–26.
[54] Bettina Knapp sees the musicians in *Deirdre* in a 'space/time continuum where past, present, and future are experienced simultaneously'. *Women, Myth and the Feminine Principle* (Albany: State University of New York Press, 1998), p. 189.
[55] Villiers de l'Isle Adam, *Axël*, pp. 124–9.

of the palace long closed and clean the steps. Standing on the threshold, one of the maid-servants becomes bathed in the dawn light coming over the sea.[56] In the moment the mother dies at the end of *The Intruder*, light floods the stage from the door opening to the room where she has lain ill. Simultaneously, a nun appears on the threshold, making the sign of the cross to announce the mother's death. Similarly, the pivotal moment of *Deirdre* takes place when the messenger, standing on the threshold, reveals that the king will not admit 'the traitor' Naoise into his presence (*VPl*, 369–70). The pervasive nature of this spatial representation in Symbolist drama of the period gives pertinence to Gaston Bachelard's notion of threshold as 'one of the most clearly objective ideas in modern psychology'.[57] Foucault's argument for the symbolic importance of threshold space in medieval Europe, the space to which the insane were confined within the city gates, is of particular relevance to Seanchan in *The King's Threshold*. Banished from the court and immobile on the steps to the palace, the poet grows ever more disconnected from those round him, a threat to those who bid him be reasonable.[58]

Richard Cave points out that, in Yeats's designs for *The King's Threshold*, all the attention was brought to focus on the steps upon which Seanchan lies, midway between the portico and the forestage.[59] James Flannery notes that Yeats had designed a scenic arrangement for the Abbey Theatre tours of 1913–14 closely resembling Craig's screens and incorporating, within the proscenium opening, an inner proscenium, constructed from two upright rectangular pillars upon which a third rested. It appears that *The King's Threshold* was the only play during this period to have been performed within the inner proscenium.[60] This suggests the degree to which Yeats's work with Craig was influenced by the highly interiorised theatre of Maeterlinck in the 1890s. In his 1913 publication, *Towards A New Theatre*, Craig included a number of sketches for a drama he had in mind in 1905, provisionally entitled 'The Steps', steps being the architectural creation he most admired.[61] These drawings and Yeats's sketches for

---

[56] Maeterlinck, *Pelléas*, p. 19.
[57] Gaston Bachelard *The Poetics of Space*, trans. Maria Jolas (Boston: Beacon Press, 1969), p. 174.
[58] Michel Foucault, *Madness and Civilization: A History of Insanity in the Age of Reason*, trans. Richard Howard (London: Tavistock Press, 1967), p. 11.
[59] Cave, 'Staging', p. 166. Cave's observation is based on a reproduction of Yeats's sketch for a ground plan of a setting for *The King's Threshold* using the Craig design method in Liam Miller, *The Noble Drama of W. B. Yeats* (Dublin: The Dolmen Press, 1977), p. 158.
[60] Flannery, 'W. B. Yeats', pp. 106–7.
[61] Edward Gordon Craig, *Towards a New Theatre: Forty Designs for Stage Scenes with Critical Notes* (London: J. M. Dent & Sons, 1913), p. 38.

Figure 1 Sketch for lighting plan for the steps in *The King's Threshold*. W. B. Yeats Collection, Stony Brook. Published with the permission of A. P. Watt Ltd on behalf of Gráinne Yeats.

the lighting for the steps in *The King's Threshold* bear remarkable affinity to one another in conception, a marked emphasis upon the drama as a spatial configuration concentrated upon the steps in both instances (*see* Figure 1 *and* Figure 2). Craig also revealed his idea of a scene suggesting upper and lower classes; this consisted of a palace on one side, severe in form, a slum on the other and, in between, a stairway, 'the magic spot where the whole world meets practically in harmony'.[62] Some idea of utopia was then at work in Craig's obsession with steps, of direct relevance to the representation of threshold space in *The King's Threshold*.

Concentrating on the space of threshold, Yeats was representing historical change through psychic disturbance. A reminder of the merchants who first appear on the threshold in *The Countess Cathleen*, the threshold upon which the poet starves in *The King's Threshold* marks a historical transition from feudal to modern through Seanchan's isolation and the struggle of those round him to wean him from his protest. In this sense, the play illustrates how fundamental space is to the exercise of power, a point Foucault emphasises.[63] By making the threshold central to the play,

---

[62] *Ibid.*, p. 66.
[63] 'Space, Knowledge, and Power', interview with Michel Foucault by Paul Rainbow, in Michel Foucault, *Power: Essential Works of Foucault 1954–1984*, vol. III, ed. James D. Faubion, trans. Robert Hurley *et al.* (London: Penguin Press, 2001), p. 361.

Figure 2 Edward Gordon Craig, 'The Steps' (1905), *Towards a New Theatre: Forty Designs for Stage Scenes with Critical Notes* (London: J. M. Dent & Sons, 1913). Publication is with the consent of the Edward Gordon Craig Estate.

Yeats designated it as a site of power struggle between the king and poet, the poet and pupils. The threshold marks off the terrain of this struggle, setting limits to the manner of its articulation; the king never occupies the forestage, the pupils never enter the portico, yet both king and pupils descend and ascend the steps at certain points in the play.

Seanchan's obstinate refusal to move from the steps reflected the static form of theatre Yeats sought, emanating from debates around the reform of the theatre at the turn of the century. In *The Dome* of 1898, Arthur Symons had praised the movement in Wagner's *Parsifal* as 'slow, deliberate, as if automatic', creating a pictorial effect. Symons admired this for the subordination of action on the stage to rhythm: 'After all, action, it has been said, is only a way of spoiling something.'[64] Laurence Binyon

---

[64] Symons, 'Ballet, Pantomime, and Poetic Drama', *The Dome*, 1 (1898), 69.

responded critically, taking issue with Yeats's suggestion that the prospects for a poetic drama were being damaged by the power of stage-managers over playwrights in contemporary England:

> Action is decried now as uninteresting, being confounded with incident. But we may be quite sure that plays in which there is no action will never live; portray souls and states of emotion by all means, but let them be portrayed through act and gesture, otherwise why use the stage?[65]

In his essay on the theatre published in the following issue of *The Dome*, Yeats defended his attack on 'the theatre of commerce', suggesting, however, that the problem lay not with poetic dramatists or stage managers, but with audiences and the willingness of dramatists and managers to serve their tastes. The selectivity of the audience he envisaged for an Irish Literary Theatre at that point was founded upon a view that the general public, absorbed as it was in the affairs of commerce, had taste only for incident and excitement.[66] Behind this lay Yeats's belief that contemporary audiences had learned 'from the life of crowded cities to live upon the surface of life, and actors and managers, who study to please them, have changed'.[67]

These exchanges anticipated the heated debate on the direction of modern theatre in the pages of *The New Age* in 1910, to which Yeats also contributed, debate anticipated in Ireland in the responses to *The King's Threshold* and Synge's *In the Shadow of the Glen* in *The United Irishman*.[68] Literally refusing to move in the play, Seanchan's static position on the threshold embodied that adopted by Yeats in these debates, an insistence upon drama not carried along by the hurried surfaces of modern society but faithful to a pursuit of the highest levels of artistic integrity. Responding to criticism provoked by his and Synge's play in 1903, he wrote, 'I would sooner our theatre failed through the indifference or hostility of our audiences than gained an immense popularity by any loss of freedom.'[69] Seanchan's unbending assertion of artistic autonomy, represented by his refusal to move from the steps, was here embodied in the actual circumstances Yeats found himself in Ireland in 1903.

---

[65] Laurence Binyon, 'Mr Bridges' "Prometheus" and Poetic Drama'. Binyon took issue with the admiration Yeats expressed for B. W. Leader's landscapes as a model for modern stage scenery, believing it would, in fact, nullify the effect of acting. *The Dome*, 2 (1899), 203–4.
[66] W. B. Yeats, 'The Theatre', *The Dome*, 3 (1899), 49.
[67] *Ibid.*, p. 49.
[68] See Yeats, 'The Theatre, the Pulpit', pp. 1–2, and James Connolly, 'National Drama', *The United Irishman*, 10:243 (1903), 2–3.
[69] W. B. Yeats, 'An Irish National Theatre', *The United Irishman*, 10:241 (1903), 2.

The estranging effect Yeats sought through the spatial arrangement in *The King's Threshold* derived in the first instance from this stance of protest. In so doing, he sought to incorporate into Maeterlinck's interiorised theatre the power of protest and indomitable will typical of protagonists in Ibsen's later plays. Seanchan's refusal to accommodate himself to changes in the prevailing social order meets with the same mixture of cajoling and threat to which Dr Stockmann is subject in *An Enemy of the People* when he, likewise, refuses to placate the majority, instead exposing the physical and spiritual corruption poisoning his community. *The King's Threshold* shared with *An Enemy of the People* a virulent criticism of the unholy alliance of the Press, the Church and the State in the respective nations of Norway and Ireland, one mediated through an old Irish story in Yeats's case. King Guaire declares to Seanchan's pupils that he yielded to his courtiers, 'Bishops, Soldiers, and Makers of the Law', who declared it beneath their dignity to sit in government with 'a mere man of words' (*VPl*, 259). Here Yeats was borrowing directly from John Ruskin, who took 'Bishops, Soldiers, Lawyers and Squires' to task in *Fors Clavigera* for their roles in maintaining the appalling conditions of the English industrial working classes.[70]

In particular, the Mayor in *The King's Threshold* bears striking affinity to the Mayor in *An Enemy of the People*. We first encounter him rehearsing a speech he has prepared to deliver to Seanchan in an effort to wean him from his protest, a sign of his insincerity from the outset (*VPl*, 269). The same insincerity is evident in Dr Stockmann's brother Peter, mayor of the town in *An Enemy of the People*. From a desire to secure his own reputation and that of the town as a health resort, he demands that Thomas Stockmann suppress the evidence he has discovered of the contamination of the town's waters. In both plays, the mayors invoke their authority and the material interests of the community at large in attempting to persuade the protagonists away from the course of action they intend. The mayor announces his authority as one of Seanchan's pupils pushes him away from the poet, asserting that he represents the king himself (*VPl*, 279). The mayor impresses upon Stockmann the importance of his moral authority in ensuring the 'general welfare' of the town in *An Enemy of People*.[71] The tone moves quickly from placatory to threatening in both instances, the mayor mocking Seanchan in *The King's Threshold*, stating that he never

---

[70] John Ruskin, *Fors Clavigera: Letters to the Workmen and Labourers of Great Britain*, vol. VI (London: George Allen, 1876), p. 42. Decades later, Yeats would characterise his most controversial essay, *On the Boiler*, as his *Fors Clavigera*. See Chapter 8 of this volume.
[71] Ibsen, *An Enemy*, p. 62.

understood the words of a poet any more than 'the baa of a sheep' (*VPl*, 276). Likewise the mayor in Ibsen's play accuses Stockmann of being 'amazingly reckless' and having 'a turbulent, unruly, rebellious spirit'.[72] In both plays, the protagonists experience their alienation from the society around them in a growing sense of their own lunacy. Seanchan speaks to his pupil of the mind wandering, 'moonstruck and fantastical', as his body grows weak (*VPl*, 263). Prepared to jeopardise the welfare of his wife and daughter to maintain the truth of his discovery, Dr Stockmann declares to his father-in-law in a state of hysteria at the end of *An Enemy of the People* that he is 'a madman'. During the public meeting in which he launches his attack on the townspeople, one man wonders whether there is hereditary insanity in Stockmann's family, the theme of Ibsen's preceding play, *Ghosts*.[73]

This descent into madness is a measure of how alienated the protagonists in both plays have become from their respective communities. It is a sign of the degree to which both men retain, in Dr Stockmann's phrase, 'spiritual distinction' incomprehensible to a society grown coarse through expediency and commerce.[74] The language of disease pervades both plays, set in contrast to water as source of spiritual purity. The mayor accuses his brother of jeopardising the town's chief source of prosperity in planning to expose the contamination of the source for the spas in *An Enemy of the People*. Dr Stockmann responds that it is poisoned, the town's prosperity deriving from traffic 'in filth and corruption'.[75] In *The King's Threshold*, the cripples personify the spiritual corruption into which the community has sunk in expelling the poet from the court. Anticipating the subject of Synge's 1905 play, *The Well of the Saints*, one of the cripples mentions how Seanchan spoke of the 'blessed well to cure the crippled' (*VPl*, 270). Later when Seanchan's pupil Brian attacks the mayor, accusing the king of rooting up 'old customs, old habits, old rights', the cripples join in, deriding the king for having fouled 'the holy well' in expelling Seanchan from the court (*VPl*, 279). In both plays, the spring is an emblem of spiritual purity, its corruption expressing a moral corruption of the community that draws on it for sustenance. As he nears death, Seanchan identifies this pestilence symbolically with lunacy, seeing in the light of the moon 'the white of leprosy / And the contagion that afflicts mankind' (*VPl*, 309).

Linking irrationalism, degeneracy and revolt in this manner, *An Enemy of the People* and *The King's Threshold* shared the criticism of contemporary

---

[72] *Ibid.*, pp. 63, 64.   [73] *Ibid.*, pp. 147, 172.   [74] *Ibid.*, pp. 140.

[75] *Ibid.*, p. 71.

civilisation Nietzsche developed towards the end of the nineteenth century. Attacking the majoritarianism of political democracy as the rule of the stupid over the intelligent and trumpeting the authority of 'the intellectually distinguished few', the themes of *The Will to Power* pervade Stockmann's public address in Act 4 of *An Enemy of the People*.[76] At the heart of this, however, was that belief in ugliness as destitution propounded by Morris and Wilde, Stockmann blaming 'stupidity, poverty, the ugliness of life' for the demoralisation of the community.[77] Writing his play in the light of the Symbolist revolution of the 1890s, Yeats extended Nietzsche's critique in *The King's Threshold* into the realm of language itself, taking on board his belief that 'everywhere' language was 'sick' in the modern world.[78] Describing the form of Seanchan's speech as 'connotative', Timothy Reiss contrasts this with the 'resolutely denotative' speech of the king and his representatives, a contrast that lies behind their failure to understand the nature of his protest.[79] Denis Donoghue has traced this to the influence of Maeterlinck, in whose work he observes 'an impulse to eliminate denotation, to make the words answerable only to connotation'.[80]

By the end of *The King's Threshold*, Seanchan appears to withdraw entirely into himself. Likewise Deirdre's suicide absorbs her into the narrative of the play itself as an autonomous work of art. The combination of her solemn movement, the voices of the musicians delivered according to the method Yeats sought through his psaltery experiment in 1903, and the stylised nature of spatial arrangement, create that harmonic effect Arthur Symons admired in Wagner's *Parsifal* in 1898, a harmonisation of all performative elements.[81] Similar at the level of form to Seanchan's speech patterns, the impression created expressed that liberation of language through poetic rhythm Nietzsche admired in Wagner.[82] In this way, the

---

[76] *Ibid.*, p. 137.   [77] *Ibid.*, p. 142.
[78] Friedrich Nietzsche, 'Richard Wagner in Bayreuth', *Untimely Meditations*, ed. Daniel Breazeale, trans. R.J. Hollingdale (Cambridge University Press, 1997), pp. 213–14. Suheil Bushrui views Seanchan's reference to 'God's Laughter' in terms of Nietzsche's idea of laughter announcing the advent of the *Übermensch*. Claiming that *The King's Threshold* was the nearest Yeats came to Greek tragedy, Bushrui lends credence to Nietzsche's belief that the re-birth of tragedy was taking place in his own age. '*The King's Threshold*: A Defence of Poetry', *Review of English Literature*, 4:3 (1963), 81, 92–3.
[79] Timothy Reiss, 'The Golden Cradle and the Beggar-Man: Problems of Yeats's Poetics', *Canadian Review of Comparative Literature*, 3:1 (1976), 84.
[80] Denis Donoghue, *The Third Voice: Modern British and American Verse Drama* (London: Oxford University Press, 1959), p. 28.
[81] Symons, 'Ballet', p. 69.
[82] Nietzsche, 'Richard Wagner', p. 217. Nietzsche's praise of Wagner was one element attracting Yeats to the philosopher, Yeats invoking Wagner as the model for cultural revival in *Literary Ideals in Ireland*. Another source was Édouard Dujardin, whom George Moore recalls as an avid

plays seem to characterise a subjective point of view, that sense of reality as 'a construct of the mind' Terry Eagleton observes in Yeats's work as a mark of the determination of 'a sinking Ascendancy to assert a last edge over a history which flouts them'.[83] This overlooks the integral relationship of estrangement and revolt in these plays of the 1900s, deriving from the critique of modern society outlined by Morris and extended by Wilde. Taking place offstage, Deirdre's suicide intimates a transformation as provocative as that of Cathleen ni Houlihan in St Teresa's Hall in 1902.[84] These plays bear the hallmarks of Heidegger's notion of 'the happening' in their performative enactments during the 1900s, plays the political meaning of which are intrinsic to the performative methods employed.[85] The following section explores the complex nature of the political perspectives underlying Yeats's engagement with European avant-garde theatre in his most ambitious theatrical project, the Cuchulain cycle of plays.

Wagnerite in *Ave*. See *Hail and Farewell*, ed. Richard Allen Cave (Gerrards Cross: Colin Smythe, 1976), p. 89.
[83] Terry Eagleton, *Heathcliff and the Great Hunger: Studies in Irish Culture* (London: Verso, 1995), pp. 306, 310.
[84] Christopher Morash describes Maud Gonne's dramatic intervention as Cathleen on the opening night, arriving ten minutes before the curtain went up, her eye make-up accentuating the dramatic effect of her masterful stare into space. *A History*, p. 123. Douglas Hyde thought Mrs Patrick Campbell's performance of *Deirdre* in Dublin the greatest tragic acting he had seen. See Foster, *W. B. Yeats*, vol. I, p. 392.
[85] Martin Heidegger, 'The Origin of the Work of Art', *Basic Writings*, ed. David Farrell Krell (London: Routledge Press, 1993), p. 179.

PART 2

The Cuchulain cycle

CHAPTER 3

'I'll not be bound': On Baile's Strand *and* The Green Helmet

The five plays of Yeats's Cuchulain cycle have remained enigmatic within the theatre of the Irish Revival period. The theme of the Irish mythical hero Cuchulain, brought into public consciousness through Standish O'Grady, Augusta Gregory and T. W. Rolleston in their versions of the *Táin Bo Cuailgne*, seemed the obvious choice for a national-popular theatre movement in the Ireland of the 1900s. However, the esoteric dimension Yeats put into the plays, coupled with the degree of experiment he envisaged for performance in the final three plays, convey the impression of the cycle as an exercise in cultural elitism, intended only for the sophisticated few. The time span covered was immense, from the first performance of *On Baile's Strand*, inaugurating the Abbey Theatre in December 1904 with Gregory's *Spreading the News*, to Yeats's final drafts for *The Death of Cuchulain* weeks before his death in January 1939. If this underlines the necessity of attending to distinctive historical circumstances in which the various plays of the cycle were written and performed, it also conveys the importance of the cycle as a whole to Yeats's understanding of his age and the place of his own work within it.[1] The range of theatrical forms and influences Yeats brought to these plays brings complex political perspectives to the surface for which a neat distinction between popular and elite is insufficient as a frame of interpretation. This chapter considers the two earliest plays in the cycle with this in mind.

---

[1] Several critics have observed how the five Cuchulain plays developed as a coherent cycle. See, Reg Skene, *The Cuchulain Plays of W. B. Yeats: A Study* (London: Macmillan Press, 1974); Birgit Bjersby, *The Interpretation of the Cuchulain Legend in the Works of W. B. Yeats* (Dublin: Hodges Figgis, 1950); Daniel Hoffman, *Barbarous Knowledge* (London: Oxford University Press, 1967), p. 87. Noting that Yeats began his composition of *On Baile's Strand* after attending performances of Shakespeare's five history plays at Stratford-upon-Avon in 1901, Philip Edwards strengthens the view that Yeats intended a cycle from the outset and, further, one critically attentive to a historical process of modernisation. *Threshold of a Nation*, p. 209. See also Ruth Nevo, 'Yeats, Shakespeare and Ireland', *Literature and Nationalism*, ed. Vincent Newey and Ann Thompson (Liverpool University Press, 1991), p. 183.

Like *The King's Threshold* and *Deirdre*, *On Baile's Strand* probes the themes of estrangement and revolution that preoccupied Yeats in the 1890s under the influence of Naturalism and Symbolism. As the work of the Irish National Theatre Society acquired new institutional significance with the opening of the Abbey Theatre under the patronage of Annie Horniman, the political stakes of Yeats's theatrical experiments grew higher. This was already evident in the sharp responses provoked by the performances of *The King's Threshold* and Synge's *In the Shadow of the Glen* in 1903. Criticism over recent years has been a little too quick to read in this and later controversies a struggle between competing aspirations for a theatre of nation and a theatre of art, a struggle voiced in accusations of foreign influence countered by claims of cultural philistinism. Notable in this regard is the fact that in 1900 Edward Martyn identified Irish culture with that of continental Europe as a way of bolstering distinction from England. Believing that Dublin had 'more the character of a continental than an English city', Martyn insisted that Ireland's 'foreign influences should come from the Continent, not from England'.[2] In his new admiration for Ibsen in the 1900s, Yeats adopted the same rhetoric, identifying Ireland with Norway as a way of distinguishing the country from England, though also, it has to be said, from France: 'So far as we can be certain of anything, we may be certain that Ireland with her long National struggle, her old literature, her unbounded folk-imagination, will, in so far as her literature is National at all, be more like Norway than England or France.'[3]

The distinction between artistic culture and politics commonly drawn in critical appraisal of the period leading up to the *Playboy* riots of 1907, a distinction drawn by Yeats himself in later years, insufficiently accounts for the nature of his public interventions in the 1900s. Aside from the extent to which his own Symbolist dramaturgy and poetics were underwritten by the social vision of Morris, Yeats saw in the attacks of 1903 a change in the nature of political nationalism itself, a moment of embourgeoisement reflected in the vitriol of certain sections of the Irish press. Defending *In The Shadow of the Glen*, he noted how 'extreme politics' in Ireland, once 'the politics of intellectual freedom', was now turning against ideas altogether, under the influence of 'a violent contemporary paper'.[4]

---

[2] Edward Martyn, 'A Comparison between Irish and English Theatrical Audiences', *Beltaine*, 2 (1900), 13.
[3] Yeats, 'First Principles', *Plays and Controversies*, p. 112.
[4] W. B. Yeats, 'The Irish National Theatre and Three Sorts of Ignorance', *The United Irishman*, 10:243 (1903).

The argument sounds more like an attempt to embarrass the socialist Connolly than rebuke the nationalist Gonne; Connolly's criticism of *The King's Threshold* and *In the Shadow of the Glen* appeared in the same issue of *The United Irishman*. Arguing that space for intellectual freedom could only be granted when political freedom had been achieved, Connolly's argument was a formative influence on Irish Republican socialism.[5] While in one sense it was a standard restatement of Engels's base-superstructure theory of culture, it also imposed a serious qualification on the intellectual radicalism from which the European socialist movement sprang, and set up a dichotomy within Irish Marxism that endured right into the era of the Troubles. Significantly, the position of Frederick Ryan, another Irish Marxist of the time, restated that of Yeats rather than Connolly. Writing in response to the pogrom against Limerick's Jewish community in 1904, Ryan pleaded for a spirit of intellectual freedom in Ireland; rather than substituting political for intellectual freedom, nationalist intellectuals had to acknowledge they were one and the same.[6] Defending himself and Synge, Yeats invoked the Russian anarchists Peter Kropotkin and Serge Stepniak as fitting models for a genuinely revolutionary movement, men 'who would not make a mob drunk with a passion they could not share'. Here he was giving expression to a belief that artistic freedom and virtuous leadership should be central to radical politics in Ireland.[7] This allusion to Russia was politically loaded, coming just two years before the Russian Revolution of 1905, the political direction of which was, to quote Perry Anderson, 'profoundly ambiguous'.[8]

This ambiguity derived in the Irish case from Yeats's desire to create a cultural movement at once intellectual and popular. Yeats was drawn to Ibsen and his achievement in Norway precisely for this reason. Responding in 1899 to the criticism directed at *The Countess Cathleen*, he compared the present dramatic movement in Ireland to that of Norway between 1840 and 1860, a movement that was 'at once intellectual and popular' and one which had produced in Ibsen 'a great European figure'.[9]

---

[5] Connolly, 'National Drama', *The United Irishman*, 10:243 (1903).
[6] Frederick Ryan, 'Political and Intellectual Freedom', *Dana*, 1 (1904). For a discussion of Ryan's importance to Irish socialism in the Revival period, see Terry Eagleton, 'The Ryan Line', *Crazy John and the Bishop* (Cork University Press in association with Field Day, 1998), pp. 249–72.
[7] Yeats, 'The Theatre, the Pulpit', p. 2.
[8] Perry Anderson, 'Modernism and Revolution', *The New Left Review*, 144 (1984), 105–6. Ben Levitas notes the political ambiguity to which the allusion attested in the Ireland of 1903. *The Theatre of Nation*, p. 75.
[9] Report of speech delivered by Yeats at 6, Stephen's Green, Dublin, 4 May, *The Freeman's Journal*, 6 May 1899, p. 6.

Ibsen offered a model of revolutionary individualism in *A Doll's House*, *Ghosts* and *An Enemy of the People*; revolutionary collectivism in *Peer Gynt* and *The Vikings at Helgeland*. In his own plays of the 1900s, Yeats sought to harness these twin energies to Maeterlinckian Symbolism and release them on stage through occult representations of Irish mythology. Ibsen's influence was not just thematic; Yeats's musical experiments in *On Baile's Strand* and *Deirdre* were partly inspired by *The Vikings at Helgeland*, produced by Ellen Terry and her son Gordon Craig in April 1903 at the Imperial Theatre. Coming soon after his own psaltery lectures, Yeats was most struck by the lyre to which the lead actor spoke in performance, commenting how it appeared that the whole orchestral wind instruments seemed to arise out of it.[10] Later that year he proposed a special free performance of the most popular plays of the Irish Literary Theatre, inviting members of the Dublin Working Men's organisation. Yeats had in mind here the cultivation of a People's Theatre modelled along the lines of Bruno Wille's 1890 *Die Freie Volksbühne* in Berlin, a theatre for the working classes.[11] In the same month that he attended Terry's production of *The Vikings of Helgeland*, the string band of the Workmen's Club played a selection of Irish airs at St Teresa's Hall during the interval between the performances of George Russell's version of *Deirdre* and Yeats/Gregory's *Cathleen ni Houlihan*.[12]

The tensions and possibilities within this vision of a popular intellectual theatre were evident in the first two plays of the Cuchulain cycle, *On Baile's Strand* and *The Green Helmet*, both performed at the Abbey Theatre in the 1900s. Yeats's attempts to create intellectual passion within the Irish dramatic movement of the time is evident in the tension between tragedy and farce in these plays, myth and its unmasking. The Cuchulain cycle has been critically received as a tragic representation of history through a mythic form, but as early as 1904 Yeats was reflecting on the relation of tragedy to farce. In 'First Principles' he wrote that a farce and a tragedy were alike in being 'a moment of intensest life'.[13] The sense of dissatisfaction many have felt with the Cuchulain cycle derives largely from the uncertain generic nature of the plays, uncertainty that magnifies as the cycle develops. This was not simply a failure to create drama of mythical power on Yeats's part; it testified a deliberate interrogation of such power through the medium of farce, consonant with an aspiration to evoke

---

[10] Kelly and Schuchard, *Collected Letters*, vol. III, p. 352.
[11] Yeats to Frank J. Fay, 25 Sept 1903. Kelly and Schuchard, *Collected Letters*, vol. III, pp. 432–3.
[12] *The Freeman's Journal*, 3 April 1903, p. 5.
[13] Yeats, 'First Principles', *Plays and Controversies*, p. 103.

energy in performance through symbolism having both individual and collective appeal. *On Baile's Strand* has all the elements of Idealist theatre: ritual, solemnity, the image of the hero in direct conflict with Fate. At its heart, however, is a Rite of Initiation that proves to be a charade. Rather than binding Cuchulain to the authority of the King of Ulster, Conchobar MacNessa, it acts as the catalyst for his descent into madness. A discreet hint of farce underlies the tragic image of Cuchulain fighting the waves, relayed by the Fool at the end of the play; it is accentuated five years later in the play through which Yeats responded to the *Playboy* riots of 1907, *The Green Helmet*.

Yeats drew upon 'The Only Son of Aoife' in Augusta Gregory's *Cuchulain of Muirthemne* for the plot of *On Baile's Strand*, making considerable changes to the narrative in the process.[14] While praising *Cuchulain of Muirthemne* as 'the best book that has come out of Ireland in my time', these changes show strong differences in Yeats's reception of the Cuchulain legend. Gregory's narrative carried something of the scholarly tone of the eighteenth-century antiquarian tradition. The claim to disinterest in her dedication, stating that she 'put in nothing of my own that could not be helped', was characteristic of that earlier movement.[15] Her narrative also dealt with gender aspects of the legend in a distinctively Victorian manner. The young Cuchulain (Setanta) is painfully shy in the presence of women and his motives in choosing Emer as his wife are conservative, attracted as he is to her 'six gifts' of 'beauty, voice, "sweet speech", needlework, wisdom and chastity'.[16]

The Cuchulain of Yeats's plays is a far more virile figure, in keeping with the disdain he shared with Shaw for what both regarded as the emasculating effects of Victorian English middle-class culture and its puritan undertones, taking hold in Irish society as prospects for economic security increased in the 1900s. King Conchubar encourages Cuchulain to settle and marry; the warrior responds that he had never known love but 'as a kiss / In the mid-battle, and a difficult truce / Of oil and water'

---

[14] Catherine Greene has listed these changes. See 'The Cuchulain legend in the Plays of W. B. Yeats', unpublished MA thesis, Liverpool University (1973), pp. 206–11. There is some dispute over authorship of the dialogue between the Fool and Blind Man, Mary Lou Kohfeldt attributing it to Gregory. See *Lady Gregory: The Woman Behind the Irish Renaissance* (London: Deutsche Press, 1985), p. 165.

[15] Lady Augusta Gregory, *Cuchulain of Muirthemne* (London: John Murray, 1903), p. vi. Working for two years at the British Museum, she assembled all nineteenth-century translations of the Cuchulain tales and attempted some degree of mastery of old Irish in order to read the manuscripts in their original form. See, Edward A. Kopper, *Lady Isabella Persse Gregory* (Boston: Twayne Publishers, 1976), p. 42. Kohfeldt, *Lady Gregory*, p. 30.

[16] Gregory, *Cuchulain*, pp. 20, 22.

(*VPl*, 489). An image of perpetual strife between the sexes anticipating the preoccupations of Lawrence, it is partly autobiographical. Advising Fay on how to act Cuchulain, Yeats places him at the age of forty, just a year older than Yeats himself at the time.[17] The slightly ridiculous figure of an unmarried middle-aged man still remembering the earlier love of Aoife brings Yeats himself to mind, still reeling from Gonne's marriage to MacBride in early 1903. But Cuchulain's response also brings Nietzsche's *The Birth of Tragedy* to mind, as Reg Skene has noted, and Blake's maxim that 'sexual love is founded upon spiritual hate'.[18]

Through a ritual bonding introduced to the 1906 version of the play, King Conchubar tries to bring Cuchulain's volatility under the control of the state over which he presides. The ritual enacts in performance the gender and historical forms through which supernatural power, as Yeats understood it, became manifest. In this scene of Cuchulain's bonding, three women carrying bowls of fire above them enter the stage. For Conchubar, they sing 'against the will of woman at its wildest' and the ritual in which they participate becomes an attempt to subdue feminine power (*VPl*, 495). As Angela Jenkins has shown, the ritual was a modified version of one Yeats had devised in his plans for the Celtic Order of Mysteries, put to an end by Gonne's marriage in 1903. This was the Initiation of the Spear, roughly corresponding to the 5 = 6 Adeptus Minor grade of the Golden Dawn, Yeats's grade at the time the play was written.[19] Garrigan Mattar notes that in addition to the symbolism of fire and water, the Castle of Heroes and Golden Dawn rituals were also presented in the opposition of door and threshold, further emphasising the scene as a rite of passage.[20] This also points to how power was manifested and contested in the ritual through spatial configuration, particularly with reference to the threshold.

Attempting to subdue feminine power and still the volatile warrior, the ritual becomes a charade, an attempt to subdue magic through magic.

---

[17] W. B. Yeats to Frank J. Fay, [20 January 1904]. Kelly and Schuchard, *Collected Letters*, vol. III, p. 527.

[18] Skene, *The Cuchulain Plays of W. B. Yeats*, p. 172. This confirms the extent to which Nietzsche's influence on the composition of this and other plays of the early 1900s was evidence of Yeats's determination to 'put muscle in his style'. See, Stipe Grgas, 'Tragic Affirmation in Yeats and Nietzsche', *Orbis Litterarum*, 46 (1991), 166.

[19] Angela Jenkins, 'W. B. Yeats and Irish Mythology', unpublished MA thesis, University of Kent at Canterbury (1980), p. 115. The ritual of bonding ends in the gathering of men plunging their swords into bowls of water, a gesture also taken from one of the proposed rites for the Castle of Heroes, the initiation of the sword. NLI ms. 13568.

[20] NLI ms. 13568. Garrigan Mattar, *Primitivism, Science, and the Irish Revival* (Oxford: Clarendon Press, 2004), p. 123.

Admitting that it was time 'the years put water in my blood', Cuchulain appears as both the figure of Christ and the embodiment of Nietzsche's view of Christianity as the killer of instinct.[21] Likewise the women's chorus is directed against their own power to transform the warrior through magic:

> May this fire have driven out
> The Shape-Changers that can put
> Ruin on a great king's house
> Until all be ruinous. (*VPl*, 495)

These words move quickly from expressing the hope for protection from feminine spirit to evoking its power. Maeterlinckian in style, they are full of connotation, evocative rather than descriptive, typical of the women's chorus throughout Yeats's plays. Harold Segel proposes that words mattered less in Maeterlinck's drama than 'their evocative power' and 'the sense of uneasiness they induce in the viewer'; this is borne out in the chorus for *On Baile's Strand*.[22]

The ritual of Cuchulain's bonding triggers events that lead to him killing his son and the stability of Ulster unravelling. Yeats sought to conjure the estranging effect of the ritual through a particular mode of diction in the women's chorus. In 'Speaking to the Psaltery', he talked of how his experiment with Florence Farr and Arnold Dolmetsch tried to create a new form of speech akin to music yet distinguished from it. Dissatisfied with the manner in which musical rhythm drowned out the meaning of words in song, while equally impatient with the silence of words on the page, he sought a form of speech capable of harmonising meaning with rhythm.[23] The form of dramatic speech that Yeats envisaged entailed simple musical notation that would regulate the general form of the spoken word while allowing it variety of dramatic expression, thereby achieving intellectual complexity in rhythmic simplicity.[24]

Not surprisingly, the experiment with Fay and Dolmetsch encountered considerable scepticism. After attending Yeats's lecture followed by the performance of pieces by Dolmetsch and Farr in November 1902, Frank Fay wrote in *The United Irishman* that he could only describe Farr's recitation of Yeats's verse as singing, something Yeats insisted it

---

[21] Anthony Bradley argues that Cuchulain 'betrays his very selfhood' in submitting to Conchubar's bond. *William Butler Yeats* (New York: Ungar Press, 1979), p. 120.
[22] Harold B. Segel, *Pinocchio's Progeny*, p. 50. Donoghue also notes the connotative power of Maeterlinck's drama as a precedent for Yeats. See *The Third Voice*, p. 28.
[23] W. B. Yeats, 'Speaking to the Psaltery', *Essays and Introductions* (London: Macmillan, 1961), p. 13.
[24] *Ibid.*, p. 17.

was not.[25] More acerbically, St John Ervine remarked that the single merit of Dolmetsch's psaltery was that it had only one string which was easily broken, while Shaw described the voice experiment as 'cantilating', a practice that Yeats believed was new simply because he did not go to church: 'Half the curates in the kingdom cantilate like mad all the time.'[26] Such derision notwithstanding, Yeats's experiment was a new departure of an antique kind. The comparison he drew with Tibetan music illustrates the extent to which it was an exercise in orientalist exoticism, a cultivation of a new aesthetic sensibility within contemporary European culture drawing on antique forms:

> But this new art, new in modern life, I mean, will have to train its hearers as well as its speakers, for it takes time to surrender gladly the gross effects one is accustomed to, and one may well find mere monotony at first where one soon learns to find a variety as incalculable as in the outline of faces or in the expression of eyes.[27]

Here Yeats anticipated the kind of scepticism his experiment met and anticipated how strange this new form of dramatic speech would sound in contemporary theatres. It also shows the agenda of cultural reform that drove it. Yeats was trying to develop a form of delivery that would defamiliarise the theatre by emphasising its artifice, bringing into consciousness the distorting effects of realism in performance, particularly its abandonment of rhythm in speech.

The women's chorus for the fire and sword ritual in *On Baile's Strand* was a theatrical enactment of the psaltery experiment, an experiment that carried the critique of modern society in *The King's Threshold*. Ronald Schuchard identifies in the experiment and the lectures that accompanied it the expression of Yeats's hope that a 'spiritual democracy' might emerge from the Abbey and the broader cultural revival in Ireland during the early 1900s.[28]

---

[25] Fay added that were he to hear Yeats recite it, he would only have the impression of musical speech. *Towards a National Theatre*, p. 96.

[26] Cited in Robert Hogan and James Kilroy, eds., *The Irish Literary Theatre, 1899–1901* (Dublin: Dolmen, 1975), pp. 28–9. For a full account of responses to the experiment, see Schuchard, *The Last Minstrels*, pp. 76–7.

[27] Yeats, 'Speaking to the Psaltery', pp. 16, 18. It is arguable that the new medium of television could achieve through close-up shots the kind of variety Yeats envisaged here more effectively than the theatre. William Fay claimed that Yeats once told him that he wished he could send his plays directly to his audience by telepathy to their own homes. Fay observed tellingly that 'with the help of television and wireless it will soon be possible to do it mechanically'. William Fay, 'A Spot of Acting', NLI ms. 5981.

[28] Ronald Schuchard, 'The Minstrel in the Theatre: Arnold, Chaucer, and Yeats's New Spiritual Democracy', *Yeats Annual*, vol. II, ed. Richard Finneran (London: Macmillan Press, 1983), pp. 3–4. See also Schuchard, *The Last Minstrels*, pp. 191–218.

Yeats's hope that the theatre would depict great types capable of inspiring 'a great democracy' in Ireland bore the hallmarks of what George Russell would later describe as aristo-democracy in *The National Being*. The notable ambivalence that Perry Anderson identifies in revolutionary ideology of the early 1900s is evident in the syndicalist strain of Russell's thought, aspiring to a heroic individualism founded upon economic corporatism. 'Instead of being democratic in our economic life, with the aristocracy of character and intelligence to lead us', A. E. complained, 'we became meanly individualistic in our economics and meanly democratic in leadership'.[29]

Schuchard's discussion of what Yeats was trying to achieve through theatrical voice with the psaltery experiment is vital in drawing attention to its political aspect, but the kind of transformation Yeats sought at this point was decidedly anti-middle class, avant-garde, tentatively gesturing towards a revolutionary movement led by cultured elites. As late as 1934, in his introduction to *The Resurrection* published in *Wheels and Butterflies*, Yeats was observing the possibility of accommodating heroic individualism even to Marxism. Quoting Lenin, he noted that 'it is not true, according to Prince Mirski, that Marxian socialism denies the existence of great men. "Great men are the embodiment of great social movements, and it is natural that the greater the movement the greater the 'great man' produced by it." '[30] The psaltery experiments and the lecture tour on 'Literature and the Living Voice' that accompanied it was driven by a desire to arouse such a movement, but through the medium of artistic estrangement that sought to combine inspiration and intellectual seriousness.

The intellectual and populist appeal of 'Literature and the Living Voice' was constrained by the difficulty attaching to the psaltery experiment that Yeats proposed in 1902. If he intended his lectures to stimulate a popular movement, its form was to be decidedly anti-middle class, distinct from the civic democracy of Young Ireland nationalism or, more generally, the orthodoxies of contemporary mass culture. Behind the psaltery experiment lay Yeats's aspiration to estrange audiences so as to reflect inversely the spiritual alienation he felt to be pervasive in modern society. Katharine Worth has contextualised it in relation to Arnold Schoenberg's musical experiments with the drama of Maeterlinck and Georgette Leblanc's verse recitals in Paris, suggesting that Yeats's conception of non-musical music

---

[29] A. E., *The National Being: Some Thoughts on Irish Polity* (Dublin: Maunsel, 1916), p. 126.
[30] W. B. Yeats, *Wheels and Butterflies* (London: Macmillan Press, 1934), pp. 104–5.

bore affinity with the notoriously difficult experiments in atonality that Schoenberg developed in the 1900s.[31]

That Yeats himself saw the psaltery experiment in such a context retrospectively is borne out in a letter to Edmund Dulac of November 1934, over thirty years after the first performance of *On Baile's Strand*. Here he conveyed news of a recent visit from a Californian musician, Harry Partch, who had written to Yeats some years previously for permission to write a musical score for his version of *Oedipus the King* based on an entirely new system. Partch had made a viola according to his system and claimed to have discovered the foundations of Greek and Chinese music. Requesting Dulac to grant him audience, Yeats saw Partch engaging in the kind of experiment he had tried with Farr and Dolmetsch in the 1900s, 'but with a science and a knowledge of music beyond Farr's reach'.[32] That Yeats identified a similarity between Partch's chanting to his new instrument and Farr's recitations to the accompaniment of Dolmetsch's psaltery testified the deliberate tonal difficulty of chant and music in his plays from the 1900s. The chanting of the women in *On Baile's Strand* was designed to have a deeply unsettling effect on its audience, inevitably turning many off.[33] Neither song nor speech, the notation of which was developed from an instrument that was 'half psaltery, half lyre', the women's chorus in the ritual scene carried an air of solemnity disturbed by a pronounced sense of its own artifice.

The fire and sword ritual was a concentrated instance of a wider occult pattern of revelation through concealment that Yeats worked with during the 1900s.[34] We encounter it in the cloak the Young Man presents to Cuchulain as a token of friendship when he arrives on stage in *On Baile's Strand*, a gesture reminiscent of Shakespeare and bound up with the treatment of destiny in the play.[35] But the most significant instance is the sword-fight in which Cuchulain kills his son, hidden from audience view. This staging decision showed Yeats heeding Fay's judicious advice. Because the Abbey relied on amateur actors, 'simplicity and not

---

[31] Worth, *The Irish Drama*, pp. 42–5.
[32] Yeats to Dulac, 21 November 1934. W. B. Yeats Collection, Series II, HRHRC. For a detailed discussion of Partch's meetings with Yeats in 1934, see Schuchard, *The Last Minstrels*, pp. 67–77.
[33] Karen Dorn suggests that it was not until his collaboration with Gordon Craig that Yeats would achieve the combination of language and movement on the stage which he aimed at in earlier plays such as *On Baile's Strand*. *Players*, p. 16.
[34] Haskell M. Block observes that occultism in early modernist drama reflected the symbolist conception of art 'as at once concealment and revelation'. 'Symbolist Drama: Villiers de l'Isle Adam, Strindberg, and Yeats', *New York Literary Forum*, 4 (1980), 43.
[35] Ruth Nevo has laid emphasis upon the foolishness of Cuchulain's destiny in drawing attention to Aristotelian and Shakespearean precedents. See 'Yeats, Shakespeare and Ireland', p. 185.

subtlety must be aimed at'. Above all, death scenes and combats should be described rather than acted, requiring as they did experienced professionals.[36] Fay was among those sceptical of the experimental theatre Yeats was seeking to develop, blaming him for bringing 'effeminate artistry' into Ireland in a letter to W.J. Lawrence from May 1907, and declaring his loathing for 'the Wagners, Ibsens, Maeterlincks and other people with "messages" '.[37] The distance between Yeats and Fay was evident in the discrepancy between the advice Yeats gave him for an essay he was preparing in response to George Moore's attack on Willie Fay's stage-management in the September 1904 issue of *Dana*, and Fay's own reflection on acting many years after he had departed the Abbey scene. In a letter of August 1904, Yeats suggested that he acknowledge the achievement of Antoine's *Théâtre Libre* in Paris but criticise its pursuit of realism on the stage: 'Be just to Antoine's genius, but show the defects of his movement. Art is art because it is not nature, and he tried to make it nature. A realist, he cared nothing for poetry, which is founded on convention.'[38] This contrasted sharply with an observation Fay made years later in correspondence with W.J. Lawrence, writing that 'George Arliss' priceless description of acting as the art of being unnatural without being found out ought to be drummed into every stage aspirant.'[39]

Whatever their personal differences, Fay's criticism showed the thin line between drama of high artifice and clumsy amateurism, pointing to the element of farce latent within even the most symbolically intense of Yeats's plays. John Rees Moore has recognised that the economy of style Yeats first brought to the stage in *On Baile's Strand* risked slipping into wooden, one-dimensional drama; in sacrificing epic scale for intensity of impact, Yeats risked 'turning his hero into a puppet'.[40] The decision to place Cuchulain's battle with the Young Man offstage appears to bear this out. The play risked descent into pure farce if the attempt was made

---

[36] Fay, *Towards a National Theatre*, p. 76.
[37] Frank Fay to W.J. Lawrence, 24 May 1907. NLI ms. 10952(1). See also Fay to Lawrence, 27 February 1908. NLI ms. 10952(2): 'Self-consciousness ruins art and I think modern art (if there be any) will always take a back seat until it learns to be humble and its makers think less about themselves.'
[38] W.B. Yeats to Frank Fay, 28 August 1904. Kelly and Schuchard, *Collected Letters*, vol. III, p. 642.
[39] Frank Fay to W.J. Lawrence, 9 September 1930. NLI ms. 10952(2). Recognising the genius of Henry Irving, Yeats nonetheless believed he had done more than anyone to destroy poetical drama through that desire to conceal artifice that Fay saw as the hallmark of fine acting. *Playergoer*, 14 April 1904. NLI ms. 12146.
[40] Moore, *Masks of Love and Death: Yeats as Dramatist* (New York: Cornell University Press, 1971), pp. 123–34.

to combine theatrical excitement and mythic symbolism in this pivotal scene of combat. Nonetheless, placing it offstage denied the audience any taste of the vigour from which the mythic stature of the hero radiated. The result was a drama in the classical Greek mode that hovered on the edge of puppet theatre.

Rather than theatrical failure, this undercurrent of farce attaching to the occult form of *On Baile's Strand*, explored more openly in the later plays of the cycle, anticipated the experimental form of drama that would be fully developed by Pirandello, Brecht and Beckett. The manner in which the occlusion of Cuchulain killing his son hovered between profundity and simple-mindedness, tragedy and farce, brought into view a dialectic of maturity and regression that Adorno has identified as distinctive of modern art, a 'straining toward maturity as the organized and heightened aversion toward the childish in art' that eventually mutates into a primitivist aesthetics.[41] Adorno was not the first to note this agonising over the childish in the European avant-garde. Two months before it published Yeats's *At the Hawk's Well* in June 1917, Holbrook Jackson's journal *To-Day* published an essay on modernist art by G. K. Chesterton. Here, the minimalist forms of Max Ernst's Surrealism expressed an artform that belonged 'not only to the infancy of the world, but to the infancy of the individual'. This infantilism marked a process of dehumanisation, an art that sought 'to make men less than men; the rudiments and last realities of men'.[42] Yeats had already intimated a relation between the condition of childhood, fetish worship and estrangement in *The Land of Heart's Desire*. *On Baile's Strand* developed this further; in the formality of its ritual style appeared that straining towards maturity which Adorno observes, yet its simplicity carried an almost child-like quality, precisely the quality that made it feasible for an amateur group of actors.

The conclusion to *On Baile's Strand* carries a strong element of farce subverting the displays of authority in the play. A dialogue between the women forming the chorus for the earlier ritual of bonding replaces the fight between Cuchulain and the Young Man on stage, a dialogue in which they reflect poignantly on life drifting 'between a fool and a blind man' (*VPl*, 514). This is followed by the entry of the Fool and Blind Man who appeared at the play's opening, bringing the play to its concluding moment of revelation. The Fool has beaten the Blind Man because he had

---

[41] Theodor W. Adorno, *Aesthetic Theory*, ed. Gretel Adorno and Rolf Tiedemann, trans. Robert Hullot-Kentor (London: The Athlone Press, 1997), p. 43.
[42] G. K. Chesterton, 'The Hieroglyphics of Innocence', *To-Day*, ed. Holbrook Jackson, vol. 1:2 (1917), 49–50.

'left me nothing but the bones', another instance of the threat of starvation looming as it did in *The Countess Cathleen* and *The King's Threshold*. The exchange also belittles the gravity of Cuchulain killing his son, the beating administered by the Fool symbolic of the collapse of old structures of authority and the confused emergence of a new order. In some respects anticipating the full force of mockery that Synge would later employ to such devastating effect in *The Playboy of the Western World*, it hints at the raucous energy of medieval folk culture Yeats encountered through his reading of Chaucer in the early 1900s, an energy Bakhtin has identified as revolutionary and renewing. Drawing on Rabelais' colourful depiction of medieval excess in *Gargantua and Pantagruel*, Bakhtin sees in the many thrashings dished out to kings an old order giving way, the king becoming a clown to be mocked, beaten and dethroned.[43]

In personifying the destinies of Cuchulain and Conchubar, the Fool and Blind Man belittle them. Invested with the spiritual force of *daimon*, they yet reduce hero and king to the basest level of material need. This is made evident in the one moment of contact between Cuchulain and the Fool before the end. Cuchulain takes from the Fool's hair some feathers from a chicken the Blind Man has just eaten and uses them to wipe his dead son's blood from his sword. Immediately Cuchulain learns that it is his son he has killed. The sacrificial blood of the son is thus reduced to gluttonous mockery of the Fool. Once again, the symbolism had its origin in a rite for the Celtic Order of Mysteries, the Initiation of the Sword, during which the first Initiator presented the candidate with a long eagle's feather, speaking of man as a feather in the wind until the mind could conquer material experience.[44] As employed here, the prospect of such mastery is mocked. Awaking to his own blindness, Cuchulain is seen by the Fool and Blind Man rushing to the sea waving his sword in frenzy while they make haste to steal bread from ovens now unguarded.

Borrowing from Shakespeare and Chaucer, Yeats concluded his first play of the Cuchulain cycle in a way that reveals the profound ambivalence shaping his aspiration for a popular cultural movement in Ireland that might connect into larger patterns of cultural and social reform in Europe. Choosing the legend of Cuchulain as its topic, the broad influence of Wagner on *On Baile's Strand* is discernible, coloured significantly by the work of Nietzsche. As Frances Oppel observes, the manner of its

---

[43] Mikhail Bakhtin, *Rabelais and His World*, trans. Helene Iswolsky (Cambridge, MA: MIT Press, 1968), p. 206.
[44] NLI ms. 13568.

ending bears all the hallmarks of tragic ecstasy: the Blind Man scurrying to steal bread deflates the tragic aura of Cuchulain fighting the waves; this same bread, however, intimating Cuchulain as Christ, the man with water in his blood.[45] Yeats's treatment of the heroic theme was distinguished from the Wagnerian mode, however, in subverting tragic heroism to symbolise historical change. Whether through the almost amateurish quality of the play's simplicity, the primitive nature of Fool and Blind Man or the return to childhood trauma in the killing of the son (a catastrophic reversal of the Oedipal structure), the play is obsessed with the power of the primitive. In this it deepened and expanded that ambivalence between totemism and commodity fetishism first evident in *The Land of Heart's Desire*. Leon Surette observes that 'the historical sense of key modernists was very strongly touched by occult political and cultural historical speculation'.[46] But just as the sheer simplicity of *On Baile's Strand* threatens to collapse into farce, so its occult pattern borders on mere charade, belittling Cuchulain himself. The manner in which the play ends shows how seriously Yeats entertained this prospect of an anti-heroic drama expressing the tumult of modernity through farce. In its proto-Surrealist mode, Yeats's next play in the cycle, *The Green Helmet*, demonstrated this more emphatically, extending the anarchism of Cuchulain's madness to the form and energy of the play itself.

First performed in the Abbey Theatre in 1908 and rewritten in verse form for the 1910 performances, *The Green Helmet* was the most experimental play Yeats had yet directed. John Rees Moore compares it to Eliot's *Sweeney Agonistes* while James Flannery and Katharine Worth have drawn attention to the techniques of total theatre employed, Worth regarding in its form an attempt to draw the symbolism of the 1890s into 'the modern theatre of surrealist farce'.[47] The immediate inspiration was undoubtedly the *Playboy* disturbances at the Abbey Theatre in 1907, and the controversies that shadowed performances in England and the United States in the years to follow. Offering his own theatrical response to the riots, Yeats reached back to the year of his first encounter with Synge, and the opening night's performance of Alfred Jarry's *Ubu Roi* on 11 December 1896.

---

[45] Frances Nesbitt Oppel, *Mask and Tragedy: Yeats and Nietzsche, 1902–10* (Charlottsville: Virginia University Press, 1987), p. 156.

[46] Leon Surette, *The Birth of Modernism: Ezra Pound, T.S. Eliot, W.B. Yeats, and the Occult* (Montreal: McGill-Queen's University Press, 1994), pp. 37, 41–51.

[47] Worth, *The Irish Drama of Europe*, p. 153. Moore, *Masks of Love and Death*, p. 159. Flannery recognises how the limitations of the Abbey stage made it difficult for Yeats to realise the theatrical vision he intended for *The Green Helmet*. *Yeats and the Theatre*, p. 93.

A performance also interrupted by a disruptive audience, Jarry's play heralded the birth of Surrealist theatre. Concluding his autobiographical volume *The Tragic Generation*, Yeats memorably recalled his impressions of that night:

> Feeling bound to support the most spirited party, we have shouted for the play, but that night at the Hôtel Corneille I am very sad, for comedy, objectivity, has displayed its growing power once more. I say: 'After Stéphane Mallarmé, after Paul Verlaine, after Gustave Moreau, after Puvis de Chavannes, after our own verse, after all our subtle colour and nervous rhythm, after the faint mixed tints of Conder, what more is possible? After us the Savage God.[48]

That invocation was a further instance of Yeats's sense of the modern as a reawakening of the primitive, object of terror and awe, at once mesmerising and repellent. However limited *The Green Helmet* seemed in the aftermath of the devastating impact of *The Playboy*, it pointed to his sense of contemporary theatre as a space for revolutionary experimentation. If *On Baile's Strand* concentrated primarily on the mythic hero as barometer of historical change, *The Green Helmet* sought to convey some sense of the seething tumult of the modern in attending to energies generated from the rise in mass culture. Considered a pair, they illustrate that aspiration to harmonise revolutionary individualist and collectivist energies dating back to Ibsen and Morris.

It is customary to regard the poetry collection that accompanied *The Green Helmet* as further evidence of Yeats's retreat into aristocratic solitude as his hopes for cultural reform appeared quashed with the *Playboy* riots and Synge's death in 1909, paving the way for the openly elitist sentiments of his last years. Marjorie Howes draws attention to Yeats's obsession with the crowd mentality in poems from *The Green Helmet* collection in which crowds are those 'middle-class materialists' Yeats had berated since the early 1900s.[49] Reg Skene sees in Yeats's description of the play as 'heroic farce' a desire to contrast the nobility of Cuchulain with the pettiness of his rivals in the play.[50] Howes considers the influence of Gustav le Bon's *The Crowd* (1895) in shaping Yeats's response to the rise of mass culture, while Conor Cruise O'Brien has made the case powerfully for the reactionary nature of Nietzsche's influence on Yeats's from the 1900s.[51]

---

[48] Yeats, *Autobiographies*, pp. 348–9.
[49] Howes, *Yeats's Nations* (Cambridge University Press, 1996), p. 97.
[50] Skene, *The Cuchulain Plays*, p. 147.
[51] Howes, *Yeats's Nations*, pp. 80–3. Conor Cruise O'Brien, *The Suspecting Glance* (London: Faber, 1972), pp. 82–3.

Le Bon's work appears to have influenced Yeats significantly, bearing the hallmarks of social Darwinism. Several features he attributed to leaders of crowds characterised some of the leading protagonists in Yeats's plays of the 1900s. Le Bon asserted that these leaders were more men of action than thought, lacking in the foresight that would induce doubt and 'recruited from the ranks of those morbidly nervous excitable, half-deranged persons who are bordering on madness'.[52] Cuchulain is an obstinate man of action lacking all foresight in *On Baile's Strand*, eventually descending to madness. But the figure closest to le Bon's image of the deranged leader is Paul Ruttledge from Yeats's spiritual anarchist work of 1902, co-written with Moore and Hyde, *Where There is Nothing, There is God*, the most instructive play for evaluating the political meaning of *The Green Helmet*. A visionary mystic, Ruttledge leaves a life of comfort to live with the travellers before exciting revolt in a monastery after delivering a sermon on spiritual nihilism.[53] Yeats had Morris in mind, a man 'too busy and absorbed to give himself much to persons'.[54] Ruttledge anticipates the confusion and dissent that the arrival of the Red Man generates in *The Green Helmet*, expressing a sentiment in a 1904 letter Yeats wrote to George Russell where he declares, '[l]et us have no emotions, however abstract, in which their [sic] is not an athletic joy'.[55]

Le Bon identified in the crowd leader an impulse to martyrdom, sacrificing all family and personal interest in the process.[56] Ruttledge conforms to this type; leaving the comforts of his upper middle-class background to live among the travellers, his mother is convinced that he has gone mad.[57] Michael Gillane of *Cathleen ni Houlihan* also comes to mind, as does the hunger-striking Seanchan of *The King's Threshold*. As *Where There Is Nothing* progresses, emotions become ever more extreme. Respectable friends of the Ruttledge family are stripped of their clothes and subjected to ritual humiliation, echo of the Fool beating the Blind Man in *On Baile's Strand*, with its undertones of travesty and revolt. The spiritual bond between Paul and the monk Jerome is torn apart following his heretical sermon and Paul is finally beaten to death by a hysterical mob intent on destroying his breakaway religious community. A disaster on stage, the play nonetheless expressed certain features le

---

[52] Gustave le Bon, *The Crowd* (London: T. Fisher Unwin, 1896), p. 134.
[53] Yeats, *Where There Is Nothing / The Unicorn from the Stars*, ed. Katharine Worth (Washington DC: The Catholic University of America Press, 1987), pp. 101–2.
[54] Yeats to Quinn, 6 Feb. [1903]. Kelly and Schuchard, *Collected Letters*, vol. III, p. 312.
[55] Yeats to A. E., April 1904. Kelly and Schuchard, *Collected Letters*, vol. III, p. 578.
[56] Le Bon, *The Crowd*, p. 135.   [57] Yeats, *Where There Is Nothing*, p. 67.

Bon attributed to the sentiments of crowds with striking intensity. His sense of the 'simplicity and exaggeration of the sentiments of crowds' and the speed with which they spread like 'contagion' was evident not just in the violent conclusion of *Where There Is Nothing* but in the general extremity of feeling Paul arouses. The influence of le Bon's belief that 'an individual in a crowd resembles primitive beings' was demonstrated in Paul's immersion in the ancient beliefs and practices of the travellers.[58]

Howes's claims for le Bon's influence on Yeats are borne out in his plays of the 1900s but its political significance was highly ambivalent. Le Bon regarded the contemporary age as one of 'transition and anarchy', regarded literature as a far more reliable source of historical accuracy than works of history proper, and warned against 'the profoundly conservative instincts of crowds'.[59] Adrian Frazier and Spurgeon Thompson have characterised Yeats's behaviour during the *Playboy* disturbances as colonialist, characteristically Anglo-Irish in calling in the police to arrest rioters.[60] The provocative nature of *Where There Is Nothing* suggests something more complex; an automatic response to an embryonically totalitarian power beginning to shape nationalist revival in Ireland into militant dogma. Moreover, le Bon's hypotheses raises an interesting conundrum for assessing Yeats's politics at the end of the 1900s – the irrationality of the leader, through which Yeats distinguishes the hero from the conformity of the common mass, flows directly from crowd energy in the argument of *The Crowd*. Lauding the irrationality of Cuchulain as he does in *On Baile's Strand* and *The Green Helmet*, Yeats gives vent to that power of the crowd le Bon describes.

A new departure in Yeats's drama, *The Green Helmet* is crowded and noisy: charioteers, stable boys, and scullions jostle and roar, drowning out Cuchulain's shouting at one point (*VPl*, 442). It is difficult to overlook here the image of Yeats's voice being drowned out by the rioting crowd at the Abbey Theatre in January 1907. Behind it lay the ghost of Charles Stuart Parnell; in 'The Tragic Generation', Yeats recalled a remark by Goethe quoted extensively in the press at the time of Parnell's death: 'The Irish seem to me like a pack of hounds always dragging down some noble stag.' In 1905, Joseph Holloway claimed that Yeats had told him that he had Parnell in mind when writing *On Baile's Strand*: ' "People who do aught for Ireland", he said, "ever and always have to fight with the waves

---

[58] Le Bon, *The Crowd*, p. 56.   [59] *Ibid.*, pp. 14, 54, 62.
[60] Frazier, *Behind the Scenes*, pp. 213–18; Thompson, 'Yeats and Eugenicism', pp. 35–6.

in the end".[61] The concluding lines of *The Green Helmet* point to Parnell as a type of Nietzschean *Übermensch* mediated through the figure of Synge:

> When heart and mind shall darken that the weak
>   may end the strong,
> And the long-remembering harpers have matter for
>   their song. (*VPl*, 453)

Patrick Keane notes the praise of heroic individualism as virtuous folly in the Red Man's praise of Cuchulain in his final speech, marking him off from the crowd around him.[62] When the mob come to finish off Paul Ruttledge at the end of *Where There Is Nothing*, he asks that they give him 'a good death', a Nietzshean twist, perhaps, to the death of Parnell.[63] Echoing Ibsen, *The Will to Power* lamented the herd mentality that had gradually come to dominate European culture, a hatred of the individual expressing itself in ethical prescription.[64]

Drawing on the literature of farce in Chaucer and Shakespeare and engaging the Surrealist motifs of Jarry, *The Green Helmet* moved beyond this lament to ridicule Cuchulain in a situation of general turmoil. Taking its source from the stories of the feast of Briciu and the championship of Ulster in Gregory's *Cuchulain of Muirthemne*, the play seeks to generate a climate of lunacy. Like Jarry, Yeats wanted to create a stage where the visual impact would be 'intentionally violent and startling' (*VPl*, 421).[65] As Worth has observed, everything in the play was intended to shock: the violent colour scheme, the noisy sound effects and the 'first surrealist explosion' when three black hands come through the windows, plunging the scene into total darkness.[66] It shared with *Ubu Roi* the raucous qualities Peter Brook has identified with the 'rough' theatre.[67] Moon and sea are dominant presences, symbolising destiny and a voracious collective libidinal power. There is a full moon at the outset (*VPl*, 422), the daimonic Red Man who has come from the sea tells Conall he was so thirsty he could have drunk up the sea (*VPl*, 428), and the full moon reappears at the end (*VPl*, 451). Typical

---

[61] Yeats, *Autobiographies*, p. 316. Hogan and O'Neill, *Joseph Holloway's Abbey Theatre*, p. 58. This justifies the belief that *The Green Helmet* identifies in the fall of Parnell a source for the instincts motivating the *Playboy* riots. See also Foster, *Yeats*, vol. I, p. 336.
[62] Patrick Keane, *Yeats's Interactions with Tradition* (Columbia: University of Missouri Press, 1987), pp. 260–1.
[63] Yeats, *Where There Is Nothing*, p. 116.
[64] Friedrich Nietzsche, *The Will to Power* (London: Weidenfeld & Nicolson, 1968), p. 157.
[65] Jarry had wished his play to appear 'horrific' to its audience. 'De l'inutilité du théâtre au théâtre', *Mercure de France*, September (1896).
[66] Worth, *The Irish Drama*, p. 153.
[67] Peter Brook, *The Empty Space* (London: Penguin Press, 1990), pp. 73–4.

of reactions to the earliest Surrealist experiments on stage, Holloway was utterly bemused, complaining that the 'talkative group of chattering men and women who filled the stage was confused and unpicturesquely disposed'.[68] Like Jarry, Yeats intended *The Green Helmet* to mirror the Abbey audience, riling it through ridicule in recollection of *The Playboy*.[69]

The transgressive pretensions of the play are evident early on when Conall attempts to prevent the Young Man from entering the house, telling him he was ordered to protect it from the 'Shape-Changers' till dawn. The Young Man – Cuchulain's son in *On Baile's Strand* – pushes him aside, announcing his determination to 'unmake the law'.[70] When Cuchulain enters the stage for the first time, Conall tells him how the Red Man had visited on the same night twelve months previously and demanded a head for a head. Conall's response is both macabre and farcical, the effect of which is to caricature Cuchulain more as fool than hero:

> But he stood and laughed at us there, as though his sides
>   would split,
> Till I could stand it no longer, and whipped off his
>   head at a blow,
> Being mad that he did not answer, and more at his
>   laughing so,
> And there on the ground where it fell it went on
>   laughing at me. (*VPl*, 429–30)

This is reminiscent of farcical combat scenes in *Ubu Roi*, as when the young Buggerlas tries to defend Queen Wencelas against Père Ubu in Act II. At first Cuchulain does not believe Conall's story, thinking him to be drunk, to which Conall responds by ridiculing Cuchulain's insistent claims to heroic superiority (*VPl*, 430). The entire proceeding of the play, the pursuit of the Green Helmet, becomes a clownish charade akin to Ubu's quest for the Polish throne.[71] The final crowning of Cuchulain

---

[68] Nonetheless, he did praise the performances of Ambrose Power as the Red Man and J.M. Kerrigan as Cuchulain in the 1908 Abbey performance of the play's prose version. See Hogan and O'Neill, *Joseph Holloway's Abbey Theatre*, p. 107. Holloway's complaint marks the considerable distance Yeats had travelled since the 1890s; characteristic of his attitudes in that decade, he would complain to the poet Robert Bridges of Ibsen's friend Georg Brandes praising 'all manner of noisy persons'. Frayne and Johnson, *Collected Letters*, vol. II, pp. 64–5.
[69] Maya Slater, ed., *Three Pre-Surrealist Plays* (Oxford University Press, 1997), p. xxiii. The various competing factions in *The Green Helmet* seem a direct image of 'the tyranny of cliques' that Yeats suspected behind the *Playboy* riots in his opening speech at the Abbey Theatre debate on Synge's play of 4 February 1907. See, Frayne and Johnson, *Uncollected Prose*, vol. II, p. 351.
[70] Frayne and Johnson, *Uncollected Prose*, vol. II, p. 425.
[71] In Kenneth McLeish's robust translation of *Ubu Roi*, the Queen of Poland dreams that her husband's crown was taken from him and placed upon the head of the rebel Ubu by the lion and unicorn. Martin Hearne intends to gather 'the lawbreakers, the tinkers, the sievemakers,

acquires a farcical quality intended to pre-empt the charade of the ritual in *On Baile's Strand*, Yeats writing *The Green Helmet* retrospectively as a prologue to the earlier play.

This pronounced sense of farce owes much to Yeats's reading of Chaucer in the 1900s, giving expression to the transgressive and transformative power of laughter Bakhtin identifies in medieval literature. Reg Skene has noted the influence of 'The Nun's Priest's Tale' from *The Canterbury Tales*. In a telling letter to Florence Farr in August 1905, Yeats suggested that Morris would have done well to heed the practice of Chaucer in following the noble with the bawdy. 'Chaucer for instance follows his noble 'The Knight's Tale' with an unspeakable tale told by a drunken miller. If Morris had done the like – everyone would have read his *Earthly Paradise* for ever.'[72] Yeats was adopting this pattern in the first two plays of the Cuchulain cycle; the Wagnerian pretensions of *On Baile's Strand* are mocked in *The Green Helmet* farce. Through this Chaucerian influence, the play attempts to revive 'the grotesque tradition of laughter' that Bakhtin traced through Rabelais to medieval folk culture, laughter in its most universal and radical form.[73]

This transgressive power is represented through the Red Man who 'laughs like the sea', offering the Green Helmet to the bravest in the kingdom. A shape-changer of drunkenness, he jests 'too grimly when the ale is in the cup' (*VPl*, 435). Recalling Wilde's *Salomé*, a play that exercised an enduring influence on the later drama of Yeats, he has been beheaded. In this motif of decapitation, Yeats's preoccupations with virility and impotence as expressions of the historical forces shaping his age come into view. The Green Helmet itself is symbol of sanctity and profanity; an echo of the holy Grail that enthralled Eliot in *The Waste Land*, it is yet the Bacchanalian vessel of drunken Dionysian excess, a parody of the sacred in the manner of Bakhtin's caricature of medieval festival, an occasion of revelry and orgy.[74] Like Christy Mahon in *The Playboy*, the Red Man triggers dissent and passion in this community of warriors, wives, stablemen and servants. Laeg and Laegaire squabble over which of their masters is greatest, Conall or Cuchulain, bringing heroic virtue down to the level

---

the sheep-stealers' under the banner of the lion and unicorn, raised up by the beggar Johnny, in *The Unicorn from the Stars*'. Alfred Jarry, *The Ubu Plays*, trans. Kenneth McLeish (London: Nick Hern Books, 1997), p. 12; Yeats, *Where There Is Nothing*, p. 143.

[72] W. B. Yeats to Florence Farr [?4–5] August, 1905. Kelly and Schuchard, *Collected Letters*, vol. IV, p. 152. Steve Ellis argues that Chaucer's influence on Yeats was far from populist, though he leaves *The Green Helmet* out of account. See 'Chaucer, Yeats and the Living Voice', *Yeats Annual*, vol. XI, ed. Warwick Gould (London: Macmillan Press, 1995), pp. 45–60.

[73] Bakhtin, *Rabelais and His World*, pp. 72, 101.   [74] *Ibid.*, p. 83.

of a courtyard cockfight in a manner reminiscent of exchanges between Chanticleer and Pertelote in 'The Nun's Priest's Tale' from *The Canterbury Tales* (*VPl*, 439). The insults traded between their wives cast aspersions on the warriors' virility, sharply echoing the exchanges between Pegeen Mike and the Widow Quinn in Act I of *The Playboy*.[75]

Drawing on medieval traditions, subversive and transgressive forces in *The Green Helmet* owed much to Nietzsche. Making the case for Cuchulain as *Übermensch*, Patrick Keane traces the Red Man's talk of Cuchulain's 'laughing lip' to Zarathustra's 'laughter from the heights'.[76] In a poem from *The Green Helmet* collection, 'Upon a House Shaken by the Land Agitation', Yeats draws laughter and ceremonial imagery together:

> And the sweet laughing eagle thoughts that grow
> Where wings have memory of wings, and all
> That comes of the best knit to the best? (*VP*, 264)

The poem concludes with the lines, 'a written speech / [w]rought of high laughter, loveliness and ease'. The subversive power of laughter here appears tempered by aristocratic poise. Nonetheless, in placing it within writing, Yeats draws laughter into rhetoric, a decidedly Nietzschean move, particularly in light of Paul de Man's reading of Nietzsche's work as a testament to 'the rhetoric of tropes'.[77]

Nietzsche's influence bears strongly upon a political evaluation of *The Green Helmet* in the light of Conor Cruise O'Brien's argument for the reactionary turn in Yeats's politics from 1900, O'Brien regarding Nietzsche as a latter-day Machiavelli, riding roughshod over quotidian political realities.[78] In a perspective influenced profoundly by the democratic conservatism of Edmund Burke, O'Brien saw in Nietzsche's rhetoricity, admired by de Man and the deconstructionist school, the basis for a political fanaticism indifferent to practical social considerations.[79] Adorno and Horkheimer have argued strongly against the position on Nietzsche we encounter in O'Brien, claiming that Nietzsche's refusal to disguise the impossibility of deriving from reason any sustainable argument against

---

[75] J.M. Synge, *The Playboy of the Western World*, *The Complete Plays* (London: Methuen, 1981), pp. 177, 190–2.
[76] Keane, *Yeats's Interactions*, p. 156.
[77] Paul de Man, *Allegories of Reading: Figural Language in Rousseau, Nietzsche, Rilke and Proust* (New Haven: Yale University Press, 1979), pp. 82–3.
[78] O'Brien, *The Suspecting Glance*, p. 83.
[79] This is why O'Brien insists that Yeats misrepresents Burke. *The Suspecting Glance*, pp. 82–3. For O'Brien's reading of Burke, see *The Great Melody: A Thematic Biography and Commented Anthology of Edmund Burke* (London: Sinclair-Stevenson, 1992).

murder had fuelled the hatred of liberal democrats. Far from expressing a blind Romantic revolt against Enlightenment rationality, they see Nietzsche as 'one of the few after Hegel who recognised the dialectic of enlightenment'.[80]

However we read Nietzsche's influence, the mark of history is evident in *The Green Helmet* in this tension between laughter as self-delight, expression of the capacity of the *Übermensch* to live triumphantly in the consciousness of language as rhetoric, and laughter as mockery, including mockery of all pretension to elevated distinction. Cuchulain finally becomes an expression of that collective force against which he seeks to distinguish himself in *The Green Helmet*, embodying Yeats's desire to harmonise collective passion and revolutionary individualism. The limitations of the play lie in the incongruence of its raucous tone with the cadence of its verse form. But they also testify how difficult it had become to achieve Yeats's broader cultural project in Ireland in the aftermath of the *Playboy* riots. He continued to work towards its imaginative representation in subsequent plays of the Cuchulain cycle, engaging Expressionist techniques and the Absurdist mode of Pirandello in the process. Within the supernaturalist and mystical ponderings of these later plays lay a persistent tension between the images of the mythic hero separated from or expressive of his historical moment, figure of tragedy or farce. The following chapter explores this tension in the plays of the Cuchulain cycle that Yeats staged in the Japanese Noh form, *At the Hawk's Well* and *The Only Jealousy of Emer*.

[80] Theodor Adorno and Max Horkheimer 'The Concept of Enlightenment', *Dialect of Enlightenment* (London: Allen Lane, 1973), p. 44. Jameson traces the Nietzschean roots of *Dialectic of the Enlightenment* and *Negative Dialectics*, See *Late Marxism* (London: Verso, 1990), pp. 94–110.

CHAPTER 4

The turn to Noh: At the Hawk's Well *and* The Only Jealousy of Emer

It would be another six years before Yeats's next play on Cuchulain was performed, by which time the circumstances, style and audience for the production had altered dramatically from those of *On Baile's Strand* and *The Green Helmet*. Yeats employed the medieval Japanese Noh form of dance theatre for the performance of *At the Hawk's Well* in Lady Cunard's drawing room in April 1916. Interest in Japanese art was marked in London bohemian circles from the 1890s, particularly through the pages of *The Dome*, and Yeats was long familiar with the fad of *Japonisme* when he came to compose *At the Hawk's Well* and *The Only Jealousy of Emer* soon after in 1917. The turn to Noh has been generally received as Yeats's manner of withdrawing his energies from the cultivation of a popular movement in the Irish theatre shaped by a renewed faith in artistic vitality. The aristocratic patronage of these plays evident in the drawing room settings Lady Cunard and Lady Islington offered for the performances, along with their stylised quality and their concentration upon supernatural themes, point to an elitism on Yeats's part advanced in the level of its self-consciousness.

These Noh plays were quite obviously forms of high art presented before a select audience. There are, however, other aspects pertinent to evaluating their political meaning at a time when Europe was engulfed in the ravages of the First World War. Whatever the relative silence in Yeats's poetry on the subject of the war, the crisis in values it precipitated in Europe is felt everywhere in these plays. The second performance of *At the Hawk's Well* was staged at Lady Islington's drawing room for a war benefit, the Social Institute's Union of Women and Girls. Yeats turned to the Noh form of drama at this time because those plays 'arose in an age of continual war and became a part of the education of soldiers'.[1] Through

---

[1] Yeats, 'Certain Noble Plays of Japan', *Essays and Introductions* (London: Macmillan Press, 1961), p. 235. On the second performance of *At the Hawk's Well* see Hone, *Yeats*, p. 297, and Saddlemyer, *Becoming George: The Life of Mrs W. B. Yeats* (Oxford University Press, 2002), pp. 140–1.

the Noh form, Yeats was developing the kind of theatre he learned from Maeterlinck to imagine the war as regression to primitive totemism in the machine age. In so doing, he was following a path Strindberg took in *The Ghost Sonata* and Oskar Kokoschka in *Murderer, Hope of Woman*, both from 1907. In developing the pattern of 1890s Symbolism and its Wagnerian undercurrents, these plays laid theatrical foundations for the development of Expressionism as the dominant form through which Germany's experience of the war was represented.

Yeats's experiments with Noh were part of that desire to reform the theatre dating back to the 1890s. In 1899, he recalled advising a friend to write a pastoral play that succeeded admirably in a little theatre before suffering ridicule when transferred to a major London theatre. He blamed the rise of commercial theatre for this failure, through which managers substituted painted landscapes for the descriptions of poetry, the canvas becoming as important as the story itself.[2] In 1904, he called for a wholesale reform of the theatre, believing there was 'nothing good about it at present'.[3] The range of Yeats plays during the 1900s were not only composed and performed in opposition to the theatre of commerce, but they also contrived to convey through the mood of estrangement they evoked the stupefying effect of such theatre, seeking to stimulate in audiences a sense of the dehumanising aspect of modern culture. In a 1917 essay published alongside Yeats's introduction to *At the Hawk's Well*, Holbrook Jackson recognised the radical nature of Yeats's theatrical vision, aiming at 'Ibsen's revolution in the spirit of men' that, 'far from being insular ... hoped to add to a renascent folk-spirit the culture of the modern world'.[4]

Yeats's collaboration with Edward Gordon Craig, son of the actress Ellen Terry, illustrates the ambivalence in the political nature of that vision. Described by the Hungarian dramatist Alexander Hevesi as 'the truest revolutionist I have ever known', Craig exerted profound influence on Yeats's theatrical development from 1910.[5] This influence was felt most dramatically in Yeats's decision to use masks for *At the Hawk's Well* and *The Only Jealousy of Emer*, a decision that owed much to the ideas discussed in Craig's journal *The Mask*, first published in March

---

[2] Yeats, 'The Theatre', *The Dome*, pp. 48, 50–1.
[3] W. B. Yeats, 'The Reform of the Theatre', *Plays and Controversies* (London: Macmillan Press, 1923), p. 49.
[4] Holbrook Jackson, 'Men of To-Day and To-Morrow', *To-Day*, ed. Holbrook Jackson, 1:3 (1917), 95.
[5] Alexander Hevesi, 'A Tribute to Craig from Hungarian Theatre', *A Living Theatre: The Gordon Craig School: The Arena: Goldoni: The Mask* (Florence: Edward Gordon Craig, 1913), p. 65. For an excellent discussion of Yeats's collaboration with Craig, see Dorn, *Players*, pp. 13–33.

1908.⁶ In his 1911 essay, 'The Actor and the Über-marionette', Craig envisaged a theatre in which all trace of human character would be erased through a puppet-like acting style, the 'Über-marionette'.⁷ Craig sought to combine the subversive power of Alfred Jarry's puppet theatre with Nietzsche's revolutionary individualism. He was attracted to the Noh form as an effective means of staging the kind of non-human theatre he envisaged, discussing it extensively in the 1910 issue of *The Mask*, an issue that also included Yeats's essay 'The Tragic Theatre'.⁸

It is true that Craig's unease with realism lay partly in its political influence, each 'whisper of Revolt' finding 'an echo in the Theatre of Realism'.⁹ In certain measure, however, this distinguished him from Yeats, given the persistent sense of disturbance in Yeats's plays of the 1900s and the explicit connection made to political revolt in *Where There Is Nothing* and *Cathleen ni Houlihan*. Craig's main complaint against realism was not sedition, but parsimony, the public's concern with 'the quest of money', being for him a 'class of monstrous meanness' that encouraged realism on stage, 'the short measure or meanness of the artist'.¹⁰

These sentiments here were close to those Yeats expressed to Lady Gregory in an open letter published in *The Irish Statesman* in Autumn 1919:

All exploitation of the life of the wealthy, for the eye and the ear of the poor and half poor, in plays, in popular novels, in musical comedy, in fashion papers, at the cinema, in *Daily Mirror* photographs, is a travesty of the life of the rich; and if it were not would all but justify some Red Terror; and it impoverishes and vulgarises the imagination, seeming to hold up for envy and to commend a life where all is display and hurry, passion without emotion, emotion without intellect, and where there is nothing stern and solitary.¹¹

This typified the sentiments emanating from *The Mask*. Dorothy Nevile Lees, for example, made exactly the same complaint about contemporary culture in 1913, when reflecting on the reforms Craig proposed:

Among the evils which *The Mask* attacks to that end are Realism, Vulgarity, Commercialism and the trade spirit, Pedantry, Theatricalism, the aggressive

---

⁶ Miller, *The Noble Drama*, p. 147.
⁷ Edward Gordon Craig, 'The Actor and the Über-marionette', *On The Art of The Theatre* (London: Heinemann, 1911), pp. 81–2.
⁸ See Flannery, 'W. B. Yeats', p. 98.
⁹ Craig, 'Foreword', *A Living Theatre*, p. 5.
¹⁰ Edward Gordon Craig, 'Realism and the Actor', *On The Art* (London: Heinemann, 1911), p. 288. Elsewhere Craig describes realism as 'the blunt statement of life, something everybody misunderstands while recognizing'. 'The Actor', p. 89.
¹¹ W. B. Yeats, 'A People's Theatre: A Letter to Lady Gregory' (1919), *Explorations* (London: Macmillan Press, 1962), pp. 244–5.

personality of the actor, the star systems, badly built theatres, the invasion of the theatre by other artists, the system of actor managers, the representation of ugliness ... the selfish cowardice which would oppose all progress or reform lest it should militate against personal prosperity and personal ease.[12]

Craig's collaboration with Yeats was born in significant measure from a sense that only a revolutionary transformation in the forms of contemporary art might withstand this relentless process of commercialisation. Whatever his conservative bent, Craig nonetheless gave wholehearted endorsement to Eleonora Duse's declaration that 'to save the Theatre, the Theatre must be destroyed, the actors and actresses must all die of the plague'.[13] This was one of the earliest statements of anti-theatre developed subsequently by Pirandello, Brecht and Beckett, and Yeats himself would use the title 'Instead of a Theatre' for his introduction to *At the Hawk's Well* published in May 1917.[14]

Yeats's departures from the classical conventions of Noh in *At the Hawk's Well* were deliberate choices made in the creation of one of the earliest instances of anti-theatre. Masaru Sekine has identified the distortions in Ernest Fenollosa's translations of Motokiyo Ze-Ami's original versions of Noh dramas that formed the basis to *Noh, Or Accomplishment*, arising in large measure from Fenollosa's misunderstanding of religious meaning in the plays, and the even greater distortions in Ezra Pound's editing of Fenollosa's versions.[15] Comparing *At the Hawk's Well* with the Noh drama *Yoro* (that Pound left out of *Noh, Or Accomplishment*), Richard Taylor observes how Yeats inverts myth in his play. Rather than expressing cosmic harmony, the symbols of tree and well are destitute of creative force: the tree is bare, the well is dry.[16] This describes precisely Adorno's definition of the modernist aesthetic as 'myth turned against itself' in which 'the timelessness of myth becomes the catastrophic instant that destroys temporal continuity'.[17] In his account of the personality of Phase

---

[12] Dorothy Nevile Lees, 'About "The Mask" ', *A Living Theatre: The Gordon Craig School: The Avenue: Goldoni: The Mask* (Florence: Edward Gordon Craig, 1913), p. 13.

[13] Craig, 'The Actor', p. 79. For Craig's royalism see also in the same volume 'God Save the King', pp. xix–xxiii.

[14] W. B. Yeats, 'Instead of a Theatre', *To-Day*, 1:3 (1917), 98–102. See also Preface to *Four Plays for Dancers* (London: Macmillan Press, 1921).

[15] The versions of Fenollosa and Pound were, of course, the sources from which Yeats was working. Masaru Sekine, 'Noh, Fenollosa, Pound and Yeats – Have East and West Met?', *Yeats Annual*, vol. XIII, ed. Warwick Gould (London: Macmillan Press, 1998), pp. 176–94. See also Okifumi Komesu, '*At the Hawk's Well* and *Taka No Izumi* in a "Creative Circle" ', *Yeats Annual*, vol. v, ed. Warwick Gould (London: Macmillan Press, 1987), p. 111.

[16] Taylor, *The Drama of W. B. Yeats*, p. 128.

[17] Adorno, *Aesthetic Theory*, p. 23.

23 in the occult system outlined in *A Vision*, Yeats anticipated this perspective on the early avant-garde. Here the iconoclasm of Joyce, Pound, Pirandello and Eliot is presented as the complete sundering of myth and fact 'united until the exhaustion of the Renaissance'. For the first time, man recognises 'the rigidity of fact', calling up myth – 'the Mask – which now but gropes its way out of the mind's dark but will shortly pursue and terrify'.[18] Notwithstanding crucial differences in taste and disposition, Yeats shared with these leading figures in European modernism a propensity to literary and theatrical experiment through medieval forms and themes.[19]

Discussing his engagement with the Noh form, Jeffares and Knowland note how extensively Yeats modified it.[20] In so doing, *At the Hawk's Well* anticipated the stoic minimalism of *Waiting for Godot*: a bare tree, two men awaiting the arrival of Godot as the Old Man and Cuchulain await the flowing of the well.[21] The modernism of Yeats's play is further testified by the way it worked out Craig's idea of body of the actor as 'a machine'.[22] Through a sense of the unhuman he sought by the way of mask, dance and movement, Yeats was inversely representing processes of dehumanisation within industrial capitalism most traumatically evident in the slaughter in the trenches. In this way, the stylised stasis of *At the Hawk's Well* anticipated the manner in which the silence of *Waiting for Godot* would be received as meditation on the silence of Auschwitz. If Yeats's idiosyncratic deployment of the Noh form looked forward to Beckett, it also, like Strindberg in *The Ghost Sonata*, looked back to the Maeterlinck of *The Blind*, *The Intruder* and *Pelléas and Mélisande*.[23]

---

[18] George Mills Harper and Walter Kelly Hood, eds., *A Critical Edition of Yeats's A Vision (1925)* (London: Macmillan Press, 1978), p. 212. Foster detects hard-right undertones here, reading the passage in the context of Yeats's discussions with Joseph Hone in the mid-1920s on the prospects for an anti-democratic political movement in Ireland. *Yeats*, vol. II, p. 290. But the broad spectrum of the European avant-garde, from the Italian Futurists to Soviet Constructivists, were anti-democratic at this time, regarding the dominant forms of bourgeois culture as evidence of the exhausted state of modern society.

[19] Chesterton identified the avant-garde in this way, describing Futurism, for example, as 'pastism' in disguise. 'The Hyeroglyphics of Innocence', p. 51.

[20] A. Norman Jeffares and A. S. Knowland, *A Commentary on the Collected Plays of W. B. Yeats* (London: Macmillan Press, 1975), p. 83. For a full discussion of Yeats's departure from Noh conventions, see Ofikumi Komesu, *The Double Perspective of Yeats's Aesthetic* (Gerrards Cross: Colin Smythe, 1984).

[21] For a discussion of the ways in which *At the Hawk's Well* anticipated *Waiting For Godot*, see Anthony Roche, *Contemporary Irish Drama: From Beckett to McGuinness* (Dublin: Gill & Macmillan, 1994), pp. 26–7.

[22] Craig, 'The Actor', p. 70.

[23] For comparison between Strindberg and Yeats see Block, 'Symbolist Drama', p. 45.

Engaging the audience structurally through experiments in perception was a crucial element of the Noh plays. The original performances were designed for audiences composed of patrons and like-minded artists, though Edmund Dulac would later take the play successfully to wider audiences in New York. If Yeats appeared elitist in composing a deliberately 'unpopular' theatre, he was also bringing the audience more directly into the composition of the play itself. From the earliest, Yeats sought forms of revelation in performance through concealment. Through the explicit use of mask in *At the Hawk's Well*, he pursued this in a way that made the audience central to the play itself. Maeterlinck's work was an important precedent here, particularly in its treatment of perception. The audience of *The Blind* was obliged to conjure the landscape the blind men describe, stirring the powers of imagination dulled by those painted landscapes of commercial theatre derided by Yeats and Craig. The landscape suggested is arid, however, commenting upon the sterility of contemporary civilisation.

At the Hawk's Well makes perception crucial from the outset:

> I call to the eye of the mind
> A well long choked up and dry
> And boughs long stripped by the wind. (*VPl*, 399)[24]

This recalls the subject of Synge's *The Well of the Saints* and the blind couple whose eyes are opened only to witness their own decrepitude. But Yeats was reaching back further to Maeterlinck's *Pelléas and Mélisande*. At the beginning of Act II, we encounter both figures together at 'the Fountain of the Blind', so named because of a belief in the power of its waters to heal blindness.[25] The 'eye of the mind' is opened in *At the Hawk's Well*, but to a barren world. This echoes any number of passages from *The Blind*:

THE SIXTH BLIND MAN: We must be very far from home; I can't understand any of the sounds here.
THIRD MAN BORN BLIND: I've been smelling the smell of dead leaves for ages!
THE SIXTH BLIND MAN: Does anyone remember seeing the Island in the past, and can they tell us where we are?
THE OLDEST BLIND WOMAN: We were all blind by the time we got here.[26]

---

[24] Natalie Crohn Schmitt claims that Yeats probably had in mind an actual well on Tullagan Hill near Hawk's Rock in Co. Sligo when writing the play, while T. R. Henn notes the significance to the play of the legend that a spring appeared there during the prayer of St Patrick, 'whose waters ebb and flow mysteriously', and of the hazel tree that stood beside such wells. Crohn Schmitt, ' "Haunted by Places": Landscape in Three Plays by W. B. Yeats', *Comparative Drama*, 31:3 (1997), 345. T. R. Henn, *The Lonely Tower: Studies in the Poetry of W.B. Yeats*, 2nd edn (London: Methuen, 1965), p. 3.

[25] Maeterlinck, *Pelléas*, trans. Ervine Winslow, p. 36.

[26] Maurice Maeterlinck, *The Blind. Three Pre-Surrealist Plays*, ed. Maya Slater (Oxford University Press, 1997), p. 16.

Yeats's boughs 'long stripped by the wind' recalls this 'smell of dead leaves'; like the well that is choked in Yeats's play, so the senses are stifled in Maeterlinck's.

Richard Taylor argues that the efficacy of *At the Hawk's Well* depends in large measure on the producer's fidelity to Yeats's original scheme, thrusting character and action into the real world of the audience rather than drawing spectators into the fictional world of the play.[27] Joseph Hone notes that for the first performance in Lady Cunard's drawing room, the players came in by the same door as the audience and in his preface to the first published edition of the play in *Harper's Bazaar* of March 1917, Yeats stated that the decision to use masks was motivated practically by the absence of any special lighting and the nearness of the audience.[28] If this indicates the intimacy of that first performance, it was an intimacy employed to heighten the sense of estrangement epitomised in the sterile landscape conjured. In his preface to *Noh, Or Accomplishment*, Yeats recalled how witnessing the dance by Michio Ito performed on a small stage or in a drawing room, devoid of lighting technique or stage-picture, convinced him of the possibility of his new theatrical endeavour. He was struck by the extraordinary sense of distance Ito generated in such intimate surroundings. Ito's achievement renewed Yeats's faith in the estranging power of art, anticipating the explosion in theatre of alienation that would mark continental drama of the inter-war years.[29] The more intimate the setting, the greater the sense of estrangement achieved: *At the Hawk's Well* sought to draw its audience into a situation it could not recognise.

That this alienating effect was critically responding to the circumstances of the First World War is testified by the significant parallels with what yet was a very different play, Oskar Kokoschka's *Murderer, Hope of Women*. First published in 1907, a new version of this play appeared in 1917, the same year as the first publication of *At the Hawk's Well* under the title *The Well of Immortality*. With its publication in 1910 in Herwarth Walden's major Expressionist journal, *Der Sturm*, *Murderer, Hope of Women* aroused controversy and became known to a wide audience.[30] If not through his brother Jack, a great admirer of Kokoschka's painting,

---

[27] Taylor, *The Drama of W. B. Yeats*, p. 135. For further consideration of audience role in the play, see K. P. S. Jochum, 'W. B. Yeats's *At the Hawk's Well* and the Dialectic of Tragedy', *Visra-Bharati Quarterly*, 31:1 (1965–6), 27.

[28] Hone, *Yeats*, p. 297. Jeffares, *A Commentary*, p. 85.

[29] See, Yeats 'Certain Noble Plays of Japan', p. 224. For further consideration of Yeats's technique, see Natalie Crohn Schmitt, ' "Separating Strangeness" and "Intimacy" in W. B. Yeats's Drama', *Journal of Dramatic Theory and Criticism*, 15:2 (2001), 85–94.

[30] Karl Leydecker, 'Afterword', *Oskar Kokoschka: Plays and Poems*, trans. Michael Mitchell (Riverside CA: Adriadne Press, 2001), p. 247.

Yeats would certainly have been made aware of the play through Craig or Ashley Dukes, London expert on German avant-garde drama whom Yeats sought to engage to produce *The Player Queen* in the 1930s.

Notwithstanding Yeats's reservations about Expressionism evident later when he rejected O'Casey's *The Silver Tassie*, *At the Hawk's Well* shared with *Murderer, Hope of Women* features pointing to a shared sense of the war as the manifestation of certain dispositions overtaking European society in the first decades of the twentieth century. Names are depersonalised: *Murderer, Hope of Women* gives us the Man, the Woman, warriors and maidens; in *At the Hawk's Well* we encounter an Old Man, a Young Man, the Guardian of the Well and three musicians, all wearing masks. In Kokoschka's play, the Old Man brands the Woman; in Yeats's, the Old Man regards the Woman of the Sidhe as his mortal enemy, victim of her curse. Both plays are set in antiquity at nightfall and, personifying destiny, the warriors of Kokoschka's play mirror Yeats's musicians. In contrast to *At the Hawk's Well*, theirs is a raw physical presence on stage, but like the musicians in Yeats's play, they chant the opening lines, speaking fatalistically of the Man whom they follow and try to tear from his horse:

We were the blazing wheel around him. We were the blazing wheel around you, stormer of sealed strongholds![31]

The maidens of Kokoschka's play seek to guard the Woman in the Tower from the Man just as the female Guardian of the Well protects its waters from the Young Man through the allure of her Hawk dance in *At the Hawk's Well*.

Behind these similarities lay a shared meditation on sex, power and violence as primitive urges laid bare in the orgiastic destruction of the war. Developing Blake's idea of sexual love founded upon spiritual hatred, the sexual symbolism of the flowing water and the Hawk dance in Yeats's play stirs in Cuchulain a lust for war while perpetuating the Old Man's paralysis. Power resides at the level of a blind instinctual willing here in which its relentless pursuit ultimately leads to a complete loss of agency, evident in the hypnotic effect of the Hawk dance on Cuchulain. The influence of Schopenhauer, a figure central to German Expressionism, is evident in this regard. In 1901, Yeats claimed that some of Schopenhauer's essays provided the best account of literature's role in human affairs;

---

[31] Oskar Kokoschka, *Murderer, Hope of Women*, *Oskar Kokoschka: Plays and Poems*, trans. Michael Mitchell (Riverside, CA: Adriadne Press, 2001), p. 31.

in the 1930s, he makes a number of telling references to Schopenhauer, addressed in Chapter 7 in this volume.[32]

The representation of power through aquatic and lunatic symbolism receives its most concentrated expression in Yeats's play in the symbol of the well. Dried up, it embodies that draining of imaginative vitality Yeats identified in a middle-class propensity for conformity, recalling the contaminated spring of *An Enemy of the People*.[33] A decrepit figure who hypnotises the Young Man, the Guardian of the Well recalls Cathleen ni Houlihan and the spell she casts on Michael Gillane. The Hawk cry she emits, however, is not her own, the Old Man revealing that she is 'possessed'. Following her Hawk dance, the First Musician calls on God's protection '[f]rom a horrible deathless body / Sliding through the veins of a sudden' (*VPl*, 408–10). Images of living death equally abound in *Murderer, Hope of Women*. The Man's appearance strongly suggests a ghost from among the dead of the trenches in the 1917 production, Kokoschka himself having been wounded in the war. His face is white and a bandage covers a wound on his forehead. When he touches the Woman at the play's end she turns white and rigid.[34] In the visually striking opening, the warriors feed off the hero in vampiric fashion as they now seem to follow him, now drag him down. Striking is the similarity of both plays in their obsession with parasitic existence; characters feed off one another compulsively, draining their energy or having their lives drained from them. Neither the Old Man nor the Guardian of the Well are capable of life away from 'the barbarous spot' where their vitality has been sapped. The warriors in Kokoschka's drama feed off the Man, while the Woman is drawn inexorably towards him as towards her death. The branding of the Woman is the most violent and theatrically daring moment in *Murderer, Hope of Women*; beyond its sexual violence, it also presents her acquisition of identity as a painful congealment, a permanent mark of possession.

The flow of waters in *At the Hawk's Well* holds out the promise of the return of imaginative power in a sterile world. The Old Man has sunken

---

[32] To the editor of *The United Irishman*, 7 December 1901. Kelly and Schuchard, *Collected Letters*, vol. III, p. 133.
[33] Birgit Bjersby traces the well image to a record of three visions seen by members of the Order of the Golden Dawn, while Helen Vendler identifies a source in a piece from Standish O'Grady published in *Selected Essays and Passages* (1918) that was based on material originally included in *History of Ireland* (1880). Bjersby, *The Interpretation of the Cuchulain Legend*, p. 43. Vendler, *Yeats's Vision and the Later Plays*, pp. 204–5. These identifications, however, do not discredit T. R. Henn's observation of the 'intense interest in all aspects of virility' in the later Yeats plays, the well symbol being one instance thereof. See, *The Lonely Tower*, p. 280.
[34] Kokoschka, *Murderer*, pp. 31, 36.

from vitality to destitution, one who has 'eaten grass / And drunk the rain' (*VPl*, 405–6). The curse of the Woman of the Sidhe hangs over him:

> That curse may be
> Never to win a woman's love and keep it;
> Or always to mix hatred in the love;
> Or it may be that she will kill your children,
> That you will find them, their throats torn and bloody,
> Or you will be so maddened that you will kill them
> With your own hand. (*VPl*, 407–8)

The images of violence here recall *On Baile's Strand* and Cuchulain's account of love 'but as a kiss / In the mid-battle'. Yeats comes close to the raw metaphysical horror of Kokoschka's play at this point, in which the Man, in convulsions, laments with a bleeding, visible wound:

Senseless desire from horror to horror, Insatiable gyration in the void. Labor without birth, sunfall, heaving space. End of those who praised me.[35]

The dominant motif of both plays is that of futility and suffering as primary conditions of human existence. The Old Man's image of the woman who murders her offspring in *At the Hawk's Well* echoes the Expressionist violence of *Murderer, Hope of Woman*.

Daniel Albright notes how important an influence Otto Weininger's *Sex and Character* (1903) was on Kokoschka, a work in which sex was conceived as a kind of damnation and women as formless, corporeal creatures 'who have no interest in anything except phallus worship and sexual intercourse'. Central to his reading of *Murderer, Hope of Women* is the moment of branding, in which Weininger's idea of woman as a 'signless' creature devoid of identity is enacted. It symbolises Weininger's notion of sex as a man's attempt to possess and name a woman, and a woman's attempt 'to kill a man, drink his blood, incorporate his force'.[36] This vampiric image of Kokoschka's archetypal Woman further underlines the Expressionist influence on *At the Hawk's Well*, given the vampiric nature of the archetypal Woman of the Sidhe who takes possession of the Guardian of the Well as 'a horrible deathless body'.

Behind this lay the fetishism of the commodity haunting Yeats's drama from its inception, and the antagonism of the gender relations it intensified. The curse of infanticide that the Old Man imagines looks back to *On Baile's Strand* and ahead to *Purgatory*. Like the branding in Kokoschka's

---

[35] Kokoschka, *Murderer*, p. 35.
[36] Daniel Albright, *Untwisting the Serpent: Modernism in Music, Literature, and Other Arts* (The University of Chicago Press, 2000), p. 25.

play, the curse is a symptom of the fetish character of commodification, reducing its subject to the static form of the object. Faced with circumstances in which commodification had saturated culture itself, both Kokoschka and Yeats turn to primeval images of branding and curse in the attempt to imagine the deadening impact of reification in modern European society, manifested most brutally in the catastrophe of the war.

Given the influence of Maeterlinck's treatment of audience on *At the Hawk's Well*, and its consonance with that of *Murderer, Hope of Women*, the Hawk dance is conceivable as a performative representation of the forces unleashed in the First World War. Sylvia Ellis has brought to light the revolution in dance taking place in London society from the 1900s as the backdrop to Yeats engaging Michio Ito for the 1916 performance of *At the Hawk's Well*. Drawing attention to the 'free' interpretation of the Hawk dance performed by Ninette de Valois in 1921, Ellis points to the contribution the play made to a revolution in practices across the arts taking place during the war years. Following Ito, de Valois's performance was hugely indebted to the revolutionary impact of Isadora Duncan in the field of dance and the iconoclastic achievement of Diaghilev's *Ballets Russes*. In later years, de Valois revealed that she performed the Hawk dance in the manner of Abstract Expressionism.[37]

Albright points out that Ito, who performed the dance in the 1916 productions, had been trained in eurhythmics, a system of movement and gesture devised by Émile Jaques-Dalcroze, within which the entire body was employed to represent a single musical phrase.[38] Helen Caldwell argues that Ito's dance, first performed on 3 April 1916, though indeed a modified form of Noh dance, involved a faster increase of tempo than that of Noh, with more dramatic arm movement designed to convey Egyptian representations of the Hawk with spread wings.[39] Ito notoriously practised his dance technique by imitating the gestures of birds at the London Zoo, with Yeats observing, following the method that led him to devise the 'Fox Dance' in 1915.[40] Approximating to the method acting developed from Konstantin Stanislavski's revolution at the Moscow Art theatre, the

---

[37] Sylvia Ellis, *The Plays of W. B. Yeats: Yeats and the Dancer* (London: Palgrave-Macmillan, 1994), pp. 227–8. .
[38] Albright, *Untwisting the Serpent*, p. 71. Ellis adds that Ito knew the conventions of Noh in his youth before leaving Japan. *The Plays of W. B. Yeats*, pp. 225–7.
[39] Helen Caldwell, *Michio Ito: The Dancer and His Dances* (Berkeley, CA: University of California Press, 1977). Quoted in Ellis, *The Plays of W. B. Yeats*, p. 227. Ellis also notes that Ito shared Yeats's interest in Greek and Egyptian dance and experimented with choreography based on sculptural friezes or on figures of ancient Greek amphorae. *Ibid.*, p. 227.
[40] *Ibid.*, p. 226.

practice suggests how Ito saw the dance as at once corporeal and artificial; through this combination, the intense sexual energy we encounter in Kokoschka's *Murderer, Hope of Women* becomes concentrated and disciplined, precisely the dynamic of Abstract Expressionism.

Typical of Yeats's later drama, the Hawk dance combined sexual and supernatural power.[41] Yeats's relationship with Gonne was certainly at play here; Ann Saddlemeyer draws attention to the claim Gonne made upon the Hawk symbol in a letter to Yeats of March 1916 when she learned of *At the Hawk's Well*.[42] However, the dance was more than an expression of frustrated desire; Yeats was taking his personal struggle with impotence as a point of departure for a much broader sense of the sterility and destruction he discerned everywhere in contemporary civilisation. The dance frustrates the usurpation of the old generation by the new, thereby breaking a natural course of descent. Cuchulain is mesmerised by the Guardian of the Well and the Old Man misses the flow of its waters once more. Faced with this failure, Cuchulain rushes to war in the hills at the end of the play, while the Old Man remains condemned to slow decay. The war is not renewal but distortion, born from a failure to release creative vitality through a slaying of the father.

The Noh dance form attracted Yeats because the dancer's body acquired a machine-like rigidity, with the upper body completely still.[43] This recalls Arthur Symons's argument for the abstract thinker's love of dance, describing it in 1898 as part of 'that natural madness which men were once wise enough to include in religion'.[44] Yeats found in that combination of rigidity and movement a religious image of iconic coldness that paradoxically articulated the force of mechanical abstraction driving an industrial-scale war. Inhabiting the Oedipal dynamic while yet subverting it, the order of conflict expressed through the Hawk dance glosses the war as a form of primitive regression manifesting itself as a break from Nature.

De Valois's Abstract Expressionist interpretation of the Hawk dance was, following Ito, an entirely appropriate expression of the historical agony concentrated in *At the Hawk's Well*. The rigour of the Hawk dance carried a geometric abstraction even as it revolted against the mechanism of a scientific age; its energy expressed the force of the modernist

---

[41] See Nicholas Meihuizen's consideration of sanctity and sexuality in Yeats's later work. *Yeats and the Drama of Sacred Space* (Amsterdam: Rodopi, 1998), p. 147.
[42] Saddlemeyer, *Becoming George*, pp. 140–1.
[43] Yeats, 'Certain Noble Plays of Japan', *Essays and Introductions*, p. 231.
[44] Symons, 'Ballet', p. 66.

imagination unleashed even as it hesitated before the prospect of formlessness and obliteration of tradition. Emerging from the strife between a historical drive to homogenise and its irrationalist counter-force, its intensity was transformative to the extent to which it sought an idiosyncratic fusion of these polarities. In this sense, the Hawk dance was hieratic in its eroticism, anticipating the strange sexual violence of *The Herne's Egg*. The brutalising process of modernisation was inscribed in the dialectical nature of the play's ritual form.[45]

Yeats began writing his second dance play of the Cuchulain cycle, *The Only Jealousy of Emer*, in 1917, a play that quickly became an obsession, born out of his rejected marriage proposals to Maud Gonne and her daughter Iseult that year and his later marriage to George Hyde Lees.[46] Its composition grew out of the experiment in Automatic Writing that George began days after the marriage on 20 October, 1917.[47] The messages from what Yeats called his 'Instructors' would not only provide him with 'metaphors for poetry' but also form the basis for what remains his most enigmatic creation, *A Vision*, first published in 1925, a work that continues to defy critical understanding. Foster dismisses it as largely nonsensical, while Saddlemeyer describes it curiously as a 'fragmented report of their encounter with another universe'.[48]

Fran Brearton makes the case for the First World War as the 'major force' behind the creation of *A Vision*, a work that is 'preoccupied with the dead'.[49] Of course the spiritualist and occult beliefs of both Yeatses that inform the work predated the war, by two decades in the case of William. That the war was indeed a determining influence on the Automatic Writing experiment is testified by the fact that *A Vision* was not nearly as rare a volume as contemporary observers have deemed it to be. Early in 1921, just over three years after the Yeats experiment began,

---

[45] Derrida identifies the influence of Ernest Fenollosa's work on Ezra Pound as crucial to the break in Western phonocentrism in its concern for the Chinese ideogram. *Of Grammatology*, trans. Gayatri Spivak (Baltimore: Johns Hopkins University Press, 1976), p. 92. Albright points out, however, that modern scholars 'look askance' at Fenollosa's arguments in *The Chinese Written Character as a Medium for Poetry*. *Untwisting the Serpent*, p. 64.

[46] See George Mills Harper, *The Making of Yeats's A Vision: A Story of the Automatic Script*, vol. I (Carbondale: Southern Illinois University Press, 1987), p. 62.

[47] Saddlemeyer, *Becoming George*, pp. 102–4. Gregory N. Eaves is struck by how frequently the play is referred to in the Automatic Script and George Mills Harper describes how Yeats postponed its completion because he wanted further messages from the Automatic Script to fully clarify its symbolic meanings. Eaves, 'The Anti-Theatre and its Double', p. 34; Mills Harper, *The Making*, vol. I, pp. 25, 28.

[48] Foster, *Yeats*, vol. II, p. 282. Saddlemeyer, *Becoming George*, p. 343.

[49] Fran Brearton, *The First World War in Irish Poetry: From W. B. Yeats to Michael Longley* (Oxford University Press, 2000), p. 59.

The New Age reviewed *The Fellowship of the Picture*, an Automatic Script taken down by a certain Nancy Dearmer and edited by her husband, purporting to emanate from the spirit of a friend killed in action in France in 1918 who reputedly inaugurated the script in July the following year. A similar work appeared the following year, *The Survival of the Soul and its Evolution after Death*, documenting the visions and paranormal experiences of a young girl employed as an artist's model in Paris in 1912.[50]

That the Automatic Writing experiment derived in large measure from the entanglements of Yeats's love life, perpetually haunted by the figure of Gonne, is not in dispute; as a theatrical outcome of the Script, *The Only Jealousy of Emer* simply confirms this. Janis Hadwell and Rosalind E. Clark agree that the play was written with the perspective of Emer paramount, Hadwell asserting that Emer represented George whom Yeats had married in 1917.[51] This is confirmed in Yeats's *Vision* notes of this time, in which George is identified with Emer, Iseult with Eithne and Maud with Fand.[52] Through the manner in which he addressed these matters creatively, however, Yeats engaged the catastrophic pressures on European society generated from the war. The Automatic Writing experiment was not just typical of responses to the loss effected by the war in London circles, but also the esoteric experiments associated with Surrealism and Dadaism in Paris. As *The Green Helmet* showed, Yeats had already absorbed Jarry's *Ubu Roi* even as he bemoaned the arrival of the Savage God; as Yeats's first theatrical expression of the Automatic Writing experiment, *The Only Jealousy of Emer* engaged Surrealist practices through the frame of Irish myth.[53]

Placing *The Only Jealousy of Emer* in relation to Surrealism has important consequences for evaluating the political nature of Yeats's later drama. This is underlined through the importance Frankfurt School critics Adorno and Benjamin gave to the Automatic Writing experiments of Breton and his circle, and the significant disagreement in their critical evaluations of the occult. Adorno has observed a dialectic in Modernism

---

[50] Nancy Dearmer, *The Fellowship of the Picture*, ed. Percy Dearmer (London: Nisbet, 1921). Reviewed in *The New Age*, 28:10 (1921), 119. Pierre Émile Cornillier, *The Survival of the Soul, and Its Evolution after Death* (London: Kegan Paul, 1922).
[51] Rosalind E. Clark, 'Yeats's *The Only Jealousy of Emer* and the Old Irish Serglige Con Culainn', *Yeats: An Annual of Critical and Textual Studies*, 8 (1990), 44–5. Janis Tedesco Hadwell, *Pressed Against Divinity*, (DeKalb, IL: Northern Illinois University Press, 1997), p. 64.
[52] George Mills Harper et al., eds., *Yeats's Vision Papers*, vol. 1 (London: Macmillan Press, 1992), p. 177.
[53] W. J. McCormack retains too neat a distinction between the Freudianism of the Breton circle in Paris and the spiritualism of the Yeatses on this matter. See *Blood Kindred: W. B. Yeats, the Life, the Death, the Politics* (London: Pimlico, 2005), pp. 52–3.

between the work of art as finished and accidental that bears directly upon *The Only Jealousy of Emer* as the outcome of the Automatic Script. Citing the Automatic Writing of the early avant-garde, he observes how the fully integrated formally complete artwork had converged with the completely accidental artwork.[54] Yeats's second Cuchulain Noh play seems a case in point; absolutely integrated in all elements – space, voice, movement – it is yet balanced precariously on the pure immediacy of George's Automatic Writing.

Adorno's point is borne out through the Automatic Script. An entry from 21 December 1917, during which the 'Instructors' supply Yeats with information concerning the meaning of characters in *The Only Jealousy of Emer*, reveals a telling distinction that governed the play. Action was linked to destiny and free will, while passivity was connected to fate and determinism, Harper noting that this 'unusual distinction between destiny and fate runs throughout the Script'.[55] In an entry from the following evening, Yeats asked who was 'antithetical' in *The Only Jealousy of Emer*. The following response is recorded: 'Sidhe Cuchulain anti Emor Eithne E[vil] genius primary'.[56] The Woman of the Sidhe and Cuchulain were to be taken as 'antithetical', while Emer, Eithne and Briciu (represented in the play as the Figure of Cuchulain and the 'Maker of discord') were intended to be 'primary'.[57]

The terms 'antithetical' and 'primary' were part of Yeats's personal lexicon derived from medieval occultist literature, expressions of the spiritual philosophy outlined in *A Vision*. F. A. C. Wilson has related them to a tradition of subjective mysticism informing Yeats's later work; the pursuit of spiritual perfection through purification gave rise to the objective personality, whereas the subjective or antithetical personality sought visionary experience through joyful self-sufficiency.[58] In Wilson's account, the Upanishads opened this second 'antithetical' road to enlightenment, Yeats identifying himself with the subjective personality. A Script entry of 22 December suggests that he identified in the play with the 'antithetical' Cuchulain, the Woman of Sidhe a possible reference to Gonne. However, both Script and play reveal that the meaning of the terms 'antithetical' and 'primary' were not as clear-cut as Wilson has suggested. One of the

---

[54] Adorno, *Aesthetic Theory*, p. 26.   [55] Mills Harper, *The Making*, vol. 1, p. 82.
[56] *Ibid.*, p. 88.
[57] Reg Skene and Janis Hadwell identify the significance of Briciu as the maker of discord and Hadwell also notes his importance as the enemy of Fand. Skene, *The Cuchulain Plays*, p. 204. Tedesco Hadwell, *Pressed Against Divinity*, p. 65.
[58] F. A. C. Wilson, *W. B. Yeats and Tradition* (London: Victor Gollancz, 1958), p. 21.

most intriguing aspects of the 22 December entry is that the Evil Genius is 'primary' or the objective type. This disrupts any argument laid for the purely spiritual meaning of the terms 'primary' and 'antithetical' in the later plays, since this Evil Genius would implausibly have to be at one with the ascetic personality, both being 'primary'. The confusion that arises here stems from Wilson's assumption, commonly made, that Yeats was concerned purely with a subjective drama in the Noh plays.[59]

The meaning of primary and antithetical was further complicated by the identity of the figure of the Evil Genius in *The Only Jealousy of Emer*. In an entry from the Script of 21 December 1917, the Evil Genius is recorded as the 'false' Cuchulain – Briciu – introduced in the play as the Figure of Cuchulain. The same entry identifies this figure not with the 'sin of primary' or the 'fall' into objectivity, but with 'the nature of the phase tenanted by the sun whether primary or anti'.[60] The figure of the Evil Genius was recorded in the same entry as the temptation of the cessation of desire, or the desire to escape desire. The Figure of Cuchulain in the play manifests not objectivity as such but subjectivity distorted in a period dominated by objectivity – his mask is a distorted face (*VPl*, 543). The 'discord' he generates is not in the nature of objectivity itself but in the subjection of the interior life to external, objective form.

The Automatic Script, then, allows us to trace the figure of Briciu, the Evil Genius in *The Only Jealousy of Emer*, back to the Demon Merchants of *The Countess Cathleen*, who represented not materialism against idealism, but materialism in its distorted spiritual form. Like the merchant's gold, the petrificating effect of commodification is represented inversely through Briciu's totemic nature, evident when Eithne kisses him:

> It is no man.
> I felt some evil thing that dried my heart
> When my lips touched it. (*VPl*, 541)

Representing that 'desire to escape desire' recorded in the Automatic Script, this Figure encapsulated a compulsion to objectification – the reduction of passion to object – that Yeats had long identified in the rise of the middle-class society.

The political meaning of *The Only Jealousy of Emer* lies in the role of Briciu. If Yeats intended him merely as a plot function, then the play can be seen as an evasion of contemporary historical realities through art. This implicates the play in Adorno's attack on the reactionary anti-historical

---

[59] Wilson, *Yeats*, p. 34.   [60] Mills Harper, *The Making*, vol. 1, pp. 76–7.

nature of occultism in twentieth-century culture.[61] Benjamin's alternative reading of occultism, relating directly to Surrealist practices, is worth bearing in mind here. Benjamin recognised in Breton's automatic writing experiments the potential for ideology critique of the type he himself developed, while equally cognisant of its potential for delusory mysticism. Recognising how Surrealism and occultism could be conceived as flaccid mysticism, he nonetheless observes their value in perceiving, through 'a dialectical optic', the 'everyday as impenetrable, the impenetrable as everyday'.[62]

In Briciu, the everyday is presented in *The Only Jealousy of Emer*, embodiment of that impenetrability which Benjamin describes. His distorted image, unhuman nature and the discord he creates, inversely reflects the commodification of human beings within modern society as a form of regression to primitive totemism. The Automatic Script indicates how the play carried Yeats's sense that the power technology was exercising over people was akin to that of the totem in pre-modern society. The following revelation was recorded on 7 January 1918 in response to a question on the symbolic meaning of the four figures in the play: before sex, Emer represented Race, Eithne, passion, and Fand, love. After intercourse, Emer represented love and Eithne continued to represent passion.[63] Having located a card file headed 'Automatism', Harper takes Emer to represent the character of George, but more significant here is the link Yeats makes between automatism and race: 'Instinctive automatism preserves the race element.'[64]

The history of Yeats's plays before the Automatic Script is persistent enough in their treatment of automatism to indicate that he had something more than his marriage to George in mind here. Automatism describes the rigid condition that overcomes several characters in the earlier plays: Mary Bruin under the spell of the Fairy Child in *The Land of Heart's Desire*; Michael Gillane under the spell of Cathleen ni Houlihan; Paul Ruttledge in a state of visionary ecstasy. In the cold rigour of its form and its mesmeric effect, transcendent vision in *The Only Jealousy of Emer* gives mythic shape to patterns of industrial mechanisation in Yeats's age.[65] Identifying George with Emer, his ambivalence towards automatism

---

[61] Theodor Adorno, 'Theses Against Occultism', *The Stars Down to Earth and other Essays on the Irrational in Culture*, ed. Stephen Crook (London: Routledge Press, 1994), p. 129.
[62] Walter Benjamin, 'Surrealism', *One-Way Street and Other Writings*, trans. Edmund Jephcott and Kinglsey Shorter (London: New Left Books, 1979), p. 237.
[63] Mills Harper, *The Making*, vol. I, p. 123.   [64] *Ibid.*, p. 125.
[65] Alan Ramon Clinton notes how Yeats's later retreat into art registered historical processes in the fascination with 'zombification' evident in 'Sailing to Byzantium'. *Mechanical Occult: Automatism, Modernism, and the Specter of Politics* (New York: Peter Lang, 2004), p. 103.

comes strikingly into view: a force repellent in reducing people to instruments, its sheer intensity is yet a source of fascination. This becomes apparent later in *A Vision* when Yeats employs the phrase 'instinctive automatism' to describe the personality who, in his primary lunar phase, refused conflict with his mask. Crucially, this evasion of conflict did not imply a weak personality as we might expect of Yeats, 'the most powerful natures' being those who, in his view, most often needed automatism as a rest.[66]

Margaret Mills Harper examines the gender ideology of the Automatic Writing by noting how automatism frustrates the desire to control a text, a specifically male desire within the history of Western philosophy since Plato. Harper extends this gender perspective further in noting the relationship between the Automatic Writing and the emergence of the typewriter as a new communication technology that was quickly designated to women's employment in office clerical work.[67] Like George's Automatic Script, the typewriter disturbed the Romantic idea of the text as the expression of the author's intention. Considering Friederich Kittler's major study of the typewriter and its impact at the end of the nineteenth century in *Discourse Networks*, Morag Shiach notes how important it was to the kinds of experiments writers of the avant-garde were developing – the typewriter becoming 'the archetypal modernist technology, staging language as process, as structure, and as in a distant and a contested relation to the self'.[68] These observations are hugely significant, particularly if we consider the Yeatses' experiment in terms of those of the Breton school in Paris, greatly influenced as they were by Freud's theories of unconscious process. In showing the relevance of the Automatic Script as a process to what was happening in the wider culture, however, Margaret Mills Harper also opens up for examination the ways in which it also signified Yeats's sense of the estranging nature of human experience in a machine age. The spontaneity of the immediate in George's Automatic Writing is countered by the transformation of writing itself into a mechanical process.

Gregory Eaves observes that nothing happens in *The Only Jealousy of Emer* that is not reciprocal, and this is certainly true of relations between Emer and Eithne.[69] Symbolising fire and water, both stand in polar opposition as wife and mistress. If Emer is the estranged wife of Cuchulain,

---

[66] W. B. Yeats, *A Vision*, 2nd edn (London: Macmillan Press, 1937), p. 95.
[67] Margaret Mills Harper, *Wisdom of Two: The Spiritual and Literary Collaboration of George and W. B. Yeats* (Oxford University Press, 2006), p. 177.
[68] Shiach, *Modernism, Labour and Selfhood*, p. 60.
[69] Eaves, 'The Anti-Theatre', p. 55.

Eithne is one of those who, 'the violent hour passed over', are flung to one corner (*VPl*, 538–9). Both Eithne and Emer desire what the other lacks: Eithne, the durability of marital love, Emer, the frenzy of fleeting passion. Fand, the Woman of the Sidhe, appears the synthesis of these contraries, but in the perfection of her beauty all trace of humanity has vanished. Claiming that both she and Eithne are 'but two women struggling with the sea', Emer reveals how the perfection of Fand offers them not liberation, but the condemnation of fate; like the Red Man of *The Green Helmet*, Fand has come from the sea. If Emer is to save Cuchulain from Fand, she must renounce the possibility of ever possessing his love as a husband. Having known his passion, she desires to harness it to the durability of marriage. But following his struggle with the waves, the warrior's passion is now directed to the superhuman, the perfection of Fand. Margaret Mills Harper shows how Emer's struggle with Fand came out of George's struggle to rescue Yeats from his own 'sterile desire for absolute beauty' personified in the figure of Maud Gonne.[70]

Yeats signifies the relationship between history and the supernatural in *The Only Jealousy of Emer* in granting Emer victory over Fand. Fand comes from the moon's 'fifteenth night', the lunar phase in *A Vision* representing complete beauty and unity of being (*VPl*, 551).[71] Gonne may be the ultimate personification of this, but Fand is essentially a supernatural figure. George Mills Harper makes the plausible case that whatever interpretation we bring to the play's mythology, its meaning finally resides in the mystical cosmology that was the genesis for the play. He notes that by 31 January 1918, when Yeats discussed the seven planes of existence with his wife, he had come to see the outline of *The Only Jealousy of Emer* as a symbolic mirror of the 'Invisible', the seventh plane, finally regarding the circle of life as 'a microcosmic image of the circle of civilization'. However, the play does not present a vision of 'divine man united with ideal woman', but of man suspended between historical and transcendent conditions.[72] In attributing 'instinctive automatism' to Emer, Yeats's attitude to the advent of modern technology as an omniscient power had taken a new direction. In part from that fascination with trance evident in the earlier plays, this power is now understood in relation to race; Emer's 'instinctive automatism' refers to the 'race element'.

---

[70] Mills Harper, *Wisdom of Two*, p. 196.
[71] Eaves, 'The Anti-Theatre', p. 551. Yeats, *A Vision*, pp. 97, 135–7. Ellis, *The Plays*, p. 289.
[72] Mills Harper, *The Making*, vol. I, p. 152.

Emer's relation to Fand is a crucial element in the play's manner of addressing historical forces through supernatural imagery. The Script from 7 January 1918 records that before sexual intercourse with Cuchulain, Emer represented race, and after, love; before intercourse with Cuchulain, Fand represented love, and after, simply disappears. This suggests that Fand is the projection of Emer's sexual desire, vanishing when Emer realises it. Freud was in mind during the composition of the play; on 12 November 1917 Georgie asked the 'Instructors' for clarification of the relation between the terms primary/antithetical and Freud's idea of the subconscious.[73] Emer's relation to Fand was certainly not intended to express Freud's notions of displacement and condensation; the Script record of 7 January, however, suggests that the relation took on some of the characteristics Freud had first elaborated in 1899 in *The Interpretation of Dreams*.

Yeats's decision to grant Emer victory, however pyrrhic, reverses a trend in previous plays. Through the idea of race as instinctive automatism, Yeats had arrived at a formulation through which he could regard the historical processes of commodification as something other than degenerative. This relationship of race to history would remain uncertain. There are moments in Yeats's late drama where it appears conflictual and others where it appears to epitomise his understanding of modern civilisation. He certainly had George in mind when coining the phrase 'instinctive automatism', bringing together her roles as medium, wife and mother. But it also draws on the images of figures hypnotised in earlier plays and carries his sense of a general petrifaction in modern society. Often considered an expression of aristocratic pugnacity in the face of bourgeois culture in early twentieth-century Europe, Yeats's treatment of race in *The Only Jealousy of Emer* was more a means of responding to large-scale processes of mechanisation in contemporary European society. In reducing agency to the determinism of genealogy, the human subject becomes an automaton; herein lay the most explicit point of contact between race and historical process.

In renouncing her love of Cuchulain so as to save him from Fand, Emer becomes a kind of machine. In the song of the Musicians for the unfolding and folding of the cloth with which the play concludes, the paradox of her sacrifice is evoked through the uncanny image of a statue that beats with a human heart:

> Why does your heart beat thus?
> Plain to be understood,

[73] *Ibid.*, p. 33.

> I have met in a man's house
> A statue of solitude,
> Moving there and walking;
> Its strange heart beating fast
> For all our talking.
> O still that heart at last. (*VPl*, 563)

Alluding to Cuchulain's possession, this statue also conveys the dehumanising effect of Emer's sacrifice. In this 'statue of solitude', we are presented with an emblem of humanity reduced to object, the persistent theme in Yeats's reponses to contemporary history. It suggests why he chose George Antheil to write a musical score for the 1929 prose version of the play, *Fighting the Waves*. Albright describes it as a score in which a type of Irish folk tune is brought into the 'implacabilities' of Stravinsky's *Oedipus Rex* (1927).[74] Incorporating folk ballad into an experimental piece of music in a manner akin to Bartok, Antheil conveyed that strange intimacy of modern and pre-modern forms of alienation which Yeats sought to express through totemic power. Addressing the modern phenomenon of reification through race, the constraint upon Emer's desire as wife is magnified to the point of evoking the mesmeric power of Fand herself. In this way, Yeats's sense of contemporary history became more pronounced in its fascination.

Was this articulation of modernity in racial terms indeed reactionary? The relation Adorno draws between occultism and totalitarianism suggests so. Here, cosmic determinism becomes the image of the bureaucratically administered state, 'hypnotic power of things occult' a reflex of totalitarian terror, and number mysticism a 'preparation for administrative statistics and cartel prices'.[75] Key to determining whether or not Yeats stands rightly accused here is the figure of Briciu. In spite its title, Briciu dominates the play's proceedings. Cuchulain utters just two lines prior to the closing song of the musicians when free from possession; otherwise, he is merely an instrument for Briciu's spirit to appear on stage. Furthermore, it is ultimately he who has rescued Cuchulain from the lure of Fand by imploring Emer to renounce her love for Cuchulain.

The mesmerising effect Briciu exerts over Cuchulain exemplifies the hypnotic power Adorno describes. A link to totalitarian terror would appear justified if Briciu is seen as puppet-master rather than mere plot device. Drawing on Yeats's idiosyncratic interpretation of the *Commedia*

---

[74] Albright, *Untwisting the Serpent*, p. 88.
[75] Adorno, 'Theses Against Occultism', p. 129.

dell'arte in the 1925 version of *A Vision*, Gregory Eaves describes Briciu as the Stage Manager who sets in train the contraries from which the action of the play develops.[76] Briciu is a link back to the figure of the Old Man originally intended for the 1903 version of *The King's Threshold* and forward to the Old Man in *The Death of Cuchulain*. Both stand on the threshold of these plays, existing outside the action yet part of the structure. Briciu pushes this liminal position further by entering into the action he himself, as the figure of Stage Manager, sets in motion. Eaves makes the point that the term 'discord', of which Briciu is the 'maker' in the play, is a technical one deriving from the *Commedia dell'arte*. Whatever its provenance, it expresses more than simple conflict between characters; it names a discordance in the very structure of the play itself. Participating in a plot that he himself has inaugurated, Briciu subverts the very idea of theatre even as he generates its action.

The Only Jealousy of Emer thus diverges from Adorno's reading in troubling the exclusively determinist perspective of the occult that he adopts. As the Stage Manager of *Commedia dell'arte*, Briciu resembles the power of a modern-day super agent guiding the course of historical development through the instruments of state and market, pervasive yet invisible, exerting hypnotic effect. Yet he simultaneously refuses that resemblance through his participation in events he himself has set in motion. In his double role as author and actor, Briciu confounds the distinction between fate and freedom, thereby indicating why the Automatic Script maintains a distinction between fate and destiny, this latter term referring to that which synthesises the fate–freedom antithesis.[77] In his 1917 essay 'Per Amica Silentia Lunae', Yeats's surrealistic record of a dream indicates how intentionally the double role of Briciu was conceived:

> I dreamed very lately that I was writing a story, and at the same time I dreamed that I was one of the characters in that story and seeking to touch the heart of some girl in defiance of the author's intention; and concurrently with all that, I was as another self trying to strike with the button of a foil a great china jar.[78]

In this double role, Briciu is not the surrogate of Yeats the author, but the Automatic Script itself; his presence is that of the Script in the play.

---

[76] Eaves, 'The Anti-Theatre', pp. 39–41. The phrasing in the passage in 1937 is virtually identical to that in the 1925 edition of *A Vision*. See Mills Harper and Hood, eds., *A Critical Edition*, pp. 17–18, and Yeats, *A Vision*, pp. 83–4.
[77] Yeats clarifies the distinction in *A Vision* in regarding Fate as something from without, Destiny as something from within. Mills Harper and Hood, *A Critical Edition*, p. 15.
[78] W. B. Yeats, 'Per Amica Silentia Lunae', *W. B. Yeats, Later Essays*, ed. William H. O'Donnell, *Collected Works of W. B. Yeats*, vol. v (New York: Charles Scribner's Sons, 1994), p. 26.

As noted already, Adorno viewed modernist art as a dialectic of the well-made and the spontaneous; this captures precisely the relation of *The Only Jealousy of Emer*, in its theatrical formality, to the spontaneity of the Script. As the puppet-master who becomes his own puppet, Briciu embodies the dialectic at the structural level in *The Only Jealousy of Emer*. He is at once the supreme agent who connives the fate of Emer, Eithne and Cuchulain, and a character who is subject to the pattern of fate that has been set in motion.

The structural centrality of Briciu to *The Only Jealousy of Emer*, drawing together the play's formal determinism with the spontaneity of the Script, brings to the fore the undercurrent of farce in the play, obliging the audience to consider whether or not the performance they are witnessing is a charade. In its connection to the Automatic Writing experiment, the play engages the subversive practices of Surrealism, carrying with it the critique of reification and the rigidifying effect it was seen to exert on the human spirit in a time of unprecedented war and revolution. If the proximity intimated between race and reification in the play points to a change in the nature of Yeats's attitude to conditions in modern society, *The Only Jealousy of Emer* further underlined the depth of his awareness of the historical forces shaping the age and their profoundly discordant impact on the quality of human experience and social relations. Like *At the Hawk's Well*, it is torn between lament and laughter, the abstract and the somatic, laying the ground for Yeats's final theatrical dramatisation of the Cuchulain legend in 1939, *The Death of Cuchulain*.

CHAPTER 5

'When everything sublunary must change':
The Death of Cuchulain

Written in the months before his own death in January 1939, *The Death of Cuchulain* is a poignant conclusion to the Cuchulain cycle. Critical opinion on its merits is sharply divided: F. L. Lucas dismissing it as largely ineffectual, Frank Kermode regarding it as probably Yeats's finest play.[1] A. S. Knowland complains that, without the opportunity to revise it, Yeats left us with a play that carries too many uncertainties, yet Richard Taylor asserts that of all Yeats's later plays, it was the one that accorded most closely with the Noh form.[2] Coming as it did at the end of his life, it is quite easy to regard in Cuchulain the figure of Yeats himself, determined to hold fast to a sense of virtuous nobility in the face of illness, approaching death, and a world unrecognisable from that he knew in his youth. A striking feature of the play, however, is its experimental form; even in his last months Yeats was continuing to engage new kinds of theatre, responding to developments elsewhere and anticipating some of the most radical innovations of post-war drama, particularly those of Beckett. For all the heroic iconography of the play, *The Death of Cuchulain* carries in form and theme a subversive undercurrent of farce. Significant is its refusal to grant Cuchulain a noble death, Yeats offering instead his final contribution to the new form of anti-theatre emerging in response to the crises visited upon European society in the first decades of the twentieth century.

This chapter explores the anti-heroic form of the play through the influence of Luigi Pirandello. Though rarely considered a significant influence, several of Yeats's later plays display techniques and address concerns similar to those of Pirandello. Yeats's *Calvary* of 1922 and Pirandello's *Lazarus* of 1927 engaged the same subject, and the following chapter looks at

---

[1] F. L. Lucas, *The Drama of Chekhov, Synge, Yeats and Pirandello* (London: Cassell & Co., 1963), p. 328. Frank Kermode, *Romantic Image* (London: Routledge & Kegan Paul, 1957), p. 82.
[2] A. S. Knowland, *W. B. Yeats: Dramatist of Vision* (Gerrards Cross: Colin Smythe, 1983), p. 238. Taylor, *The Drama of W. B. Yeats*.

the strong parallels between *The Words upon the Window-pane* and *Six Characters in Search of an Author*. A performance of Pirandello's play was given at the Abbey Theatre in late 1934 under the direction of Bladon Peake, who had been trained by the old Abbey producer Nugent Monck, not long after the 1934 publication of Yeats's play.[3] Writing to Wyndham Lewis in 1930, Yeats described Pirandello as the only living dramatist with 'unexhausted, important material', one who 'portrays the transformation from individualism to universal plasticity'.[4] In the 1925 edition of *A Vision*, Yeats identified Pirandello, Joyce, Eliot and Pound with Phase 23 of the lunar cycle. Like 'The Waste Land' and *Ulysses*, Pirandello's *Henry IV* characterised this phase with 'the physical primary' set alongside 'the spiritual primary'.[5] Though Yeats did not place himself in this phase, *The Death of Cuchulain* conformed to its terms. His description of 'the physical primary' in *Henry IV*, 'a lunatic among his keepers', also describes the Old Man in the prologue of Yeats's play. Both the prologue and the Harlot's song that concludes *The Death of Cuchulain* gave voice to Yeats's hatred of the tyranny of social conformity evident in what he called in November 1930 'the opium of the suburbs': science, separated from philosophy, expressing middle-class common sense in which any connection of objective fact to subjective intention was denied or obscured.[6] Confounding the distinction between tragedy and farce, *The Death of Cuchulain* sits in an uneasy yet undeniable sympathy with the Absurdism of Pirandello.

The phrase 'physical primary' was a term Yeats used to denote material necessity; 'spiritual primary' identified material necessity in its spiritual form, or a distorted spirituality, bringing to mind the discordant presence of Briciu in *The Only Jealousy of Emer*, the Stage Manager in the version of *Commedia dell'arte* Yeats offers in *A Vision*. A play in keeping with the description of Phase 23 in Yeats's system, *The Death of Cuchulain* was a structural development of *The Only Jealousy of Emer*, a form of *Commedia dell'arte* as Yeats understood it. Pirandello was equally indebted to this native Italian theatrical tradition, as F. L. Lucas has observed.[7] In the 1925

---

[3] Welch, *The Abbey Theatre*, pp. 118–19.
[4] Yeats to Wyndham Lewis, [?] September 1930. *The Letters of W.B. Yeats* ed. Allan Wade (London: Rupert Hart-Davis, 1954), p. 776.
[5] Mills Harper and Hood, *A Critical Edition*, pp. 211–12. Discussing the search for a poetic theme that is itself the subject for many of Yeats's later poems, Daniel Albright draws attention to Yeats's reference to Pirandello in this passage, suggesting that his search for a theme might find its motto in Pirandello's *Six Characters in Search of an Author*, the poem about poetry reflected in the drama about drama. 'The Fool by the Pool', *Yeats Annual*, vol. VII, ed. Warwick Gould (London: Macmillan Press, 1990), p. 60.
[6] Yeats, *Pages from a Diary Written in Nineteen Hundred and Thirty*, p. 58.
[7] Lucas, *The Drama of Chekhov*, p. 416.

edition of *A Vision*, 1927 was given as the year in which the 'Will' of Phase 23 reigned, with its 'Mask' at the year 900. However arbitrary these selections appear, they illustrate Yeats's sense of the importance of the medieval to the avant-garde of the inter-war years, whether through the Dantesque and Thomist dimensions of *Ulysses*, the morality form of *Murder in the Cathedral* or the farcical nature of *Six Characters* as *Commedia dell'arte*. The politics of medievalism he learned from Morris continued to inform his perspective on art and society at this time.

Yeats's sense of the avant-garde in his later years was one in which medieval influences were received in distorted form, Briciu's discordant spirit being the governing influence. Pirandello's work was compelling here because it seemed to bear this out. As far back as *On Baile's Strand* the theatre fascinated Yeats as a space both capable of mesmerising its audience while yet threatened by the reality of its own pretence; Pirandello gave these preoccupations new vitality in the daring experiments he undertook from the 1910s. *Henry IV* interested Yeats because it took his own themes of myth and mask to new levels. Its protagonist was one who played on the conceit of his mask to such an extent the audience was left unsure as to whether or not he identified in it his true self. Yeats recollected this in a humorous aside to Olivia Shakespear, writing from Rapallo in March 1930 on the subject of his newly acquired beard: 'Certainly I need a new career for I cannot recognise myself in the mirror – if Pirandello is right, my friends, taking their impulse from my appearance, which they see so much more steadily than I can, will connect me with something reckless and dashing.'[8] Pirandello's character undoubtedly made its lasting impression because of the astonishing performance given by Lennox Robinson in the lead role of *Henry IV* in a Dublin Drama League production of the play at the Abbey Theatre in late April 1924. The performance prompted a glowing review by Mary McHugh in *The Irish Independent*; Robert Hogan and Richard Burnham describe it as one of the finest pieces of acting in modern Irish theatre. Significantly for Yeats, Robinson adopted 'Paul Ruttledge' as pseudonym for this performance, directly connecting *Henry IV* to Yeats's spiritual-anarchist play of 1902.[9] In this way, the politics of Morris's radical medievalism came into an interpretation of Pirandello at the Abbey, Yeats having originally modelled the Ruttledge of *Where There Is Nothing* on Morris.[10]

[8] Yeats to Shakespear, 4 March 1930. Wade, *The Letters*, p. 773.
[9] Robert Hogan and Richard Burnham, *The Years of O'Casey, 1921–1926: A Documentary History, Modern Irish Drama*, vol. VI (University of Delaware, 1992), pp. 213–14.
[10] Yeats to John Quinn, 6 Feb [1903]. Kelly and Schuchard, *Collected Letters*, vol. III, p. 312.

Towards the end of Act II of *Henry IV*, the lead character reveals to those acting as his servants that he has been deliberately pretending to be the delusional figure who believes he is King Henry. During the course of this revelation, however, he implores them to believe that they were indeed living in the year 1100 in the court of Henry IV. Further entangling the complex play of delusion and reality, he asks that they tell themselves that, eight centuries from then (the actual period in which the play is performed), men were 'torturing themselves in agony' to find out what lay in store for them, while they were with him in history, where all was 'fixed for ever'.[11] Up to this point, the play has operated on two levels: that of attendants at the court of Henry IV and that of contemporary characters believing they were bound to play the roles of attendants to sustain the delusion of the lead character and prevent his mental collapse. The anxious modern world in which, Yeats believed, myth had been separated from fact, sat side by side with 'the spiritual primary' in Pirandello's play – the ideal world of the medieval court. The end of Act II presents a distorted medievalism, raising the difficult issue as to how Henry IV's sense of the past connected to actual historical process.

Yeats addresses the same problem through the Old Man's prologue in *The Death of Cuchulain*, what Worth has described as a 'flamboyantly anti-illusionist device'.[12] Critics have regarded in the Old Man the figure of Yeats himself, appearing, like Pirandello's protagonist, as the Stage Manager subject to his own plot.[13] This heightens the performative self-consciousness of the play, creating the impression of history itself as performance. If indeed we find in the Old Man the image of the ageing Yeats, it is a final piece of self-dramatising and self-belittlement. His relationship to the other characters of *The Death of Cuchulain* bears notable affinity to the structure of Pirandello's *Six Characters*. He occupies the same position as the manager and the company of actors in *Six Characters*, while the six characters of Pirandello's play bear the same relationship to those actors as that of the six characters in Yeats's play – Cuchulain, Eithne, Aoife, Emer, the Morrigu, the Blind Man – to the Old Man. Yeats's Old Man and

---

[11] Luigi Pirandello, *Henry IV*, *Collected Plays*, vol. 1 (London: John Calder, 1987), p. 56.
[12] Worth, *The Irish Drama of Europe*, p. 187.
[13] Worth, *The Irish Drama of Europe*, p. 187; Francisco Javier Torres Ribelles, 'Predetermination and Nihilism in W. B. Yeats's Theatre', *Revista Alicantina de Estudios Ingleses*, vol. v (1992), p. 148. Gertrude Patterson, 'W. B. Yeats in the Theatre: the Challenge of the Poetic Play', *Yeats Eliot Review*, 6:2 (1979), 38. Barton R. Friedman, *Adventures in the Deeps of the Mind: the 'Cuchulain Cycle' of W. B. Yeats* (Guildford: Princeton University Press, 1977), p. 132. A. S. Knowland challenges this, regarding the Old Man as a parody rather than a paradigm of Yeatsian subjectivity. *W. B. Yeats: Dramatist of Vision*, p. 239.

Pirandello's company of actors exist between the world of the play and the world of the audience, bringing rehearsal into the live performance.

The prologue to *The Death of Cuchulain* was not the first Yeats wrote, but it was the only one retained for performance. His 1903 version of *The King's Threshold* also had a prologue, the text of which was printed in *The United Irishman* in September of that year. This was also to be performed by an Old Man, who was to be robed in a red dressing gown, red slippers and red nightcap, holding a brass candlestick. While included in published versions of the play prior to 1922, it appears to have been included in performance on one occasion only, Austin Clarke claiming to have witnessed it, though no one else remembered it. This was not insignificant, suggesting as it does that Yeats may have suppressed some experiments early in his theatrical career under pressure to sustain a more Romanticist profile.[14] *The King's Threshold* prologue was highly meta-theatrical and deliberately farcical. The sense of tired obligation in the Old Man's opening line, 'I've got to speak the Prologue', anticipates that of *The Death of Cuchulain* over thirty-five years later; 'I have been asked to produced a play called *The Death of Cuchulain*' (*VPl*, 313–14, 1051). Pirandelloean farce abounds: he complains of a draught at one point, drawing the curtains of the stage closer together to protect himself. He says that his nephew had taught him to say what the poet had taught his nephew to say about the play. When a trumpet-blast interrupts his speech, he announces, in Brechtian fashion, that it means the curtain was about to rise. This anticipates the prologue of Yeats's last play again: when a drum and pipe are heard behind the scene in *The Death of Cuchulain*, the Old Man tells the audience that he asked the musicians to 'do that' if he was getting excited (*VPl*, 313, 1052). Manuscript versions show that Yeats originally intended the Old Man to announce that he would play one of the characters in his last play and the audience would have to discern from the context whether it was himself or another character.[15] This echoes the 1903 prologue to *The King's Threshold*, in which the Old Man proclaims that his nephew had approached him to deliver the prologue because the full company was required for the parts that were in the play.

---

[14] Austin Clarke, *The Celtic Twilight and the Nineties* (Dublin: the Dolmen Press, 1969), p. 86. Worth claims that the story had 'a truly Pirandellian twist' in that the Old Man states in the prologue that he is obliged to deliver it because the company could not spare an actor. This proved to be true in reality, resulting in the prologue being dropped. *The Irish Drama of Europe*, p. 151.

[15] W. B. Yeats, *The Death of Cuchulain: Manuscript Materials including the Author's Final Text*, ed. Phillip Marcus (Ithaca, NY: Cornell University Press, 1982), p. 29.

It thus appears that Yeats returned to the 1903 prologue when drafting that for *The Death of Cuchulain*. It is true that the figure of the Old Man had been employed in the 1916 production of *At the Hawk's Well*, and Yeats certainly had him in mind when composing the prologue, as the manuscripts reveal that he originally intended the Old Man to wear a mask in the manner of the Old Man of the earlier Cuchulain play.[16] However, he had also published a new version of *The King's Threshold* five years after the 1916 production to end the play with the death of Seanchan. Yeats may have been inclined to turn back to *The King's Threshold* because it dealt with the problem of the artist misunderstood in his age. Believing that few would understand what followed, he asks for an audience of no more than fifty or a hundred 'in this vile age'. They 'must know the old epics and Mr. Yeats' plays about them' and, above all, they must not include those 'who are educating themselves out of the Book Societies and the like, sciolists all, pickpockets and opinionated bitches' (*VPl*, 1052). In presenting the idea of the artist cut off from his time through this prologue, he is set up for ridicule, Yeats undercutting tragedy with farce once more.

In his last play then, Yeats continued to develop those experiments with the audience he had originally encountered in Maeterlinck. If the sentiment was elitist, it was no more so than Brecht in the 1920s who sought 'an extremely classical, cold, highly intellectual style of performance' not intended 'for the scum who want to have the cockles of their hearts warmed'.[17] Certainly, Brecht's hope for an audience who came to the theatre for fun and 'don't hesitate to keep their hats on' contrasted with the Old Man's plea in *The Death of Cuchulain* for the audience not to shuffle their feet or talk. Yet even here a certain facetiousness deflated the matter, particularly if we consider him as a later version of that more ludicrous figure from *The King's Threshold*, who appears as if he just got out of bed, dressed in a red night-robe and red hat holding a candlestick. The 'guiding principles' for *The Death of Cuchulain* that the Old Man belligerently shouts out have, after all, been written down on a scrap of old newspaper (*VPl*, 1051).

This improvisational, knockabout quality works against the tone of bitter lament in the Old Man's scolding. He says that he picked the musicians up 'here and there about the streets', intending to teach them 'the

---

[16] *Ibid.*, p. 27.
[17] Bertolt Brecht, *Brecht on Theatre: The Development of an Aesthetic*, ed. and trans. John Willet (London: Methuen Press, 1964), p. 14. On the similarity to Yeats, see Josephine Johnson, 'Yeats: What Method? An Approach to the Performance of the Plays', *Quarterly Journal of Speech*, 57 (1971), 71.

music of the beggar-man, Homer's music' (*VPl*, 1052). This recalls the opening scene of *Six Characters*, in which the producer, stage manager and prompter try to organise the stage and actors for Act II of *The Rules of the Game* – an earlier Pirandello play – prior to the arrival of the six characters. The Old Man's reference to 'the plays of Mr. Yeats' in the prologue is a similar throwaway reference and an instance of that practice Brecht adopted in the 1920s of glibly including references to himself in his plays.[18] These street singers that the Old Man has gathered to perform the Harlot's ballad recall not just the bawdy force of Yeats's 'Crazy Jane' sequence. As a method of theatrical estrangement, they bear a distant affinity to Brecht's more fulsome use of ballad, most famously in *The Threepenny Opera* of 1928, a work that looked back to John Gay's satire *The Beggar's Opera* two hundred years earlier, originally prompted by Swift, a figure with which Yeats became obsessed in the 1930s.[19]

The Old Man's calls for dance, for severed heads and for the tragic dancer are improvisational, conveying the sense that he is making use of materials immediately to hand in constructing the play:

I promise a dance. I wanted a dance because where there are no words there is less to spoil. Emer must dance, there must be severed heads – I am old, I belong to mythology – severed heads for her to dance before. I had thought to have had those heads carved, but no, if the dancer can dance properly no wood-carving can look as well as a parallelogram of painted wood. But I was at my wit's end to find a good dancer; I could have got such a dancer once, but she had gone; the tragi-comedian dancer, the tragic dancer, upon the same neck love and loathing, life and death. (*VPl*, 1052)

Here we find him making the play up as he goes along. His determination that there be a dance and severed heads sounds unpremeditated; manuscript materials show that the phrase 'Emer must dance' was left unchanged from the first draft and the idea of the severed head came with equal immediacy.[20] The hieratic solemnity of dance and severed head is shadowed by the meta-theatrical farce typical of Pirandello.

---

[18] Luigi Pirandello, *Six Characters in Search of an Author*, Collected Plays, vol. II (London: John Calder, 1988), pp. 3–8. On self-reference in Brecht, see the Interlude to *Man Equals Man* or the ballad sung by Jenny in Act III of *The Three-Penny Opera*, 'Solomon Song'. Bertolt Brecht, Collected Plays, vol. II, ed. John Willett and Ralph Mannheim (London: Methuen Press, 1994), pp. 38, 155.

[19] Szilvia Barta identifies aspects of Brechtian *Verfremdungseffekt* in the function of the Old Man's prologue. 'The Comedy of the Tragic: Anticipations of the Theatre of the Absurd in William Butler Yeats's *The Death of Cuchulain*', *Anachronist* (1999), p. 141.

[20] Yeats, *The Death of Cuchulain: Manuscript Materials*, p. 43. The Old Man's complaint that he lacked a good dancer was nothing new. Writing forty years earlier in *The Dome*, Yeats stated that

Critics have observed the bitter irony in the play that seems particularly concentrated in the prologue, most attributing it to an absolute distinction Yeats drew between the glories of a mythical past and the degeneracy of the modern world.[21] This seems undeniable in the hysteria of the Old Man's closing remarks, railing against the modern age as ugly and ignoble, spitting upon the painting of dancers by Degas and 'that chambermaid face' history (*VPl*, 1052). Drawing on Kermode's notion of the Yeatsian dancer as 'a speaking body', Donald Gutierrez sees in this passage Yeats's despondency at the stiffness, the 'restricted expressiveness' and 'prosaic faces' of Degas's dancers.[22] Yeats may have been recalling George Moore's remarks on the 'intellectuality' of Degas many years previously in *Hail and Farewell*, standing in contrast to what Moore saw as the pure instinct of Manet; at one point Moore describes how, though Degas painted *Semiramis* again and again, its subject remained 'unnatural as a cockatoo', dressed in 'pink tights, clumsy shoes, and bunched skirts'.[23] The attack on Degas had another early precedent, testament to the extraordinarily acute memory informing *The Death of Cuchulain*. Over forty years earlier, Yeats wrote in *The Dome* of 'men like Mr. Degas, who are still interested in life, and life at its most vivid and vigorous, picture it with a cynicism that reminds one of what ecclesiastics have written in old Latin about women and about the world'.[24]

The Old Man's invective articulates Yeats's sense of a historical process driven by intellectual abstraction that would render human conduct increasingly mechanical. As evident in the automatism of *The Only Jealousy of Emer*, however, Yeats's manner of imagining this process did not simply evince an attitude of contempt. He detected in the doll-like form of Degas's dancers that condition of alienation Morris had attributed to the nature of contemporary industry. Yet a mechanistic sense of fate governs the play as a whole, heightening Cuchulain's stature perhaps, but also implicating him in the very process of mechanisation for which

---

it might take generations before a theatre of art could be restored. In the meantime, actors and scenery must be taken 'from the theatre of commerce'. Yeats, 'The Theatre', *The Dome*, 3 (1899), 51.

[21] See Bradley, *William Butler Yeats*, p. 189, and Knowland, *W. B. Yeats*, p. 246.

[22] Donald Gutierrez, 'Ghosts Benefic and Malign: The Influence of the Noh Theatre on the Three Dance Plays of Yeats', *Forum*, 9.2 (1971), 43–4.

[23] George Moore, 'Vale', *Hail and Farewell*, pp. 532–8, 655.

[24] W. B. Yeats, 'A Symbolic Artist and the Coming of Symbolic Art', *The Dome*, 1 (1898), 234. A sense of what Yeats disliked in Degas is conveyed in J. B. Manson's contention that he was more draughtsman than painter. Commenting on 'Le Foyer de la Danse' (1872), he states: 'Each detail is beautifully drawn and painted; but each figure is, perhaps, too carefully studied, treated too much as a separate thing'. J. B. Manson, *The Life and Work of Edgar Degas*, ed. Geoffrey Holme (London: The Studio, 1917), p. 19.

the Old Man derides Degas's dancers, spinning 'like peg-tops' (*VPl*, 1052). It is hardly coincident that this calls to mind the spinning gyres of *A Vision*, the ultimate sign of historical determinism in Yeats's system.

The improvisational mode of the Old Man's prologue, taken up again in the Harlot's song with which *The Death of Cuchulain* concludes, counters his denunciations of modern life. This indicates the complex nature of Yeats's final representation of his age for the theatre. Attempts to consider the mythic action of the play separate from the contemporary settings in which it begins and concludes create the false impression of a clear distinction between the mythic and the modern. Augustine Martin has rightly pointed out that Yeats's theory of recurrence arose in large measure from a debate concerning heroic sacrifice and its effect on human beings, a debate that was itself a response to a revolutionary period in Ireland and Europe that included the First World War, the 1916 Rising, the Russian Revolution and the rise of Fascism.[25] Rather than absolute contrast between a heroic mythic past and a degenerate present, *The Death of Cuchulain* offers myth as a way of addressing dehumanisation within modern culture while deflating its own authoritarian pretensions in the process. If Yeatsian myth is centrally concerned with the power of determinism, as Francisco Torres Ribelles suggests, such power is not exclusively a question of the poet's own 'bodily decrepitude' in this play, the mechanistic determinism of modern industrial society or the transhistorical determinism of myth itself, but the interaction of all three dimensions.[26]

This is evident in several aspects of Cuchulain's death. Culminating in Emer's dance, the self-conscious nature of performance is pronounced throughout. The effect intended through the prologue, that what the audience witness is a consciously constructed illusion, is borne out in the gestures of the play itself. In the spirit of Pirandello, deception is all-pervasive. Eithne, Cuchulain's mistress from *The Only Jealousy of Emer*, tries to deceive him into believing that Emer, his estranged wife from that play, wished him to charge into battle immediately; the letter Eithne holds instructs otherwise. The Morrigu, the image of Fand from the earlier play, appears on stage between her and Cuchulain but neither he nor Eithne can see her. When Eithne becomes aware of her presence, she is awakened to the fact that she has been under a spell cast by Maeve, Cuchulain's enemy in the War of the Bull of Cooley. Cuchulain

---

[25] Augustine Martin, 'Kinesis, Stasis, Revolution in Yeatsean Drama', *Gaeliana*, 6 (1984), 159.
[26] Torres Ribelles, 'Predetermination and Nihilism', pp. 143–53.

is incredulous, however, at Eithne's description of a woman with an eye in her forehead and a head like a crow.

There is a double-play of illusion and reality directly involving the audience in this opening sequence. When the Morrigu first appears, she is visible only to the audience. When Eithne becomes aware of her supernatural presence, she is awakened to the fact that she has been acting in a trance, signalled through her description of the Morrigu's distorted features, to which Cuchulain responds with incredulity. These exchanges do not depict the supernatural power of these mythical characters but test their credibility. If the mythical hero could not see the goddess nor believe in her existence, his own supernatural prowess was questionable. Eithne herself sees the signs of a man about to die in Cuchulain's incredulity, his unwillingness to kill her though believing her a traitor, and his fear that they may be overheard by someone outside (*VPl*, 1055). These might equally be signs of scepticism towards supernatural heroism. The play of reality and illusion that Yeats achieves at the formal level through the movement from the Old Man of the prologue to the arrival of Eithne on stage is replicated in this opening exchange between Eithne and Cuchulain.

Cuchulain's scepticism surreptitiously draws attention to the role of the audience on which the Old Man of the prologue is explicit. His unwillingness to believe in the reality of the Morrigu's presence on stage carries with it the audience's disbelief – provisionally suspended – in the reality of the mythical event being performed. When Eithne laments that he was no longer the man she loved in having lost the instinct for vengeance, Cuchulain's response is highly resonant of Pirandello, a stage direction that yet remains part of the drama:

> Spoken too loudly and too near the door;
> Speak low if you would speak about my death,
> Or not in that strange voice exulting in it.
> Who knows what ears listen behind the door? (*VPl*, 1055)

The sinister presence beyond the door in Maeterlinck's *The Intruder* comes to mind here. Cuchulain's command also functions as a directorial instruction to Eithne to modify her performance, the listening ears being those of the audience. The death of the mythical hero represents the death of delusion generated in part by the actors wilfully forgetting the presence of the audience in the theatre. Cuchulain's words draw attention to the materiality of the theatre, those 'Players and painted stage' lovingly recalled in 'The Circus Animal's Desertion' (*VP*, 630). Out of these the mythic narrative is conjured, just as the Old Man's image of a 'parallelogram of painted wood' in the prologue starkly emphasises the materiality of symbol.

Of all the plays in the cycle, *The Death of Cuchulain* is the most explicit in representing the failings of the hero in gender terms. Janis Hadwell observes that Cuchulain is confronted by a host of female enemies in the play.[27] As with *The Only Jealousy of Emer*, femininity takes transcendental form here in the guise of the Morrigu and historical form in the persons of Eithne and Emer, mistress and wife. Through Aoife, it also returns to the first play in the cycle, *On Baile's Strand*. The complex interplay of reality and illusion shaping Cuchulain's opening dialogue with Eithne lays its theatricality open before the audience in a way that implicates them in its narrative. The manifestation of transcendental feminine power in the figure of the Morrigu during this exchange is entirely consequent upon the meta-theatrical mode of its articulation.

This relationship between the play as theatrical experiment and critique of gender relations bears upon its representation of contemporary history. Critics have struggled to make sense of the Harlot's song with which the play concludes as it reverts to present-day Ireland, most regarding the song as Yeats's final pronouncement on the debasement of the modern world.[28] F. A. C. Wilson and Augustine Martin have disputed this, Martin citing Yeats's 1897 story 'The Adoration of the Magi', a tale in which three Irish sages travel to a brothel in Paris to witness the birth of a new dispensation.[29] In an essay published in *The New Age* in September 1907, Yeats's friend and collaborator Florence Farr contrasted the veneration of prostitutes in ancient Egyptian society with their degraded status in the contemporary Western culture.[30] All critical readings to date, however, overlook the fact that Eithne herself is most likely a prostitute, drawing immediate direct connection between the heroic time of Cuchulain's death and the present day in which the Harlot sings her song to the Beggar Man. In *The Only Jealousy of Emer*, Eithne strongly hints her at profession:

> Women like me, the violent hour passed over,
> Are flung into some corner like old nut-shells. (*VPl*, 537–39)

---

[27] Tedesco Hadwell, *Pressed Against Divinity*, p. 58.
[28] A. S. Knowland sees in the closing song the image of Cuchulain's death debased into the world of beggar and prostitute. Peter Ure sees the Harlot's song as ironic testimony to the nature of the hero's death. Knowland. *W. B. Yeats*, p. 246; Ure, *Yeats the Playwright*, p. 78; Wilson, *W. B. Yeats and Tradition*, p. 163.
[29] Martin also notes the precedent of Crazy Jane. 'Kinesis, Stasis, Revolution in Yeatsean Drama', pp. 160–1.
[30] Florence Farr, 'The Rites of Astaroth', *The New Age*, 1 (1907), 294–5.

'When everything sublunary must change' 121

In *The Death of Cuchulain* she has been sent by Emer to be Cuchulain's bedfellow on the night before his battle (*VPl*, 1054). Eithne subverts the idea of a mythic time standing aloof from the degeneration of modernity. Rather than some absolute gap between mythic and modern, the image of Eithne in the figure of the modern-day Harlot shows how directly Yeats intended the play's mythical sequence to relate to its contemporary setting. This is also evident in the relationship between the Blind Man who administers the final death-blow to Cuchulain and the Beggar Man to whom the Harlot has sung her ballad in the play's conclusion. Thus, the mythic and the quotidian interrupt one another in the play somewhat in the manner of Eisensteinian montage technique favoured by Cocteau and the Surrealists.[31] The result is a drama in which the temporal order was suitably disturbed to express the monumental turbulence of the historical moment – eight months before the start of the Second World War – in which it was composed.

Most critics have come to regard the manner of Cuchulain's death in Yeats's last play as a theatrical and thematic failure. The aged Aoife appears on stage and everything is set for the moment in which she would kill Cuchulain in vengeance for the death of her son many years earlier. This would have completed the Cuchulain cycle perfectly, perhaps even pointing to harmony restored; the order broken open through the killing of the son in *On Baile's Strand* now finally returned to itself in Aoife's vengeance. But Yeats's theatrical move at this point in his last play refuses this closure, indicating the nature of his theatrical vision not just for *The Death of Cuchulain* but the overall cycle. Instead of inflicting the death wound, Aoife suddenly leaves the stage, at which point the Blind Man from *On Baile's Strand* enters. Feeling Cuchulain's body, it is he who kills Cuchulain with a kitchen knife, but at a moment in which the stage is fully darkened.[32]

Yeats had already employed this device in the cycle in *At the Hawk's Well*. Rather than seek water from the Well as would have been in keeping with his role as warrior-hero, the Young Man Cuchulain suddenly drops his spear and leaves the stage. Critics have not considered the possibility that Yeats was rejecting the authority of myth within a mythic frame here, quite deliberately disturbing the circular completion of mythical pattern. Conceding the disconnected nature of the play's structure, Richard Cave

---

[31] For discussion of Yeats's later poetry in relation to cinematic technique, including that of Eisenstein, see Clinton, *Mechanical Occult*, pp. 100–4.
[32] Ure has claimed this to be a brilliant instance of meta-theatre but Knowland finds it clumsy in refusing 'majestic pattern'. Ure, *Yeats the Playwright*, p. 81; Knowland, *W. B. Yeats*, p. 242.

contends that it was 'purposefully so', pointing to its consonance with the methods of Ernst Toller, the German Expressionist playwright to whom Yeats responded with notable enthusiasm in 1935.[33] However much the Blind Man may have epitomised 'the greasy till' of modern middle-class Ireland, Yeats nonetheless represented him as Conchubar's *daimon* in *On Baile's Strand*. Cuchulain discovered through the Blind Man that it was his son he had killed in the first play of the cycle. The nature of Cuchulain's death at this man's hands thus confounds an absolute distinction between mythic and modern as a basis for reading *The Death of Cuchulain*.

The Blind Man's intervention is thematically and theatrically disruptive. Not only does he prefigure the Beggar Man in the Harlot's closing song, he recalls the Old Man in the prologue. He carries the same cantankerous tone in his voice, 'fumbling' with his stick since dawn, an echo not just of those who 'fumble in the greasy till' in 'September 1913' but equally the Old Man dithering as he introduces the play. Most of all, the improvisational nature of the prologue is mirrored in the highly tenuous circumstances that have led to this last confrontation with the wounded warrior:

> Somebody said that I was in Maeve's tent,
> And somebody else, a big man by his voice,
> That if I brought Cuchulain's head in a bag
> I would be given twelve pennies; I had the bag
> To carry what I get at kitchen doors. (*VPl*, 1060)

The noble head of the mythic hero is to end up in a bag for kitchen scraps, situating Cuchulain's death precariously between accident and destiny. If these twelve pennies are twelve pieces of silver, they also belittle the absolutism of myth.[34] The short exchange between the Blind Man and Cuchulain just before his death refuses the closure of determinism, pointing instead to the contingent as the basis from which historical destiny springs.[35] Yeats had already suggested this Nietzschean idea in *On Baile's Strand*, the accidental manner through which Cuchulain discovered what he had done being an occult mode through which his destiny was revealed to him. The Blind Man interrupts rather than concludes the

---

[33] Richard Allen Cave, *Yeats's Late Plays: 'A High Grave Dignity and Strangeness'* (London: The British Academy, 1983), p. 320.

[34] Observing how the idea of apocalypse is revised in Yeats's last plays, Lynn Haimes describes these revisions as 'the noble exertion of creative energy by the artist-type to offset the attrition of a culture and the exhaustion of its values'. 'Apocalyptic Vision in Three Late Plays by Yeats', *Southern Review*, 14 (1978), 60.

[35] Taylor sees in the manner of Cuchulain's death a post-human vision, the 'death of man'. *The Drama of W. B. Yeats*, p. 193.

cyclical pattern, disrupting the order of mythic and quotidian time in colliding them together.

Under cover of darkness, the manner of Cuchulain's death comments on the form of the play as a whole, a 'happening' structured according to a series of interruptions, situational rather than teleological. The influence of Surrealism was evident here, and as early as 1900 Yeats had given public expression to a situationalist perspective, paving the way for his later attack on utopian socialism as the culmination of a nineteenth-century faith in progress. In an essay on the Irish Literary Theatre published in *The Dome* that year, he rejected the Enlightenment presumption of education as the source of progress, writing instead of progress as 'miracle' and 'sudden'.[36] *The Death of Cuchulain* kept faith with this idea of transformation as a sudden break rather than culminating outcome.

In restoring portentous symbolism to the play following Cuchulain's death, the Morrigu's speech and the dance of Emer seem to confound this interpretation. The Morrigu appears as the incarnation of destiny and Emer's dance as the embodiment of the cyclic pattern and tragic ecstasy. It would seem that we could not be further from the Blind Man's decrepit state and the fortuitous nature of his intervention. Alone on a bare stage before the audience, the opening words of the Morrigu weigh heavily with a mood of solemnity:

> The dead can hear me, and to the dead I speak.
> This head is great Cuchulain's, those other six
> Gave him six mortal wounds. (*VPl*, 1061)

Less than three years before *The Death of Cuchulain* was written, the English version of Maeterlinck's *The Hour-Glass* was published, the title borrowed from one of Yeats's earlier plays. Here Maeterlinck compares the life of the dead within the living to 'a negative obtained by means of invisible radiations from the most secret depths of our psychology', adding that the living were nothing apart from the dead spirits who lived through them.[37] Addressed to the dead, the Morrigu's speech suggests Yeats may have had Maeterlinck's work in mind, a book of reflections certainly at one with Yeats's long interest in para-psychology. If Maeterlinck was indeed a significant voice behind her speech, then it is evident that it was addressed to the audience, the living shaped by the dead of those wars and revolutions, local and national, that had altered Irish history since 1914.

[36] Yeats, 'The Irish Literary Theatre, 1900', 1899–1900, p. 235.
[37] Maeterlinck, *The Hour-Glass*, pp. 47–8.

The Morrigu's presence on stage at this moment in the drama was fundamentally an act of displacement, however. At the very least, the audience might expect some noble image of the dead warrior to follow his death. Instead, the intervention brings its audience to the edge of theatre, beyond which it would be difficult to sustain. Barren but for the Morrigu herself and six parallelograms, this moment prefigures the radical minimalism of the later Beckett. On the stage appears an Egyptian image at this point, the woman figure with the head of a bird surrounded by six parallelograms, a hieroglyph most likely from *The Book of the Dead* with which Yeats was long familiar, given the nature of the Morrigu's address. An entry in Yeats's notebooks is telling here. Reflecting on the Masonic significance of the building, he noted that the 'Egyptian hierophant was given a square headdress', an image resonating in the parallelograms used here and the cubes employed earlier for *The King of the Great Clock Tower*.[38]

How was an audience expected to respond to this? The parallelograms recall again the Old Man's prologue, and the quality of improvisation informing the play. Yeats's reading of scripture through Egyptian mystical, Masonic and Kabbalist perspectives offered well-known sources, Psalm 118 and Matthew 21, verse 42: 'The stone which the builders rejected has become the corner-stone.'[39] Once more, the contingent became invested with the full weight of historical necessity, but only through the play's self-referential theatricality: these parallelograms were, first and foremost, stage props. But they were also spatial geometric figures drawing attention to the stage itself as a pure spatial configuration, final testimony of Craig's experiments with stage design in Yeats's drama.

It is significant that Yeats chose Emer to perform the dance that follows the Morrigu's speech. The dance before the severed head was originally inspired by Wilde's *Salomé* and the subject of Yeats's 1934 play *A Full Moon in March*, an updated version of *The King of the Great Clock-Tower* staged at the Abbey Theatre in June 1934 with Ninette de Valois performing the dance.[40] In earlier Yeats plays, dances were performed by supernatural beings: the Guardian of the Well in *At the Hawk's Well* and the Woman of the Sidhe in *The Only Jealousy of Emer*. Again, his

[38] Page no. 1100198, Box 87, I.3 B, W. B. Yeats Collection, Stony Brook.
[39] In an undated notebook entry, Yeats comments on the disciple Peter as the rock of the church: 'Peter Rock – The Logos (or Interpreter) Petra – the Rock Temple where the Mystery [?] performed is also a name for a *Hierophant* or finished intiate'. Page no. 1100195, Box 87, I.3 B, W. B. Yeats Collection, Stony Brook.
[40] For discussion of the influence of Wilde's *Salomé* on these plays, see Doody, 'An Echo of Some One Else's Music'.

last play confounds expectations: Emer, the estranged and belittled wife of Cuchulain in *The Green Helmet* and *The Only Jealousy of Emer*, performs the dance in *The Death of Cuchulain*, the supreme act of ecstasy in Yeatsian theatre. In so doing, she appropriates the power of goddess for woman within material history, transforming its significance in the process. The automatism through which Yeats understood Emer in *The Only Jealousy of Emer*, connecting race and mechanisation, now appears transformed into the self-abandoning mesmerism of the dance at the end of which she becomes a static object. For all the Old Man's spitting upon Degas in the prologue, we are not far from his 'spinning peg-tops' at this point. The discreet relation between Yeats's horror at the mechanisation of human relations in a commodity-driven culture and his fascination with the body in a mesmerised state becomes explicit once more.

Yeats's manner of concluding the play illustrates its extraordinary sensitivity to the pressures of contemporary history. Rather than the entire narrative of the Cuchulain cycle becoming absorbed conclusively into dance, there is another, final interruption. Szilvia Barta describes the dance in plays such as *The Cat and the Moon* and *A Full Moon in March* as points of climax in the plot that inaugurate the cycle of life and death, but sees in the conclusion of *The Death of Cuchulain* a breaking of this illusion.[41] The three Musicians reappear, acting as balladeers singing the Harlot's song. The pressures of contemporary Irish history – Pearse, Connolly and the Easter Rising – rudely interrupt the elevated histrionics of what the audience has just witnessed. The element of farce returns; reference to Oliver Sheppard's statue of Cuchulain is made in the ballad, recently installed in the General Post Office to commemorate the 1916 Rising. Worth perceptively observes this as a 'Brechtian footnote', disturbing the high-artistic illusion of the performance of Cuchulain's death.[42] If the reality of events outside were breaking into the theatre at this point, like Pirandello's six characters emerging from the audience, the normative frame of historical understanding of those events was troubled in the process. Through the Musicians' presence the self-reflexive nature of the narrative of Cuchulain's death intersects with the improvisational mode of the Old Man's prologue. Commenting upon the play in which they perform, they exaggerate the artifice of *The Death of Cuchulain*, while in their ragged appearance and the ballad form of the Harlot's song, they remind us that in the prologue, the Old Man claimed he had picked them up off the

---

[41] Barta, 'The Comedy of the Tragic', p. 142.
[42] Worth, *The Irish Drama of Europe*, pp. 191–2.

streets (*VPl*, 1052). In this concluding ballad, stylised *l'art pour l'art* meets hand-to-mouth travelling theatre.

Knowland has remarked on the tone of deep bitterness in the ballad, but it was more than just a dying man's rage against the present times.[43] Yeats neither mythologised history nor set a debased modernity against elevated mythology in those final verses. His allusions to 1916 certainly stood in relation to the mythic figure of Cuchulain but, again, they functioned as interruption. From the celebration of '[a]ll that most ancient race', we are suddenly transferred to the General Post Office and the figures of Pearse and Connolly. The enigma of Connolly's role in 1916 was a fitting example of what haunted the ballad – how mythological types suddenly took possession of that most opposed to them.[44] If the Rising testified the intersection of myth and contemporary historical reality, it equally pointed up the gulf between '[a]ll that most ancient race' and 'the Post Office'.

The structure of historical representation at the close of *The Death of Cuchulain* lay precisely in the contiguous relationship between myth and historical reality. However wide their ideological differences, Yeats adapted the same mode of historical representation as developed by Brecht in the 1920s. References to an event as recent as the 1916 Rising were employed to interrupt the mythic totality of Cuchulain, even as Yeats saw his shadow cast over that event. The *Verfremdungseffekt* resulting tells much about Yeats's final theatrical pronouncement on recent history. An event such as 1916 could not be absorbed into mythic totality, remaining anchored as it was in the contingency of its moment; the references to the GPO and Oliver Sheppard's statue in the ballad accentuate the importance to Yeats of the unpremeditated and localised nature of the rebellion. On the other hand, the pattern of everyday life was suddenly suspended in the event, the temporal order of the quotidian thrown into confusion.[45] The manner in which Yeats introduced reference to 1916 in this last play not only suggested that he conceived the Rising along the

---

[43] Knowland, *W. B. Yeats*, p. 247.

[44] Foster cites a letter to Lolly Yeats written soon after the Rising in which Yeats expresses his bewilderment at events, regarding Connolly and MacDonagh as able and cultivated men. *W. B. Yeats, A Life*, vol. II, p. 46.

[45] The concept of the event intended here derives originally from Benjamin's idea of history as subject to a structure in which time is charged with the presence of 'the now'. 'Theses on the Philosophy of History', *Illuminations*, ed. Hannah Arendt, trans. Harry Zorn (London: Pimlico, 1999), p. 253. It accords more precisely, however, to Alain Badiou's notion of the event as *situated* and *supplementary*, 'absolutely detached from, or unrelated to, all the rules of the situation' in which it occurs. *Ethics: An Essay on the Understanding of Evil*, trans. Peter Hallward (London: Verso, 2001), p. 68.

lines of an event, but also that it exemplified the structure of modernity itself in this way. Considered as such, Yeats's view of history as the subject of magical power appears less aloof.[46]

The reference to the Post Office as the site of the Rising in the Harlot's song intimated the event's complicity with a destiny that retained its fortuitous character. Derrida's remarks on 'the postal' are pertinent here, a 'counting' that entertained the possibility of 'going astray', the 'place of the postal' ultimately a scanning of the 'destiny' of 'Being'.[47] Whatever we make of this as a deconstructive procedure, it suggests why the Post Office might have fascinated Yeats as the site of the Rising. The postal is the subject of destination itself even as the precariousness of delivery surrounded it at every turn, a particularly concentrated site within which the mythic was constituted yet interrupted in the everyday. Whether or not Yeats had in mind some notion of the 'message' of the Rising itself going astray here is a matter of speculation. What is certain is that the entire structure of the play laid its foundation on the stone that the builders rejected; the contingent proves to be the point from which a destiny is realised. To the degree to which Derrida's account of the postal describes this structure, the 'situation' of the General Post Office in 1916 appeared to acquire the force of necessity in its contingency. This recalls the relevance to the Yeatses' Automatic Script of Adorno's insight into the relationship between the well-made and the accidental in the avant-garde – the arbitrary receipt of messages forming themselves into the system of *A Vision*.[48] Indeed, the allusions to the Post Office at the end of the play and again in one of Yeats's last poems 'The Man and the Echo' address the Rising not just as an Irish matter. They also carried

---

[46] In agreement with Francis MacManus and William Irwin Thompson, David Ward claims that the Easter Rising caught Yeats totally unaware. Rightly observing the Rising and subsequent events as 'the historical rupture', Ward's characterisation of Yeats's reaction as despondent underplays the extent to which the temporal structure of the Rising as event came to shape his own writing subsequently. David Ward, 'Yeats's Conflicts with his Audience, 1897–1917', *ELH*, 49 (1982), 157–9.

[47] Jacques Derrida, *The Post Card: From Socrates to Freud and Beyond*, trans. Alan Bass (University of Chicago Press, 1987), p. 65.

[48] The telegram was a crucial element in some of the Abbey's most successful plays, including *Hyacinth Halvey* and *The Playboy of the Western World*. That Yeats's dramatisation of the *Playboy* riots takes as its key moment Gregory's second telegram sent on the opening night's performance is hardly coincident. In its speed of communication and its situational immediacy, the telegram offered a strong contemporary analogy for the telepathy Yeats had been practising and investigating since the 1890s, automatic writing of a sort. See W. B. Yeats, 'J. M. Synge and the Ireland of His Time', *Essays and Introductions* (London: Macmillan Press, 1961), p. 311. See also Yeats's preface to Rabindranath Tagore's *The Post Office* in William H. O'Donnell, ed., *W. B. Yeats: Prefaces and Introductions* (London: Macmillan, 1988), p. 144.

the memory of Rabindranath Tagore's play *The Post Office*, performed by the Abbey troupe in Dublin and London in the summer of 1913, along with Pearse's *An Rí* in the Dublin production, performed in Irish by the pupils of St Enda's College.[49] The modern in the form of the telegram was invested with the mystical in the form of the telepathic, the final elaboration of Yeats's sense of contemporary history moving according to hidden processes.

The Death of Cuchulain was about the death of Ireland's most celebrated mythical hero and the imminent death of Ireland's most celebrated modern poet. But it was also a play about the death of the theatre from which the form of anti-theatre emerged, a theatre that, like the Morrigu, spoke to the dead as living subjects. In this there was the ghost of history, the power by which human experience was becoming automatised in a machine age, producing the cultural reflexes we find in the play at the level of form. In its close proximity to the Absurdism of Pirandello and Brecht's drama of alienation, it was a striking conclusion to the cycle of Cuchulain plays, Yeats's last drama yet one of his most experimental. The view of the play as a final bitter lament of high culture written in a spirit of invective against the contemporary age overlooks the complex way in which history is treated and the critique of modernity developed in the theatre over the thirty years that it drew upon. The final section of this study elaborates the expansive nature of this critique in exploring a range of the later plays and the weight of historical consciousness they carried. The purpose is to offer a basis for reassessing Yeats's later politics in relation to the kinds of experiments he undertook in the theatre from the 1920s.

---

[49] Hunt, *The Abbey: Ireland's National Theatre, 1904–1979*, p. 101

PART 3
Later plays

CHAPTER 6

'The heart of a phantom is beating': The Dreaming of the Bones *and* Calvary

The Cuchulain cycle is testament to the range of theatrical innovations Yeats employed in response to the historical patterns shaping events over the decades in which the plays were composed and performed. These experiments were marked throughout by tensions between tradition and experiment, sanctity and profanity, tragedy and farce. Returning to the Cuchulain theme in his last play, Yeats drew together the energy of these struggles in evoking an understanding of history as the realisation of destiny through the contingent and the local. The play was a 'happening', treating contemporary history in the form of the event. Parallels with continental European dramatists become apparent in this regard, Pirandello in particular. This chapter explores the way Yeats brought a situationalist perspective to *The Dreaming of the Bones*, his play on the 1916 Rising that was first published in 1921 in *Four Plays for Dancers*. These plays presented the theatrical event as one in which the contingent became invested with the historical power of destiny. The historical meaning of the Rising is represented in this way, part of Yeats's larger understanding of the relationship between contingency and necessity through which he regarded the political circumstances of Europe since 1914. Comparing *The Dreaming of the Bones* with *Calvary*, another of the *Four Plays for Dancers*, it is evident how the theatrical event was a structure through which Yeats represented the historical forces shaping his age. Having its origin in the socialism he learned from Morris, Yeats's perspective had evolved in response to the complete overhaul of European society since the outbreak of hostilities in August 1914. The estranging power he sought to harness from the Naturalist and Symbolist revolutions in the theatre were taken to new levels in these plays.

In an undated letter sent from Dublin, Yeats wrote to Edmund Dulac that he would arrive in London on 21 May, that he was writing a new Noh play that was longer than the others he had already written, with a view to having it acted in his own drawing room, and that his future wife George was helping him arrange the plot.¹ Yeats travelled to London at the end of May 1917 and had been working since April on the play that would become *The Dreaming of the Bones*, the longest of the Noh plays he wrote. It seems odd that George was helping him compose the play at this point, given the turbulent months before their marriage in October of that year; Margaret Mills Harper's claim for her profound influence on Yeats's later texts certainly appears borne out in this instance.² George later claimed that Yeats suggested the possibility of marriage to her in March 1917, indicating the extent of her presence in his life at this time.³ It seems probable, then, that the letter to Dulac was composed in May 1917 and did indeed refer to *The Dreaming of the Bones*. In March the following year he wrote again to Dulac that he and George were thinking of a new play about Christ and Lazarus that would eventually become *Calvary*.⁴ Along with the two Noh plays from the Cuchulain cycle *At the Hawk's Well* and *The Only Jealousy of Emer*, these would form the 1921 publication, *Four Plays for Dancers*.

Richard Taylor and Masaru Sekine praise *The Dreaming of the Bones* for its fidelity to the principles and atmosphere of Noh theatre, Sekine regarding it as Yeats's most successful adaptation of *Nishikigi*, one of the fourteenth-century Japanese plays translated by Fenollosa.⁵ Alongside *At the Hawk's Well* and *The Only Jealousy of Emer*, both plays emerged from Yeats's excitement at the discovery of Japanese Noh through Fenollosa's translations in the latter half of the 1910s. His pursuit of total theatre reached a frenetic pitch during these years, particularly in the use of dance and mask. Aside from Fenollosa's translations and Gordon Craig, his long-standing theatrical collaborator, the key influence in much of this was Dulac, whom Yeats first met around 1912 or 1913.⁶ Dulac brought the highest standards of craftsmanship to the design of masks and symbolic cloths, also contributing the musical score for plays such as *At the Hawk's Well* in keeping with Yeats's notions of theatrical voice and musical

---

[1] W. B. Yeats Collection, Series II, HRHRC.
[2] Mills Harper, *Wisdom of Two*, p. 183.
[3] See Saddlemeyer, *Becoming George*, p. 87; Foster, *W. B. Yeats*, vol. II, p. 88.
[4] Yeats to Dulac, 12 March. W. B. Yeats Collection, Series II, HRHRC.
[5] Taylor, *The Drama of W. B. Yeats*, pp. 153, 161. Sekine, 'Noh, Fenollosa, Pound and Yeats', p. 193.
[6] Ann Saddlemeyer states that Dulac would become Yeats's 'closest male confidant' for the rest of his life. *Becoming George*, p. 139. Elizabeth Bergmann Loizeaux suggests that Yeats had a more fruitful theatrical relationship with Dulac than with Craig because Dulac allowed Yeats complete freedom in theatrical presentation, whereas Craig was less willing to compromise his stage designs. See *Yeats and the Visual Arts* (New York: Syracuse University Press, 2003), pp. 97–9, 112.

accompaniment developed years earlier with Farr and Dolmetsch. Yeats's enthusiasm for Dulac's masks was pronounced, claiming to John Quinn in April 1916 that *At the Hawk's Well* was the first occasion in which masks were used in 'serious theatre' in the modern age.[7]

The extent of Dulac's input into the design of Yeats's later drama is generally acknowledged but the presumption remains that it contributed to the creation of elite aristocratic theatre for drawing-room audiences. In fact, Dulac's views on art were anything but elitist. He certainly shared Yeats's dismay at the advent of realism in art at the time, believing its influence to be damaging aesthetically.[8] Yet he also criticised those who attacked commercialism, pointing out that commerce had always been a feature of artistic endeavour, provocatively citing Rembrandt and Bach as artists who engaged in the mass production of their works. He argued that the advent of the middleman, following the decline of ecclesial and aristocratic patronage, had led to the creation of bad art; commercialism itself was not at fault.[9] Dulac regarded as imperative the obligation of artists to engage the conditions of their day. In a review of Herbert Read's *Art in Industry*, he fully endorsed the art of the machine, the objective of Marinetti's Futurist movement in Italy. He criticised the persistence of outworn notions of Renaissance and Romantic idealism that worked in the interests of certain individuals and groups, requiring a strenuous effort to uproot.[10]

Dulac's views never appear to be a source of tension in Yeats's correspondence with him, the only significant point of difference being their understanding of the role of music in Yeats's plays. In a letter to Dulac mentioning the praise accorded him in an interview Yeats gave to *The News Chronicle*, an important distinction was drawn. Yeats valued Dulac's expertise in music, but insisted that his own mastery of words be acknowledged in their creative collaborations: 'I am an expert in words but not in musical notes. I hope and still hope that Behemoth and Leviathan may meet.'[11] The matter was vitally important to Yeats and endured over time, giving credence

---

[7] Yeats to Quinn, 2 April 1916. Wade, *The Letters*, p. 610. In a letter to Dulac granting permission for the staging of *At the Hawk's Well* in New York, Yeats stressed that the reproductions of masks and costume designs should not be retained by the New York company. Yeats to Dulac, 22 July. W. B. Yeats Collection, HRHRC. For Yeats's anxiety to keep Dulac's masks for a New York run of *At the Hawk's Well*, see Yeats to Dulac, 22 March 1920. W. B. Yeats Collection, HRHRC.
[8] Ts. 'Magic and Art'. Lecture given before the Pioneer Club, 22 May 1924. Edmund Dulac Collection, HRHRC.
[9] Ts. 'Commercial Art'. Edmund Dulac Collection, HRHRC.
[10] Ts. Review of Mr Herbert Read's 'Art in Industry'. Edmund Dulac Collection. HRHRC.
[11] Yeats to Dulac [n.d.]. W. B. Yeats Collection, Series II, HRHRC.

to Adorno's belief that the relationship between language and music had become critical in the twentieth century.[12] In the summer of 1937, while staying with Edith Shackleton Heald at Steyning in Sussex, Yeats drew on recollections of important women in his earlier career to stress once more the distinction between song and poetic delivery. He remarked that experiences with Florence Farr's pupils had taught him that a singer had first to be a speaker if he or she was to deliver a line of poetry effectively. He recollected once working weeks on end with a friend of Annie Horniman's who was a trained singer, the quality of spoken delivery failing to emerge despite his efforts. By contrast, Sarah Allgood was singled out as an actress who could do all Yeats wanted because her voice had been trained by the actor Frank Fay. Yeats went on in this letter to deflate Dulac's objections to tonal music by stating that he had already heard much of the same criticism from F. R. Higgins, one of the Abbey Theatre's directors, in the 1930s.[13] In another letter probably written the same summer from Penns-in-the-Rocks, he suggested that Dulac take the theme of modern music and singing for a public lecture he envisaged, adding that the differences between them on the subject would arouse much interest.[14]

Yeats had been experimenting with theatrical voice since the early 1900s but the musicians in the dance plays acquired a more pronounced presence than before. They not only frame the play in *The Dreaming of the Bones* but also appear within it, narrating the Young Man and the Stranger travelling to the ruins of the Abbey of Corcomroe at the time of the Rising. The musicians deliver almost one-third of the lines in *Calvary* and the line 'God has not died for the white heron' recurs as a musical motif throughout. Notwithstanding differences of opinion regarding voice and music, the heightened importance the musicians acquire in the dance plays testifies to Dulac's influence at possibly the most important period in Yeats's creative development, the latter half of the 1910s. Indeed, it was out of this collaboration between the two that some of the most effective formal experiments emerged, resonating avant-garde currents swelling elsewhere, notably the work of Schoenberg in the period between 1908 and 1914.

This pursuit of a new kind of musical form was part of the technique of total theatre Yeats was developing with Dulac; combining movement,

---

[12] Theodor W. Adorno, *Quasi una Fantasia: Essays on Modern Music*, 2nd edn, trans. Rodney Livingstone (London: Verso, 1998), p. 2.
[13] Yeats to Dulac, 17 July. No year given but letter addressed from Steyning, Sussex. W. B. Yeats Collection, Series II, HRHRC.
[14] Yeats to Dulac [n.d.]. W. B. Yeats Collection, Series II, HRHRC.

mask, light and sound, the dance plays aimed at generating a distinctive and unsettling theatrical experience that would contribute to the repertoire of continental European experimentalism. The historical form of *The Dreaming of the Bones* is articulated in this context. Set against the backdrop of the 1916 Rising, the play draws upon the story of Dermot and Dervorgilla, the lovers who purportedly betrayed Ireland by first inviting English soldiers into the country. James Moran rightly observes that in what little critical attention has been afforded the play, concern with its connection to Japanese Noh has obscured its political import at the time of its composition and, later, its first performance.[15] Indeed, the potent iconography of this play at the time Yeats composed it was such that it would not be staged in Ireland until 1931, produced in Dublin by Ninette de Valois, though it appears that Yeats may have intended it for a Dublin drawing-room performance alongside *At the Hawk's Well* as early as 1918 and certainly planned such a performance in February 1924.[16] Writing to Dulac in April 1919 from Thoor Ballylee about his intention to write a fourth Noh play and have Macmillan publish all four in a single volume in the hope of getting performances, Yeats worried that local farmers in the area had their eye on Ballylee as a place for hiding weapons.[17] Bearing out his fears, the Black and Tans occupied the residence the following year while the Yeatses were in Oxford, having 'in the wantonness of their hearts smashed all windows and stolen all locks'.[18] The *Four Plays for Dancers* emerged at a time of deep political turmoil in Ireland when historical forces appeared to be reaching a critical point. Yeats articulated this through the stress generated in the plays from the refusal of redemption, a stress intensified in the rigorously taut manner by which this refusal was represented. The Old Man is condemned to stasis in *At the Hawk's Well*, Emer saves Cuchulain from Fand only by giving up all hope of winning his love, the ghostly lovers remain trapped in perdition in *The Dreaming of the Bones* and *Calvary* reflects on a suffering that Christ has not redeemed. Through these denials, the plays bear the imprint of contemporary history, forcing the inversion in theatrical form that was anti-theatre, plays that worked within ritual drama while refusing its redeeming purpose.

---

[15] James Moran, *Staging the Easter Rising: 1916 as Theatre* (Cork University Press, 2005), p. 53.
[16] Yeats to Dulac, 23 October 1918 annotated in pencil. Letter addressed from Merrion Square, Dublin. Yeats to Dulac, 25 February 1924, from same address. W. B. Yeats Collection, HRHRC. See also Schmitt, '"Haunted by Places"', p. 353.
[17] Yeats to Dulac, 20 April 1919. W. B. Yeats Collection. HRHRC.
[18] Yeats to Dulac [n.d.]. 1920 annotated in pencil. W. B. Yeats Collection. HRHRC.

In both *The Dreaming of the Bones* and *Calvary*, history is mediated through entrapment and condemnation, addressed through Yeats's adaptation of total theatre technique to anti-theatrical ends. *The Dreaming of the Bones* is indebted to the notion of 'dreaming back' that engaged Yeats at the time of its composition, and Helen Vendler argues that, like the ghosts of Dermot and Dervorgilla in the play, the Young Man is also dreaming back.[19] This idea was not quite as unique in its time as it might seem today. Similar ideas were to be found in a work published by Lewis Alexander Richard Wallace in the same year as *Four Plays for Dancers*, a work rumoured to be co-authored by A. R. Orage, founder of *The New Age* along with Wallace and George Bernard Shaw, a journal to which Yeats had contributed on several occasions in the 1900s. In *Cosmic Anatomy and the Structure of the Ego*, Wallace attempted to synthesise Indian and Egyptian mysticism with modern physics and psychoanalysis. Drawing on terms from the *Vishnu Purana*, he accorded foundational importance to the notions *Pradhana* and *Purusha* in a manner bearing direct affinity to Yeats's concepts of Self and Anti-Self:

> Pradhana means prædatum, which gives a feeling that I cannot differentiate from Substance; while Purusha is to me identical with οὐσία or Essence, that which 'fills out' the 'lifeless' mass, the entity within, the essence which comes to existence; in fact, they are in a way the self and the not-self.[20]

Wallace's work anticipated the concerns of *A Vision* of 1925 in several aspects and may identify the source for Yeats's gyres in the *Katha Upanishad*, in which the *vedi* or temple was symbolised by two interlocking triangles, with fire, *Kunda*, placed at their intersection.[21] More specifically important to *Four Plays for Dancers* was the stress Wallace laid on the Hindu notion of *Laya*, corresponding to the condition of interference between two wave-systems in modern physics, a state in which a

---

[19] Vendler, *Yeats's Vision*, pp. 190–1. Yeats wrote that the conception of *The Dreaming of the Bones* derived from 'the world-wide belief that the dead dream back, for a certain time, through the more personal thoughts and dreams of life'. 'Note on *The Dreaming of the Bones*', *Four Plays for Dancers* (London: Macmillan Press, 1921), p. 129.

[20] M. B. Oxon, *Cosmic Anatomy and the Structure of the Ego* (London: John Watkins, 1921), pp. 53–4. The pseudonmyn Wallace uses was in acknowledgement of the nineteenth-century English Anglican priest and spiritualist, William Stanton Moses, author of the influential *Spirit Teachings* published under the pseudonym M. A. Oxon in 1883. Wallace's book prompted Katherine Mansfield to enter the Gurdjieff Institute for the Harmonious Development of Man, some months before her death in January 1923. See Alex Owen, 'The "Religious Sense" in a Post-War Secular Age', *Past and Present*, 1, Supplement 1 (2006), pp. 159–77.

[21] Oxon, *Cosmic Anatomy*, p. 50. Naresh Guha points out that the 1937 edition of *A Vision* is full of references to India and some of them were entered even before Yeats met Shri Purohit Swami in June 1931. *W. B. Yeats: An Indian Approach* (Calcutta: Jadavpur University, 1968), pp. 101–4.

change of dimension occurs.²² The study provides a context for the nature of Yeats's response to Einstein's theory of relativity as laid out in Bertrand Russell's *ABC of Relativity*, considered in Chapter 8 of this volume. Wallace compared what happened in bodily form at the moment of *Laya* to what happened in artistic and literary form during revivals, evidently regarding his contemporary age as a critical point within which a change of dimension was taking place in European civilisation.

Yeats's deployment of the idea of 'dreaming back' through the Noh form in *The Dreaming of the Bones* and *Calvary* appears strikingly consonant with this notion of *Laya*, that critical moment in which form and structure of reference undergo a fundamental alteration. Ostensibly focused upon seminal events in the distant past, both plays are really concerned with the contemporary historical moment as a 'zero point', drawing upon antique images to give expression to its intensity. While a mood of melancholy is certainly present in *The Dreaming of the Bones*, it does not dissipate the hard sense of petrifaction generated from the image of the Stranger and the Young Girl caught in a moment from which they cannot escape.²³ The melancholic undertone to the situation of the lovers might be traced back to Gregory's 1908 play *Dervorgilla*, an earlier treatment of the tale. Presented in a more conventional fashion, Gregory's was an appeal for forgiveness and love following the bitterness that ensued from the 1907 performances of *The Playboy of the Western World*. But even here, there was a quality of stasis and intense concentration upon hidden transgression that Yeats would take up and develop more rigorously in his own version.²⁴ His achievement was to express the entrapment of the lovers consequent upon their transgression through the enclosure of self-reflexive theatre. When the Young Girl explains the condition of the lovers to the Young Man, she is both performing as if she was *not* the ghost of Dervorgilla and presenting the ghostly condition of the lovers as itself performative:

> Although they have no blood, or living nerves,
> Who once lay warm and live the live-long night
> In one another's arms, and know their part

---

²² Oxon, *Cosmic Anatomy*, pp. 60–1.
²³ John Rees Moore goes as far as suggesting that the love between these two amounts to a form of 'antihumanity' while Katharine Worth sees the image of the Young Man circling the stage with them as a metaphor of his entrapment and, we might add, that of the lovers. Moore, *Masks of Love and Death*, p. 230; Worth, *The Irish Drama of Europe*, p. 170.
²⁴ For a discussion of Gregory's play, see Michael McAteer, '"Kindness in Your Unkindness": Lady Gregory and History', *Irish University Review: Special Issue: Lady Gregory*, 34:1(2004), 94–108.

> In life, being now but of the people of dreams,
> Is a dream's part; although they are but shadows,
> Hovering between a thorn-tree and a stone,
> Who have heaped up night on wingèd night; although
> No shade however harried and consumed
> Would change his own calamity for theirs,
> Their manner of life were blessed could their lips
> A moment meet; but when he has bent his head
> Close to her head, or hand would slip in hand,
> The memory of their crime flows up between
> And drives them apart. (*VPl*, 771–2)

Being 'of the people of dreams' and knowing their part in life 'is a dream's part', Dermot and Dervorgilla's only reality is the story of their lives from which they cannot find release. The calamitous consequence of their transgression is perpetual entrapment in its narrative.

This situation was strikingly parallel to Pirandello's *Six Characters*, first performed in Rome the same year as the publication of *Four Plays for Dancers* and staged at the Abbey by the Dublin Drama League in April 1923.[25] At the heart of this play lay a secret transgression, the consequence of which was to condemn the six characters to their allotted roles in its unfolding. In the scene that the six characters have come to perform, the Mother asserts to an uncomprehending producer the reality of the narrative to which she is condemned *in perpetuum*: 'My agony isn't made up! I am living my agony constantly, every moment; I'm alive and it's alive and it keeps coming back again and again, as fresh as the first time.' The Father, still in role, solemnly bears out this relation between his transgression and their entrapment in a drama of their own making: 'The eternal moment! I told you about it. She's here to catch me, to string me up before the public, fixed, hooked, chained for ever to the pillory of that one shaming fleeting moment of my life.'[26] That 'eternal moment' is the Mother encountering her daughter in an embrace with her stepfather.

Bound up with the political history of loyalty and treachery in Ireland, the source of shame is quite different in Yeats's play. The struggle of emotions that the 1916 Rising provoked in Yeats has received extensive critical consideration; he would delay publication of 'Easter 1916' until October 1920.[27] A significant feature of *The Dreaming of the Bones* is that the

---

[25] Robert Hogan and Richard Burnham, *The Years of O'Casey, 1921–1926: A Documentary History*, Modern Irish Drama, vol. VI (University of Delaware, 1992), p. 165.
[26] Pirandello, *Six Characters*, Collected Plays, p. 52.
[27] Foster puts the delay mostly down to Gregory's fears that it would jeopardise negotiations over the Hugh Lane collection. Wayne Chapman concurs. See Foster, *W. B. Yeats*, vol. II, pp. 59–66,

Rising was imagined in conflict with elevated figures of Gaelic antiquity, unlike 'Easter 1916' where the leaders enter into the elect of Irish mythology. The attitude to mythic heroism in the play is deeply ambivalent. Are Dermot and Dervorgilla heroic in enduring forever a love suspended because of the betrayal attached to it? Is the Young Man heroic in fidelity to the cause of his nation? Is Dermot named 'the Stranger' because he has invited 'strangers' into Ireland, recalling Cathleen ni Houlihan's lament at 'too many strangers' in her house; or does he recall the spectral presence of Cathleen herself, the revenant? Natalie Crohn Schmitt observes that in *The Dreaming of the Bones* and *Calvary*, ecstatic union is sought but denied. Arguing that Yeats used the dance to represent sexual union – the image of a cosmic union – she sees the soldier's dance around the dying figure of Christ as 'the antithesis of such ecstatic union'. The same might be said of the ritual circling of the stage in *The Dreaming of the Bones*.[28] This refusal of ecstasis was a way of interrogating mythic heroism rather than lamenting its decline. A gap appears between ecstasis and myth in that the Young Man's fidelity to the cause of Ireland condemns the lovers to a condition of perpetual frustration. The long history of Yeats's frustrated love for Gonne was present here but, equally, the influence of George Hyde-Lees. Ann Saddlemyer notes how George was initiated into the Second Order within the Golden Dawn, thus becoming a colleague of Yeats's, in May 1916. News of the Rising had appeared to agitate her during the ceremony of initiation – the execution of MacBride left Maud Gonne free once more for Yeats's advances and, with her visit to London, Iseult Gonne became another possible threat to George's hopes for matrimony.[29] We can see how this maps on to *The Dreaming of the Bones* – George's dream of ecstatic union suspended in the fallout from the Rising.

Within the occult rituals of the Golden Dawn, sexual union was considered a form of mystical experience; emblem of betrayal, the suspended kiss of *The Dreaming of the Bones* was also sexually potent. As Noreen Doody observes, the kiss connoted desecration as much as sanctity in Yeats's later plays. Observing the legacy of Wilde's influence, Doody

---

182, and W. B. Yeats, '*The Dreaming of the Bones' and 'Calvary': Manuscript Materials*, ed. Wayne Chapman (Ithaca: Cornell University Press, 2003), p. xxviii. Paulin argues that Yeats was worried at British Intelligence suspecting him of pro-German sympathies in 1916 and at the prospect of losing his Civil List pension. 'Yeats's Hunger-Strike Poem', pp. 133–50. See also Edna Longley's reading of 'Easter 1916' in *The Living Stream: Literature and Revisionism in Ireland* (Newcastle upon Tyne: Bloodaxe Press, 1994), pp. 71, 72, 79.

[28] Crohn Schmitt, '"Separating Strangeness" ', pp. 88–9.
[29] Saddlemyer, *Becoming George*, p. 30.

looks to notions of sacrilege and transgression in Wilde's *De Profundis* as a pretext for the carnal consummation of Queen and Swineherd in Yeats's *A Full Moon in March* of 1934. Like the idea of *Laya* in Wallace's *Cosmic Anatomy*, this was linked to the birth of a new epoch.[30] Sexual supernaturalism became the means by which a critical transformation in historical conditions was represented on stage. A story of Wilde's that Yeats recalled in 'The Tragic Generation' suggests his direct influence on the conception of *Calvary*, blurring the line between sanctity and profanity still further. It told of Jesus entering a city and encountering a drunk man, a man pursuing a harlot and a man weeping in the marketplace. The drunk had been a leper cured by Jesus, the man pursuing a harlot had been cured of blindness, and the man weeping had been raised by Jesus from the dead. To Jesus's question as to why they had fallen into vice and sadness, each of them responds that, having been cured, their subsequent lives could not have been otherwise. The story is evidently a source for Synge's *The Well of the Saints*. Dorothy Wellesley recalled that in 1936 Yeats claimed it was the finest story he had ever encountered, though she may have confused Yeats's opinion with that of Wilde himself recorded by Yeats in 'The Tragic Generation'.[31] The story encapsulated those aspects of *Calvary* examined below – the subversion of redemption, heroic revolt against an imposed destiny and the ceremonial articulation of the secular.

The line between sanctity and profanity became very thin in the last Yeats plays, in which bestiality, rape and filicide were invested with supernatural significance. Natalie Crohn Schmitt argues that the Queen's apparent regression to the lowest animal level of material existence – her adoration of the Swineherd – in *A Full Moon in March* is best understood in terms of ecstatic experience as formulated by psychoanalyst Abraham Maslow and writer Marghanita Laski.[32] However tenable this might be, the dance plays remain deeply transgressive and violent. Significant here is the fact that *The Dreaming of the Bones* anticipated Yeats's penultimate play, *Purgatory*, in linking sexual and political guilt. The ghosts in both plays are only manifest by virtue of the violation attached to the sexual intercourse they engaged in in life – for *The Dreaming of the Bones*, it is the tragic colonial history of Ireland since the Tudor conquest, for *Purgatory*, it is the final collapse of what D. George Boyce calls the Protestant Irish

---

[30] Doody, 'An Echo of Some One Else's Music', pp. 178–81.
[31] Yeats, 'The Tragic Generation', *Autobiographies*, p. 286. For Wellesley's recollection, see *Letters on Poetry from W. B. Yeats to Dorothy Wellesley* (London: Oxford University Press, 1940), p. 51.
[32] Natalie Crohn Schmitt, 'Ecstasy and Peak Experience: W. B. Yeats, Marghanita Laski, and Abraham Maslow', *Comparative Drama*, 28:2 (1994), 173.

nation and its sense of cultural distinctiveness.³³ The kiss to which Dermot and Dervorgilla reach is far from the sordid copulation of the drunken stableman and the Ascendancy lady in *Purgatory*, yet the narrative of adulterous lovers whose elopement prompted the demise of a culture anticipates that of *Purgatory* with considerable acuity.

Notwithstanding specific reference to Irish history then, the form of transgression in *The Dreaming of the Bones* mirrors that of Pirandello's *Six Characters*. Both plays are centred upon a moment of sexual encounter in which the theatre turns in upon itself. What might this similarity indicate about Yeats's understanding of the historical form of the Rising? The nature of the fourth dance play, *Calvary*, never performed in Yeats's lifetime, is telling here. Of all his later plays, this appears impossible to appreciate without reference to the Automatic Writing symbolism informing *A Vision*. Though couched in the exotic terms of Arabian mysticism, Yeats's explanation of the symbolism of the play bears this out. The sacrifice of Christ, because directed primarily towards the physical deprivation of the poor, manifested an objective solitude. Lazarus and Judas, on the other hand, personified the subjective loneliness captured in the image of the white heron, an 'intellectual despair' beyond the reach of the cross.³⁴

Nietzsche remained a crucial and expanded influence in this regard. In a series of important essays published in *The New Age* soon after *Four Plays for Dancers* in early 1922, Janko Lavrin offered a number of important insights on Nietzsche's religious understanding. Reflecting upon Nietzsche's transvaluation of values, Lavrin proposed two forms of what he termed magical ecstasy standing in contrast to ecstatic union with God, the ideal of Christian mysticism. The first he identified as 'Luciferic', by which he imagined the individual who rejects God in the absolute assertion of selfhood. The Stephen Dedalus of Joyce's *Ulysses* – also published in 1922 – comes to mind here. The second was more identifiably existentialist, within which the individual faced unflinchingly the absurdity of a Godless universe, becoming intoxicated by his own power in the process. Lavrin argued that these Nietzschean forms of ecstatic experience were inverse images of Christian mystical ecstasis. Whereas the Christian mystic enters a state of ecstasy in complete surrender to God, Nietzsche conveyed the paradoxically transcendental exhilaration of wilfully generating

---

[33] D.G. Boyce, *Nationalism in Ireland*, 3rd edn (London: Routledge, 1995) pp. 25–90. Boyce traces the Irish Protestant Nation back to first Tudor parliament and, significantly for Yeats, the Butlers, the Geraldines and the Desmonds feature as important families. For comparison of *The Dreaming of the Bones* and *Purgatory*, see, Ure, *Yeats the Playwright*, pp. 107–8.
[34] Yeats, 'Note on *Calvary*', *Four Plays for Dancers*, pp. 136–7.

meaning and value entirely from oneself, without recourse to any external system of belief.[35]

Calvary was probably the most structurally integrated of all Yeats's plays, each composite element interrelated to create a theatrical moment. Voice, movement, gesture and lighting required the utmost choreographic care and concentration of purpose if the effect of the play was to be achieved, yet at its heart lay an invocation of pure contingency. The play pivots on two brief dialogues, the first between Christ and Lazarus, the second between Christ and Judas. In the latter, Judas responds to Christ's proclamation that his betrayal was decreed from the origin of creation:

> It was decreed that somebody betray you –
> I'd thought of that – but not that I should do it,
> I the man Judas, born on such a day,
> In such a village, such and such his parents;
> Nor that I'd go with my old coat upon me
> To the High Priest, and chuckle to myself
> As people chuckle when alone, and do it
> For thirty pieces and no more, no less,
> And neither with a nod nor a sent message,
> But with a kiss upon your cheek. I did it,
> I, Judas, and no other man, and now
> You cannot even save me. (*VPl*, 785)

Judas defies predetermination here by invoking the situationally specific nature of his intervention. Thus the death of Christ anticipates *The Death of Cuchulain* in Yeats's final play. Articulating in performance a transcendental power through the contingency of a specific situation, the play takes on the character of an event. Recalling Lavrin's two forms of Nietzschean magical ecstasy, the Luciferic and the existentialist, it would seem that Judas expressed the first of these, becoming his own destiny in direct defiance of God.

The playfulness of Yeats's opening comments to the explanatory notes for *Calvary* in *Four Plays for Dancers* lays further emphasis on the contingent, mocking the profundity of subject-matter in the play, carrying the kind of flippancy we encounter in Pirandello:

I used to think that singers should sing a recipe for a good dish, or a list of local trains, or something else they want to get by heart, but I have changed my mind and now I prefer to give him some mystery or secret.[36]

---

[35] Janko Lavrin, 'Nietzsche Revisited. IV – "We Immoralists"', *The New Age*, 30:23 (1922), 189.
[36] Yeats, 'Note on *Calvary*', *Four Plays for Dancers*, p. 135.

This whimsy was not accidental. In *Calvary*, the figure of Christ on the cross appears discreetly farcical and with it, the narrative of salvation foundational to European history. Eliding divine providence through the specificity of his betrayal, Judas plays a kind of metaphysical trick intended to make Christ seem clownish, inflecting his last line with a sardonic gloss: 'My Father, why hast Thou forsaken Me?' The note of mockery is even more pronounced in Lazarus, who taunts Christ for denying him his death. Redemption becomes ridiculous in Lazarus's complaint that he had been lying dead in 'an old comfortable mountain cavern' before Jesus 'dragged' him to the light (*VPl*, 782). This would have an important bearing on Beckett, whose protagonist in *Malone Dies* imagines Christ spending the Easter weekend in hell, a satirical jibe at the doctrine of the crucified Christ descending into hell to unlock its gates.[37] Though Pirandello's 1927 play *Lazarus* was given a contemporary setting, its subversive power derived from recourse to the same image of the man for whom resurrection was catastrophe. The play is also inhabited by Cico, 'God's rent-collector', a comic figure from the *Commedia dell'arte* believed under the devil's influence, a reminder of Briciu from *The Only Jealousy of Emer*. Recalling Wilde's story of Jesus in the marketplace, the black comedy of *Lazarus* lies in the way faith in salvation is thrown into crisis rather than fortified by Diego's return from death.[38]

Whether or not the figures of Judas and Lazarus in *Calvary* are Luciferic or existentialist, their presence on stage is manifested within a tight dialectical structure of necessity and contingency embodied in both the form and the theme.[39] Recalling the cross of *The Land of Heart's Desire* – 'the tortured thing' – the cross in *Calvary* carries Yeats's paradoxical view of the machine age – a debasement of human experience to automation that yet fascinates in awakening the trance-inducing primeval power of the totem.

This Nietzschean perspective was gaining wider currency among intellectual circles as the political crisis of Europe deepened. Writing in *The New Age* in August 1910, Francis Grierson drew explicit connection between scientific materialism and Christianity when attacking materialism for the breakup of civilisation. Directly relating materialism to crime, murder and insanity, Grierson asserted that Greek and Roman civilisation

---

[37] Beckett, *Malone Dies, Molloy, Malone Dies, the Unnamable*, p. 282.
[38] Pirandello, *Lazarus, Collected Plays*, pp. 153–223.
[39] Murray Roston imagines Lazarus and Judas as twentieth-century dialecticians. *Biblical Drama in England: From the Middle Ages to the Present Day* (Evanston: Northwestern University Press, 1968), p. 269.

were brought to an end by scepticism: with the gradual erosion of philosophy, the political arena became the preserve of murderers and criminals. Christianity arose out of the ashes of 'Jerusalem, Athens, Rome', all of which ended in materialism; Christianity had ended by imposing a new science which was 'frankly and brazenly materialistic'.[40] The essay echoed Max Nordau's *Degeneration* (1892) while anticipating the themes of T. S. Eliot's 'The Waste Land' and Oswald Spengler's *The Decline of the West* (1918). Its influence on the perspectives informing *Calvary* lay in the connection Grierson drew between materialism, Christianity and political criminality. The years leading up to the publication of *Four Plays for Dancers* and *Michael Robartes and the Dancer* in 1921 were accompanied by Yeats's growing sense of the murderousness of modern political systems. Yeats was certainly of the belief that a new fanaticism had arisen from the spread of materialism, Marxism being its most explicit proponent. In 1919 he wrote to George Russell that Marxism was the 'spearhead' of materialism and would lead 'to inevitable murder'.[41]

Yeats's horror at news of the execution of the Tsar did not derive from an unremitting disdain of revolutionary politics, as some have assumed.[42] His response was entirely consistent with Wilde's rejection of state-controlled socialism over twenty years previously in 'The Soul of Man under Socialism', and the principled anarchism he related to Kropotkin and Stepniak in the early 1900s. In line with Grierson's 1910 essay from *The New Age*, Yeats specifically related Bolshevism to a species of Christian fanaticism:

Logic is loose again, as once in Calvin and Knox, or in the hysterical rhetoric of Savonarola, or in Christianity itself in its first raw centuries, and because it must always draw its deductions from what every dolt can understand, the wild beast cannot but destroy mysterious life.[43]

By this account, the 'rough beast' of 'The Second Coming' refers not to the figure of the anti-Christ but a murderous fanaticism growing out of Christianity itself that showed its face in the Inquisition and Cromwellite Puritanism. In his introduction to the first volume of *The Decline of the West*, published in 1918, Spengler cites a comparison commonly made between modern socialism and early Christianity to support his typological

---

[40] Francis Grierson, 'Materialism and Crime', *The New Age: A Weekly Review of Politics, Literature, and Art*, 17:15 (1910), 341.
[41] Foster, *W. B. Yeats*, vol. II, p. 147.
[42] See, for example, Paul Scott Stanfield, *Yeats and Politics in the 1930s* (London: Macmillan Press, 1988), pp. 78–111.
[43] W. B. Yeats, 'If I were Four and Twenty' (London: Macmillan Press, 1962), *Explorations*, p. 277.

account of history bearing close affinity to the typological framing of historical epochs in *A Vision*.⁴⁴ Yeats may have included reference to Fra. Girolamo Savonarola here in memory of Thomas MacDonagh's 1908 play at the Abbey, *When Dawn is Come*, depicting the tensions between insurrectionary leaders at a future moment of uprising in Ireland. Forced to covert intrigues to secure the integrity of plans for rebellion against the incursion of government spies, the leader of an insurgent Irish Army, Thurlough MacKieran, compares himself to the fifteenth-century Florentine monk. Savonarola's denunciation of the wealthy Medici family in the late fifteenth-century had led to the expulsion of the Medici from Florence, though he was himself later condemned by the Vatican, tortured and executed.⁴⁵ The example suggests how the objects of Yeats's fear in 1921 were not those Marxist ideas he had learned from Morris, but their petrifaction into a series of crude slogans, closing down artistic and intellectual freedom in the process.

Patrick Keane writes that Yeats's dread of Marxism 'was essentially focused on Leninist Communism and its revolutionary challenge to a European social order left reeling after the unprecedented catastrophe of the First World War'.⁴⁶ Katharine Worth notes how the actors enter the stage in *Calvary* as if sleepwalking, hypnotised by the voice of the musicians, a somnambulism reflecting a collective dulling of minds by mantra-like slogans of press, pulpit and party against which Yeats had railed since the early 1900s.⁴⁷ His rejection of the Marxist theory of value in the aftermath of the Russian Revolution was not sustained by any serious engagement with Marx's writings, much of which were still unpublished or untranslated at the time. In effect, he was reacting to Bolshevik rhetoric entering political discourse in Ireland and Britain following the First World War. Yeats's attitude to radical socialism during the course of his career was determined in large measure by the degree to which he felt it might enable or prohibit intellectual and artistic freedom. The influence of Blake in the 1890s included his searing depiction of decadent materialism and a degenerate ecclesial culture in 'Songs of Innocence and

---

⁴⁴ Oswald Spengler, *The Decline of the West: Form and Actuality*, 2nd edn, trans. Charles Atkinson (London: George Allen & Unwin, 1948), p. 4.
⁴⁵ Thomas MacDonagh, *When Dawn is Come*, *Four Irish Rebel Plays*, ed. James Moran (Dublin: Irish Academic Press, 2007), pp. 47, 70–1. Five years earlier, MacDonagh had dedicated his first volume of poems to Yeats, *Through the Ivory Gates*, and took great interest in Yeats's experiments with poetic incantation. See Schuchard, *The Last Minstrels*, p. 84.
⁴⁶ Keane, *Yeats's Interactions*, p. 75.
⁴⁷ Katharine Worth, '*The Words upon the Window-pane*: A Female Tragedy', *Yeats Annual*, vol. XI, ed. Warwick Gould (London: Macmillan Press, 1993), p. 137.

Experience'. Shelley's political radicalism was compared favourably with that of Blake. In 'The Philosophy of Shelley's Poetry' Yeats directly quotes a passage from Shelley's 'An Apology for Poetry', a blueprint for *The King's Threshold* performed three years later:

> Whilst the mechanist abridges and the political economist combines labour, let them be sure that their speculations, for want of correspondence with those first principles which belong to the imagination, do not tend, as they have in modern England, to exasperate at once the extremes of luxury and want ... The rich have become richer, the poor have become poorer ... such are the effects which must ever flow from an unmitigated exercise of the calculating faculty.

Yeats comments that the speaker here might almost be Blake, 'who held that the Reason not only created Ugliness, but all other evils'.[48]

Behind this lay the overriding influence of Morris. 'If I Were Four and Twenty' of 1919 recalls a public lecture on socialism delivered by Morris in Dublin that was greeted with derision. Yeats lamented how the socialism of Morris was now being gobbled up by young Irishmen after the execution of James Connolly just as assuredly as Morris had been scoffed in 1880s Dublin as an eccentric English fool.[49] Despite rejecting *John Bull's Other Island* in 1904, Yeats always held the radical Shaw in highest esteem since their careers in the theatre began at the Avenue in 1894; some of the most provocative eugenicist sentiments of his 1938 essay *On the Boiler* may be attributed to Shaw's influence. The controversial essay took as evidence of cultural degeneration a report in 1937 that the Galway Library Committee had decided that Shaw's books were not suitable for a public library and had them burnt.[50] 'If I were Four and Twenty' describes Shaw as a logician 'without rancour' and, with Morris, a lover of the best.[51] A further influence shaping in later years was Benedetto Croce, whose work exposed Yeats to Hegelian dialectic, probably for the first time. Besides an important influence on Pirandello, Croce's writings also proved hugely influential for the Italian Marxist Antonio Gramsci, who engaged Croce's ideas to counter the lack of a developed theory of culture

---

[48] W. B. Yeats, 'The Philosophy of Shelley's Poetry', *The Dome*, 7 (1900), 77.
[49] W. B. Yeats, 'If I were Four and Twenty', *Explorations*, p. 268. For the influence of Morris, see Schuchard, 'The Minstrel in the Theatre', pp. 3–24; Peter Faulkner, *William Morris and W. B. Yeats* (Dublin: The Dolmen Press, 1962). For the argument for Morris as an all-pervasive presence in Yeats's late poem, 'The Statues', see Edward Engelberg, *The Vast Design: Patterns in W. B. Yeats's Aesthetic*, 2nd edn (Washington DC: The Catholic University of America Press, 1988), pp. 190–4.
[50] W. B. Yeats, *On the Boiler* (Dublin: The Cuala Press, 1938), pp. 10–11.
[51] W. B. Yeats, 'If I were Four and Twenty', p. 43.

in Marx's work.⁵² Despite the fallout over *The Silver Tassie* in 1928, Yeats championed O'Casey, an outspoken international socialist, regarded Connolly as one of the most able contributors to intellectual life in Ireland, was friends early in life with the socialist Frederick Ryan, and engaged with dissenting intellectuals in 1930s Ireland such as Frank O'Connor and Peader O'Donnell, the latter a lead-figure in the Irish Communist Party. He was acquainted with a host of left-wing radicals among bohemian circles in 1930s London, including Lady Cunard's daughter Nancy, editor of the Hours Press, and Ethel Mannin, described by Foster as 'emphatically and vociferously left-wing'.⁵³

Michael Mays suggests that by 'filthy modern tide' Yeats did not mean the working classes but the economic system of which they were victims. This was precisely the position of Morris in the 1880s. Citing Yeats's letter of intervention to *The Irish Worker* at the time of the 1913 lockout and the invective directed against business leader William Martin Murphy in 'To a Friend Whose Work Has Come to Nothing', Mays argues that the value Yeats placed upon 'excess' had to be understood against the specific circumstances of the Ireland of his day. He considers Georges Bataille's theory of excess in relation to the later Yeats, an extreme philosophy specifically directed against the cultural forms of industrial capitalism.⁵⁴ The argument falls short in ignoring Yeats's debt to wealthy patrons, including John Quinn, Annie Horniman and, indeed, Gregory herself. Nevertheless, had the Dublin civic authorities backed funding for the Lane collection, it would have allowed Yeats more room to openly criticise British government policy in Ireland following the 1916 Rising. As Foster points out, he was forced to restraint, delaying open publication of 'Easter 1916' for four years, because Gregory and he were still lobbying British cabinet officials to fund a gallery for the Lane collection.⁵⁵ Dublin's refusal presaged an era in which cultural and artistic freedom would become conditional upon economic and political priorities themselves conceived within a narrow frame of reference.

---

[52] For Yeats's engagement with Croce see Donald T. Torchiana, 'Yeats and Croce', *Yeats Annual*, vol. IV, ed. Warwick Gould (London: Macmillan Press, 1986), pp. 3–11. References to Croce pervade Gramsci's prison notebooks which, while rejecting Croce's 'political morphinism', employ Croce as the point of departure for some of Gramsci's key formulations, including the role of the intellectual and national-popular culture. See Antonio Gramsci, *Selections from the Prison Notebooks of Antonio Gramsci*, ed. and trans. Quintin Hoare and Geoffrey Nowell Smith (London: Lawrence and Wishart, 1971), pp. 55–6, 270–1, 391, 436, 448.
[53] Foster, *W. B. Yeats*, vol. II, p. 512.
[54] Mays, 'Yeats', p. 302.
[55] Foster, *W. B. Yeats*, vol. II, p. 182.

Yeats's attitude to Marxism in the aftermath of the Russian Revolution derived from the complex profile of the intellectual circles he had inhabited since the 1890s, the traumatic circumstances of Ireland during the War of Independence, his relative ignorance of Marx's own writings, the lack of an adequate theory of culture within Marx's work, and the proliferation of incantatory rhetoric carrying the stamp of Communist Party approval becoming dogma under Stalin. 'If I Were Four and Twenty' is anxious about the spread of a flaccid utopianism and the neutralisation of cultural difference. Morris is taken to task for lacking a vision of evil, while Socialism imposed a uniformity as universal 'as Capital or as Calvinism', Yeats never having 'met a Socialist who did not believe he could carry his oratory from London to Paris and from Paris to Jericho and there find himself at home'.[56] Significantly, the essay was published in *The New Statesman*, successor of the Irish Co-operative organ *The Irish Homestead* and forerunner of *The Bell*, all centre-left journals originally modelled along the neo-Syndicalist radicalism of *The New Age*. Yeats admired the Irish Co-operative Movement because instead of attacking property, it aimed to distribute it as widely as possible, a movement 'content to be the midwife of Nature and not a juggling mechanist who would substitute an automaton for her living child'.[57]

Interrogating the redeeming purpose of the crucified Christ, Yeats was representing and resisting a historical process through which thought itself was reduced to quantity. In so doing, he symbolises Christ as an earlier Lenin and Lenin a later Cromwell (*The Resurrection* of 1931 would offer a very different view of Christ, to whom the followers of Dionysius the Areogapite are converted at the end of the Acts of the Apostles). In this way, the play went beyond the Faustian mode to historicise the solitary self-begetting of what would later become the existential hero in the plays of Sartre, Camus, Ionesco and Beckett. Cross and dance are held in tension as images of predestination and free will; the exchanges between Christ, Lazarus and Judas appear as Socratic dialectic, but in which the master is successfully rebuffed. The play does not repudiate history – in its guise as predestination, the Marxist rhetoric of historical necessity is presented as itself the outcome of historical process – but the structure of dialectic is reversed. The antithesis of Hegelian idealism and Marxian materialism is transcended in a new form whereby the contingent becomes the foundation of universal necessity. Yeats was explicit on this in his 'Genealogical

---

[56] Yeats, 'If I were Four and Twenty', p. 278.
[57] *Ibid.*, pp. 277–8.

Tree of Revolution'.[58] In the opening song of *Calvary*, the musicians sing of a flute carved from the bone of a heron that frightens the mockers of Christ. The white heron symbolises the loneliness of subjective man in Michael Robartes's writings. The symbol is enacted performatively in the delivery of the song of the white heron. The same pattern is evident in the throwing of dice – accident and determinism concentrated in a single emblem. Yeats places the dice-throwing moment within the dance, concluded by the three Roman soldiers forming a whirling circle about the cross. This reinforces the symbolic meaning of Judas's kiss that, like the suspended kiss of Dermot and Dervorgilla or the later kiss of Queen and Swineherd, is a transgressive moment of pure contingency from which a destiny emerges.

Considering *The Dreaming of the Bones* in relation to *Calvary*, then, it is evident that Yeats engaged the absurdist mode characteristic of Pirandello as the means most appropriate to represent the historical meaning of the 1916 Rising. This does not imply that Yeats regarded the Rising as a joke, though it is significant that farce becomes so pronounced in his later plays. *Calvary* reveals that the historical meaning of *The Dreaming of the Bones* lay in deciding who Christ and Judas allude to. The answer is clear – the Young Man is the figure of Christ the Redeemer, the Pearsean martyr, while Dermot and Dervorgilla are traitors. As the Christ-figure, the Young Man embodies materialism and, if not logic, then certainly rhetoric. However, Yeats was hinting at something more than the figure of the political criminal here. Questions of loyalty and treachery were deep-rooted in responses to the Rising and Yeats was no different in expressing his reaction in these terms:

> The Dublin tragedy has been a great sorrow and anxiety. Cosgrave, who I saw a few months ago in connection with the Municipal Gallery project and found our best supporter, has got many years imprisonment and to-day I see that an old friend Henry Dixon – unless there are two of the name – who began with me the whole work of the literary movement has been shot in a barrack yard without trial of any kind. I have little doubt there have been many miscarriages of justice … At this moment I feel that all the work of years has been over-turned, all the bringing together of classes, all the freeing of Irish literature & criticism from politics.[59]

The sense of betrayal here is deep – the decades-long effort at generating a progressive artistic culture capable of shaking Ireland out of a staid

---

[58] Norman Jeffares ed. 'Genealogical Tree of Revolution', *W. B. Yeats: Man and Poet*, 2nd edn, (London: Routledge & Kegan Paul, 1962), pp. 351–2.
[59] Yeats to Gregory, 11 May 1916. Wade, *The Letters*, pp. 612–13.

provincialism had been scuppered by an inept British military leadership that, as the letter intimates elsewhere, was making a mess of the war in France. Tom Paulin claims that Yeats was under government suspicion of pro-German sympathies in the summer of 1916 but we should also remember that *At the Hawk's Well* was performed that summer in the drawing rooms of Ladies Cunard and Islington to raise money for the war effort.[60]

Most importantly, the sympathies in both *Calvary* and *The Dreaming of the Bones* lay with the traitors. Yeats's circumstances in the period during and following the Rising play an important part here. No doubt subject to occasional comments on Irish treachery in London drawing-room circles in 1916, Yeats experienced sharp pangs of guilt at how his increased absorption in London life had detached him from circumstances in Ireland. Soon after the letter to Gregory, he wrote to John Quinn of the tragedy of events, how Ireland had lost 'the ablest and most fine-natured of our young men', whether there might have been something he could have done to turn them in 'some other direction' and how he intended to return to live in Dublin and 'begin building again'.[61] Part of what undoubtedly disturbed and fascinated Yeats about the Rising was that few anywhere saw it coming, its leaders divided over whether or not to go ahead with it, Eoghan MacNeill having issued a famous countermand. Its circumstances suggest how it was freely chosen rather than historically determined, comprehensible only in terms of its situationally specific nature. When Yeats writes of the struggle to free Irish literature and criticism from politics, what he meant by politics was the aspect intellectual life took following subjection to the mantras of political rhetoric, whether Unionist, Nationalist, Socialist or, later, Fascist. The age in which Yeats lived had become political in this sense and appeared to be degenerating into fanaticism, corrupt leadership and political murder. His anxieties over the Rising, his refusal to engage with the First World War on terms other than his own and his deep concern at the prospect of scientific socialism spreading across the world measured the degree to which he judged these events and movements bound up with rhetoric as the congealment of intellect.

The two last dance plays evinced a belief that the 1916 Rising could no more escape what Yeats saw as the degeneracy of political culture to which the First World War attested than the betrayal of Christ could

---

[60] Paulin, 'Yeats's Hunger-Strike Poem', p. 139.
[61] Yeats to Quinn, 23 May 1916. Wade, *The Letters*, p. 614.

have been forestalled. But the crucial question posed by *Calvary* and *The Dreaming of the Bones* was whether the Rising flowed with or against the current. Were 'Pearse and Connolly' benign traitors in the manner of Judas, revolting against the pressures of historical necessity through a radical act of self-begetting, carving a destiny from contingent, situationally specific circumstances? Or were they subjects to a fanaticism generated from vacuous political rhetoric, sacrificing themselves to the totemic allure of 'the cause', marching to certain death like the automatons of the trenches? Yeats could never resolve this question satisfactorily in his later dramas because they structured its historical frame, within which the determining power of history was manifested through the accidental and situational. What is certain is that within the esotericism of symbols in the dance plays, a powerful sense of the historical forces shaping events in Ireland and Europe reside. The following chapter addresses the political nature of Yeats's later vision of history in a number of his most esoteric plays from the later drama. The argument for the radical nature of their political meaning is made on the basis of their relation to German Expressionism and the representation of the equalisation of value they shared with Pirandello.

CHAPTER 7

'O self-born mockers': The Player Queen, The Words upon the Window-pane, The Herne's Egg

In *The Dreaming of the Bones* and *Calvary*, Yeats represented the force of history as situational rather than pre-determining, offering this as a frame through which the 1916 Rising might be understood. In so doing, he made will and passivity central to his later drama as it sought symbolic expression of the monumental changes visited upon European society after the First World War. This was consistent with his earlier work, particularly his attempt to combine the revolutionary individualism he observed in Ibsen with the Symbolist theatre of Maeterlinck. The recurrent theme of will in Yeats's later work pointed not simply to his consciousness of legacy as he became a father and moved into his sixties, but also marked the impact of profound changes in Irish and European political landscapes following the Rising and the end of the First World War. Within the obscure symbolism of the later plays lies a disturbing meditation on human agency during an era of spreading totalitarianism. The register of historical forces within this symbolism is most strongly felt in the aspect of farce through which Yeats articulates it in performance, particularly when the plays engage themes of will and passivity. Several aspects of the later drama orbit around the subject, including the nature of mask, the influence of marionette theatre, and the use of certain symbols, particularly that of the unicorn. Ideas of will and passivity were central to German Expressionist theatre as it expanded its influence in the years after the war. The consonance with Expressionism is most audible in *The Player Queen* and *The Herne's Egg*, plays that probe the nature of will and passivity through esoteric symbolism. The nature of Yeats's treatment of the subject in *The Words upon the Window-pane* owes its influence more directly to Pirandello's *Six Characters*, but all three plays are examined here as theatrical experiments daring and original in the perspectives on contemporary history they present.

The Player Queen is probably the most indecipherable Yeats play. First published alongside Eliot's 'The Waste Land' in *The Dial* in November

1922 and first performed in 1919 by the London Stage Society, its form was more radically experimental than anything he had yet written for the stage. Originally conceived in the year of the *Playboy* riots, Yeats abandoned redrafting it between 1910 and 1915 because he could not convert its esoteric subject convincingly into tragedy. This failure, followed by the speed with which he was able to make the play into a farce in 1915, points to the changes his theatre work was undergoing in the 1910s. His later drama is characterised by a growth in tension between the hieratic and the anarchic, the tragic and the farcical. Treating its unicorn theme in a farcical manner, the play bears strong affinity with Surrealist pieces such as Cocteau's *Orpheus* or Dali's painting *The Happy Unicorn*, recollecting late nineteenth-century works such as Gustav Moreau's *The Unicorn* of 1885.[1]

Despite rejecting O'Casey's *The Silver Tassie* in part for its use of certain Expressionist techniques, Expressionist influences were evident in the staging of *The Player Queen*. It was the first Yeats play located outside Ireland without any basis in Irish mythology and the only one set in a public space, the meeting place of three streets. The use of chiarosuro in the setting lent it an Expressionist mood, the play opening with the silhouettes of two old men against a bare wall at the end of one of the streets, leaning from upper windows and wearing 'grotesque masks' (*VPl*, 715). Introducing the play, Yeats revealed that he did not set it in Ireland because he wanted to realise the effectiveness of Craig's screens: 'My *dramatis personae* have no nationality because Mr. Craig's screens, where every line must suggest some mathematical proportion, where all is phantastic, incredible, and luminous, have no nationality' (*VPl*, 761). In Craig's 1913 work, *Towards a New Theatre*, some of the stage settings were decidedly Expressionist, in particular those for *The Masque of London* (see Figure 3). Craig lamented the parochialism of the English stage here, insisting that the English had to engage continental European drama and, beyond that, the drama of the East, Africa and America. However much Yeats claimed to dislike 'an international art', his drama mirrored everywhere the most technically innovative plays of Scandinavia, France, Germany and Italy; *The Player Queen* was but the most explicit instance.

The Expressionist aspect of *The Player Queen* is most striking in the manner in which it anticipated the work of Ernst Toller, the leading Expressionist playwright of the 1920s. The Dublin Drama League

---

[1] For consideration of the occult background to the unicorn symbol in *The Player Queen*, see Wilson, *W. B. Yeats and Tradition*, p.182, and Vendler, *Yeats's Vision*, p. 136.

Figure 3 Edward Gordon Craig, 'The Masque of London', *Towards a New Theatre: Forty Designs for Stage Scenes with Critical Notes* (London: J. M. Dent & Sons, 1913). Publication is with the consent of the Edward Gordon Craig Estate.

performed a number of Toller's plays during the 1920s but Yeats became more familiar with his work in 1935 following the publication of translations of seven of Toller's plays in a single volume.[2] Toller's direct influence was discernible in the play that bears closest resemblance to *The Player Queen* in Yeats's repertoire, *The Herne's Egg*. In November 1935 Yeats wrote to Dorothy Wellesley that he had a three-act tragi-comedy in mind that would be wilder than *The Player Queen* while carrying greater philosophical weight.[3] This was the play that would become *The Herne's Egg*. Earlier that same year, he expressed great enthusiasm for Toller's work

[2] Ernst Toller, *Seven Plays* (London: John Lane the Bodley Head, 1935).
[3] Yeats to Wellesley, Riversdale, 28 November 1935. Wellesley, *Letters on Poetry*, p. 43.

in a letter to Ethel Mannin, in particular *Hoppla, We're Alive!* and *The Blind Goddess*. Here he claimed that, like Pirandello, Toller had taken up and transformed Ibsen's drama completely, turning towards the crowds as Pirandello turned towards the individual. He also felt Toller was a greater technical innovator than Pirandello, and hoped to get Toller's *Mrs Eddy* performed in Dublin soon after Easter, with the possibility of his more difficult works being performed later.[4] Significantly, Yeats was trying to get *The Player Queen* performed that summer in London at Ashley Dukes's Mercury Theatre, a close ally of Rupert Doone's avant-garde Group Theatre. On 14 June, he wrote to Wellesley from Rathfarnham that he might not be in England for some time as Dukes had put the play off until September and two days later he wrote to Olivia Shakespear that Dukes had said he would do *The Player Queen* but Yeats did not believe him.[5] It was eventually produced later that year at the Little Theatre under the direction of Nancy Price, member of the People's National Theatre Company, along with *The Pot of Broth* and *The Hour-Glass*.[6]

That Yeats had in mind a performance of *The Player Queen* under the direction of Dukes so soon after his enthusiastic response to Toller was not coincidental. Dukes was one of the most knowledgeable figures on Scandinavian and German Expressionist theatre within London circles. In 1910, he contributed an important series of essays to *The New Age* on modern theatre in Germany, Austria and Scandinavia, including the work of Bjornson, Strindberg, Schnitzler and Wedekind.[7] Yeats was certainly aware of these essays, having contributed himself to the debate on the reform of the theatre in *The New Age* earlier that year and having his own drama reviewed by Darrell Figgis in an August issue of the paper in 1910.[8] Dukes's *The Scene is Changed*, published by Macmillan in 1942, was also one of the earliest English-language critical studies of European avant-garde theatre giving extensive consideration to the Expressionists, and his translation of Toller's *The Machine Wreckers* was published in 1923.[9] Yeats would have recognised Dukes as someone capable of lending *The Player*

---

[4] Yeats to Mannin, Savile Club, 2 April 1935. Wade, *The Letters*, pp. 833–4.
[5] Yeats to Wellesley, Rathfarnham, 14 June 1935. Wellesley, *Letters on Poetry*, p. 4. Yeats to Mannin, Riversdale, 16 June 1935. Wade, *The Letters*, p. 835.
[6] Dorn, *Players*, p. 93.
[7] Ashley Dukes, 'Modern Dramatists 1 – Bjornson', *The New Age*, 7:21 (1910); 'Modern Dramatists 2 – Strindberg', *The New Age*, 7:22 (1910); 'Modern Dramatists 5 – Arthur Schnitzler', *The New Age*, 7:26 (1910).
[8] Darrell Figgis, 'Some Living Poets 1 – Mr. W. B. Yeats', *The New Age*, 7:14 (1910), 327–8.
[9] For discussion of Dukes and the Mercury Theatre in relation to Yeats's later plays, see Dorn, *Players*, pp. 91–3.

Queen the kind of Expressionist power he admired so much in Toller. His desire to revive *The Player Queen* to this end in 1935 suggests that Yeats recognised similarities in form and intention between his 1919 play and the work of Toller, retrospectively acknowledging its Expressionist vision some years after rejecting O'Casey's *The Silver Tassie*. It was no surprise, therefore, that the Abbey revived O'Casey's play in the autumn of 1935, Yeats taking pride at having provoked clerical denunciation of the Abbey once more – 'priests, mainly country priests … calling on the government to withdraw our subsidy and institute a censorship of the stage'.[10] His letters to Mannin of March 1935 refer to friendly letters from O'Casey after years of hostile estrangement from the Abbey over Yeats's notorious rejection.[11]

W. J. McCormack's scepticism at this enthusiasm overlooks how Toller's plays articulated concerns central to Yeats's drama after the First World War, particularly the nature of agency in an era of mass politics. Believing Yeats to be solely concerned with pleasing Mannin, with whom he was romantically involved for a period in the 1930s, McCormack focuses on Yeats's refusal of Toller's request to sign a petition calling for the release of the dissident journalist Carl von Ossietzky, imprisoned for treason by the Nazis following Hitler's accession to power in January 1933. McCormack also points to the fact that, despite Yeats's statement of intent in his 1935 letter to Mannin, *Mrs Eddy* was never performed at the Abbey.[12] However misguided Yeats's reason for refusal seems in hindsight, it illustrated his deep unease at his literary reputation being shaped in his last years according to a specific political view.[13] Elizabeth Cullingford notes a degree of consistency in Yeats's decision and quotes from a letter

---

[10] Yeats to Wellesley, Riversdale, 28 November, 1935. Wellesley, *Letters on Poetry*, pp. 23–4. How far Yeats had revised his original judgement of O'Casey's play is open to question, a judgement Yeats was still defending somewhat churlishly in his diary notes of 1930, in which O'Casey is accused of catching 'the London contagion in *The Silver Tassie* and changed his mountain into a mouse'. *Pages from a Diary*, p. 50.

[11] Yeats to Ethel Mannin, 4 March, 1935, and [?] March, 1935. Wade, *The Letters*, pp. 831–3.

[12] McCormack, *Blood Kindred*, pp. 119–21. See also, Conor Cruise O'Brien, 'Passion and Cunning: An Essay on the Politics of W. B. Yeats', *Yeats's Political Identities*, ed. Jonathan Allison (Ann Arbor: University of Michigan Press, 1996), p. 41.

[13] McCormack contrasts this scathingly with the political commitment of O'Casey and considers the marked influence of Toller on O'Casey's work. See *Blood Kindred*, pp. 169–73. As Clair Wills shows, however, prior to the invasion of the Soviet Union in 1941 O'Casey held hopes that Hitler would 'go left'. *That Neutral Island: A Cultural History of Ireland During the Second World War* (London: Faber, 2007), p. 221. Furthermore, O'Casey's support for the Soviet suppression of the Hungarian uprising in October 1956 raises difficult questions that McCormack does not address. For discussion of O'Casey's response to the 1956 uprising, see Christopher Murray, *Seán O'Casey: Writer at Work, A Biography* (Dublin: Gill & Macmillan, 2004), pp. 375–8.

to Mannin justifying it on the basis that none of the dominant political forces – Communist, Fascist, nationalist, clerical or anti-clerical – stood innocent of atrocity, Yeats's 'horror at the cruelty of governments' growing greater as his 'sense of reality' deepened.[14]

Unlike Toller, Yeats never addresses this cruelty directly in his plays. However, in representing history as a force moving according to its own laws that became manifest through the submission or resistance of the will, *The Player Queen* and *The Herne's Egg* expressed in Symbolist fashion a vision of history close to that we encounter in Toller. Yeats's doctrine of mask arose essentially from a determination to submit the will to a single idea concentrated in a single image. Behind this lay his aspiration to capture afresh an elevated sense of will as destiny, leaving behind the pusillanimity of self-realisation. The vision of history in *The Player Queen*, however, lies in the mockery of this ideal as it is enacted. Yeats's opening comments in 'Per Amica Silentia Lunae' are telling in this regard:

> Some years ago I began to believe that our culture, with its doctrine of sincerity and self-realisation, made us gentle and passive, and that the Middle Ages and the Renaissance were right to find theirs upon the imitation of Christ or of some classic hero. St Francis and Caesar Borgia made themselves over-mastering, creative persons by turning from the mirror to meditation upon a mask. When I had this thought I could see nothing else in life. I could not write the play I had planned, for all became allegorical, and though I tore up hundreds of pages in my endeavour to escape from allegory, my imagination became sterile for nearly five years and I only escaped at last when I had mocked in a comedy my own thought.[15]

Yeats's 1902 essay on Edmund Spenser was a source for this struggle with allegory as literary form. Here he saw in allegory a symbolic language unique in expressing a soul's communion with God in a state of trance, an experience for which no other language was adequate. Sensing in Spenser the absence of deep religious conviction, he found the poet's use of allegory unconvincing, believing that allegorical descriptions of ordinary things had the effect of making them seem unreal.[16] Yeats was addressing will and passivity in the relation he presumed between mask and allegory at the outset of 'Per Amica Silentia Lunae'. Identifying with the mask as the form of a single idea, the individual will becomes overarching, the

---

[14] Wade, *The Letters*, p. 881. Elizabeth Butler Cullingford, *Yeats, Ireland and Fascism* (London: Macmillan Press, 1981), p. 222.
[15] Yeats, 'Per Amica Silentia Lunae', p. 10.
[16] W. B. Yeats, 'Edmund Spenser', *Essays and Introductions* (London: Macmillan Press, 1961), pp. 368–70.

embodiment of a single purpose. This could only be achieved, however, in the passivity of trance. Taking this a step further in subjecting it to the mockery of farce in *The Player Queen*, Yeats was shaping allegory to represent the force of historical process embodied in the struggle of individuals against collective power in an age of mass politics.

The allegorical mode featured heavily in the plays Toller composed at the end of the First World War, most notably *Transfiguration* and *Masses and Man*. The first, completed in March 1918, presents a montage of scenes from the war years through the Everyman figure of Friedrich, who is variously soldier, student, priest, lodger, prisoner, wanderer and rock climber. Composed in 1919 and performed at the Abbey by the Dublin Drama League in January 1925, *Masses and Man* is even more directly allegorical, all characters being representative types, without personal names. Yeats's revised version of *The Player Queen*, performed in London in 1919 by the Stage Society, likewise inclined in the direction of type. The leading figures in the play – Septimus, the Queen who prays to St Octema, Nona and Decima – are simply the Roman numbers seven, eight, nine and ten. In *Masses and Man*, the subjection of individual identity to the force of the mass movement is embodied in the Nameless One, concentrated expression of historical destiny:

> I am the Masses!
> Masses are fate.[17]

In *The Player Queen*, the turbulence of the crowd, a folkloric representation of the masses, relates directly to the appearance of the unicorn, symbolising a moment of revolutionary change in human civilisation. Rumours of the Queen copulating with the unicorn disturb the citizenry into marching on the palace (*VPl*, 723–9). Likewise, the penetration of Attracta by the Great Herne announces the birth of a new epoch in *The Herne's Egg*. The braying of a donkey in both plays signifies the transformation taking place. The beggar man tells Decima in *The Player Queen* that the mob will end the reign of the Queen when he brays like a donkey. For attempting to subdue the Herne, Congal is condemned to reincarnation as a donkey at the end of *The Herne's Egg* (*VPl*, 1040).

The bestial symbolism in both plays derives from the religious asceticism of both women in sacrificing themselves to ideals embodied in the figures of the unicorn and the Great Herne: the Queen is celibate and dresses as a nun beneath her royal attire in *The Player Queen* and Attracta

---

[17] Toller, *Masses and Man, Seven Plays*, p. 131.

is a virgin in *The Herne's Egg*. Unicorn and Herne are esoteric images of a collective libidinal energy in mass civilisation to which these women are drawn through the medium of religious sanctity. This theme of sacrifice to higher ideals pervades Toller's work. By the end of *Masses and Man* the Woman, won over to the cause of the masses, is nonetheless executed at the behest of the Nameless One, personification of its power. The play bears witness to the hypnotic allure of the mass movement and its capacity to generate a cold, inhuman, impersonal power even as it reached towards a vision of utopian freedom. Yeats intuited such cold passion as the enduring sign of the age. In 1935, he wrote to Wellesley that 'Auden, Spender, all that seem the new movement *look* for strength in Marxian socialism, or in Major Douglas; they want marching feet. The last expression of our time is not this obvious choice but in a sense of something steel-like and cold within the will, something passionate and cold.'[18] The influence of Nietzsche is evident here and, perhaps even more so, of Lawrence, but Yeats was also touching upon the blind impersonal force of Toller's play that leads the Woman to sacrificing herself to 'mankind' only to be executed as a class traitor, the idea of which is indebted most deeply to Arthur Schopenhauer's philosophy of will. The Nameless One was not simply an allegory for the Communist Party in *Masses and Man*, but expressed a blind universal will mesmerising individual agents. Schopenhauer contended that all willing sprang from suffering and the greatness of artistic masterpieces lay in the intuition of universal will beyond all individual phenomena. In the figure of the Nameless One, Toller's play carried the influence of Schopenhauer's theory, the all-encompassing will revealing itself in drama of the highest artistic intensity portraying the power of universal will.[19]

In his diary notes from 1930, Yeats praised the third book of Schopenhauer's *The World as Will and Representation* as one of those works that brought him back 'to concrete reality'.[20] Less than three years earlier he had written to Thomas Sturge Moore that Schopenhauer could 'do no wrong'.[21] Ruth Nevo has drawn attention to the intimacy between the themes of Schopenhauer's philosophy and Yeats's poetry, noting that both Yeats and Schopenhauer articulated fundamental antinomies of 'being

---

[18] Yeats to Wellesley, Riversdale, 6 July 1935. Wellesley, ed., *Letters on Poetry*, p. 8.
[19] Arthur Schopenhauer, *The World as Will and Representation*, trans. E. F. J. Payne, 2nd edn, vol. 1 (New York: Dover Publications, 1969), pp. 153–5, 195–200.
[20] Yeats, *Pages from a Diary*, p. 17.
[21] Yeats to T. Sturge Moore [after 23rd December, 1927]. Ursula Bridges, ed., *W. B. Yeats and T. Sturge Moore: Their Correspondence, 1901–1937* (London: Routledge and Kegan Paul, 1953), p. 117.

and knowing, Will and Idea, consciousness and experience', both were fascinated with the Upanishads and both saw in existence 'an unappeasable warfare of contraries'.[22] A shared interest in the Upanishads is borne out in Yeats's preface to Purohit Swami's translation, *The Ten Principal Upanishads*, in 1938. Here, Yeats claimed a turn from social criticism to myth took place in English literature between 1922 and 1925, citing the poetry of Eliot and Huxley's 'Those Barren Leaves', where there was 'a Buddhistic hatred of life, or a hatred Schopenhauer did not so much find in as deduce from a Latin translation of a Persian translation of the Upanishads'.[23]

Most revealing, however, is Nevo's skilful configuration of the influence of Schopenhauer's philosophy of will on Yeats's idea of theatre. Of immediate relevance to the *The Player Queen* as Expressionist drama is her discussion of 'The Double Vision of Michael Robartes', the last poem in the 1919 collection *The Wild Swans at Coole*. She looks to the figure of the marionette Yeats employs as an image of the power of an impersonal will overtaking his own:

> Constrained, arraigned, baffled, bent and unbent
> By these wire-jointed jaws and limbs of wood,
> Themselves obedient,
> Knowing not evil and good;
> Obedient to some hidden magical breath.
> They do not even feel, so abstract are they,
> So dead beyond our death,
> Triumph that we obey. (*VP*, 382)

Nevo observes the influence of Schopenhauer in the sense of awe expressed here before a relentless omniscient power. She draws attention to Thomas Mann's essay *Freud and the Future*, also published in 1919, where Mann employs the same theatre metaphor to identify the replication of Schopenhauer's description of Will and Idea in Freud's account of id and ego, quoting Schopenhauer's essay *Transcendent Speculations on Apparent Design in the Fate of the Individual*:

That precisely as in a dream it is our own will that unconsciously appears an inexorable objective destiny, everything in it proceeding out of ourselves and each of us being the secret theatre manager of our own dreams, so also in reality the great dream that a single essence, the will itself, dreams with us all, our

---

[22] Ruth Nevo, 'Yeats and Schopenhauer', *Yeats Annual*, vol. III, ed. Warwick Gould (London: Macmillan Press, 1985), p. 19.
[23] Shree Purohit Swami and W. B. Yeats, *The Ten Principal Upanishads* (London: Faber & Faber, 1938), p. 9.

fate, may be the product of our inmost selves, of our wills, and we are actually ourselves bringing about what seems to be happening to us.[24]

This describes the anxiety haunting a range of Yeats's later poems and plays; passive submission to an inexorable force as the delusion of an all-encompassing will acting in solitude. It also identifies the preoccupation with will central to Toller's drama and suggests why he takes recourse to dream pictures in several of his plays. The struggle of will and passivity is particularly concentrated in *The Player Queen*, not only reflecting Toller's Expressionism but also the Absurdism of Pirandello. The figure of the Stage Manager from *Commedia dell'arte* is explicit in both *The Player Queen* and *Six Characters*, first performed in 1921. So also are the actors who, within the plays, perform the roles of actors preparing to act the play within the play–Septimus, Nona, Decima and the Queen are allotted the same roles as Pirandello's six characters. This proximity of *The Player Queen* to Pirandello's *Six Characters* raises the spectre of a mechanistic determinism in which human agents are mere pawns, their identities purely performative.

Like *Six Characters*, the acting in *The Player Queen* is intentionally farcical. Septimus is a parody of a poet, the Queen looks ridiculous in the nun's habit she wears beneath her royal attire, the players seem equally absurd in their squabbling, and Decima is a 'ditch-delivered drab' who ends up as Queen.[25] Yeats's sense of farce grew noticeably from *Four Plays for Dancers* and was particularly striking in a later play that replicates the structure of the play within the play, *The Words upon the Window-pane* of 1930. The parallels with Pirandello's *Six Characters* were once again striking. The play is set in a séance room within an old Georgian Dublin mansion turned lodging-house, the seedy quality of which carries an echo of O'Casey, as Worth has noted.[26] Barton Friedman observes that within this setting, the séance functions as a play within a play.[27] Mrs Mallet reveals as much when she replies to Dr Trench that the spirits manifested in two previous séances said the same thing and went through the same drama, 'as if they were characters in some kind of horrible play'

---

[24] Thomas Mann, 'Freud and the Future', *Essays of Three Decades*, trans. H.T. Lowe-Porter (London: Secker & Warburg, 1947), p. 418. Nevo, 'Yeats and Schopenhauer', pp. 21–2.
[25] Phillip Marcus sees Septimus as a parody of Seanchan from *The King's Threshold* while Peter Ure argues that in refusing to perform the farcical role of Noah's wife, Decima embodies a struggle between dignity and ignobility in the play. Marcus, *Yeats and Artistic Power*, p. 110. Ure, *Yeats the Playwright*, p. 139.
[26] Worth, '*The Words upon the Window-pane*', p. 136.
[27] Barton Friedman, 'Yeatsian (Meta)physics: *The Resurrection* and the Irrational', *Yeats: An Annual of Critical and Textual Studies*, vol. 8 (1990), p. 151.

(*VPl*, 943). An echo of the 'horrible play' that Pirandello's six characters are condemned to repeat is audible here, in which the stepdaughter is abused and her young sister drowns. Mrs Mallet's words recall those the stepdaughter delivers to her sister in *Six Characters*: 'what a horrible play it is going to be for you'.[28] The characters of the inner play, Swift, Vanessa and the child Lulu, manifest themselves through the mediumship of Mrs Henderson and, as Worth and Ure observe, the medium comes very close to the professional actor.[29] As with *The Player Queen* and *The Only Jealousy of Emer*, a love triangle shapes the inner play of *The Words upon the Window-pane*. The sceptical scholar John Corbet observes that Swift had met Vanessa at the height of his fame in London but that Stella had loved him all her life (*VPl*, 941). The Cuchulain–Eithne–Emer triangle of *The Only Jealousy of Emer* or the Septimus–Nona–Decima triangle of *The Player Queen* is employed again. The play's form raises two questions about the séance: is the vision of human existence generated by the presence of the spirits tragic or farcical, and is the séance itself charlatansim?

John Corbet attends the séance as a young Cambridge don who has researched the life of Swift. His presence is that of a sceptical observer and there is enough in the play to suggest that Mrs Henderson is made insecure by it. During the course of the séance, she greets him in the voice of the child Lulu, warning that he must not laugh at the way she speaks, adding that 'Lulu does her best but can't say big long words' (*VPl*, 947). Though impressed by the accuracy of information that comes through in the sitting, Corbet is not persuaded that it is indeed supernatural in origin. Instead, he believes that Henderson has fabricated everything, being 'an accomplished actress and scholar' (*VPl*, 955). Whether or not the audience empathises with Corbet, his presence as observer characterises the entire gathering around Henderson as that of an audience attending a performance. Their passive involvement in the séance mirrors that of the audience in the auditorium, much like the actors in *Six Characters* observing the play within the play being acted out before them. Though less obviously so, the absurd nature of characters in *The Player Queen* is disernible in the gathering for the séance in *The Words upon the Window-pane*.[30]

The voices of the spirits that come through in the séance paint a terrifying picture of human relations condemned to eternal frustration. In

---

[28] Pirandello, *Six Characters, Collected Plays*, p. 63.
[29] Katharine Worth, '*The Words upon the Window-pane*', p. 141. Ure, *Yeats the Playwright*, p. 101.
[30] Derek Hand notes the comic aspect of the group. 'Breaking Boundaries, Creating Spaces: W. B. Yeats's *The Words upon the Window-pane* as a Postcolonial Text', *W. B. Yeats and Postcolonialism*, ed. Deborah Fleming (West Cornwall, CT: Locust Hill Press, 2001), p. 195.

an exchange that recalls the lovers' kiss perpetually suspended in *The Dreaming of the Bones*, Vanessa fails to consummate her love for Swift, though he touches her momentarily. Swift's reticence is expressed not just as intellectual arrogance, but also fear that his madness might pass on to a later generation. In this we are reminded of Cuchulain's madness that follows him killing his only son from *On Baile's Strand* and 'the falling sickness' that plagues Martin Hearne in *The Unicorn from the Stars*. The Old Man from *Purgatory* is also anticipated, killing his own son so as not to 'pass pollution on'. The voices of the spirits also recall Strindberg's *The Ghost Sonata*, performed by the Dublin Drama League in April 1925. Mrs Henderson speaking in the voice of the child Lulu brings to mind the colonel's wife speaking like a baby in Strindberg's play. The same horror Swift's spirit voices at being locked in with his enemy is present in the Old Man cringing in terror before the presence of the milkmaid towards the end of *The Ghost Sonata*.[31] Critics have remarked upon the uncanny atmosphere of Yeats's play, Foster regarding it as his most impressive achievement in the theatre.[32] Worth observes how the figure of the child Lulu denotes a 'sinister, surreal significance'.[33] There is the faintest echo here of the Fairy Child whose visitation brings death in *The Land of Heart's Desire* but the most abiding impression the voice of Lulu generates is that of a talking doll. Particularly when speaking in the voice of Lulu, Mrs Henderson appears to become a kind of automaton, a being whose entire body convulses under the influence of a hidden agency.[34]

Henderson's puppet-like performance throws light on the nature of that vision she mediates. It is most disturbing in the loss of agency it represents. The attacks of dizziness through which Swift's madness became manifest appear enacted in the hysterical condition of Henderson as she beats upon the door before falling to the ground exhausted. For all the intellectual arrogance that comes through in the words Swift directs at Vanessa, his voice is disturbed by the sense of a complete loss of power. This heightens the intense claustrophobia of the play that reaches a

---

[31] Strindberg, *The Ghost Sonata*, *Strindberg: Plays One*, pp. 172, 181.
[32] Foster, *W. B. Yeats*, vol. II, pp. 410–11; Worth, '*The Words upon the Window-pane*', pp. 138–9; Taylor, *The Drama of W. B. Yeats*, p. 172; Bradley, *William Butler Yeats*, p. 230.
[33] Worth, '*The Words upon the Window-pane*', p. 149.
[34] In 1921, the English translation of a book by the French artist Pierre Cornillier was published and reviewed in *The New Age*, in which he gives accounts of séances conducted with a young girl sent to him as a model in 1912. During the course of one such séance, this young girl was reported to have spoken in the voice of a man 'hoarsely, and with an automatic articulation'. *The Survival of the Soul*, p. 7. The automaton state of Mrs Henderson speaking in different voices finds a precedent here of which Yeats would have been aware.

critical moment when he suddenly feels himself imprisoned with a hostile presence:

My God, I am left alone with my enemy. Who locked the door, who locked me in with my enemy? (*VPl*, 951)?

The passive immobility to which Henderson is subject as she becomes entirely an instrument for the transference of voices not her own overtakes the vision she facilitates, the image of Swift himself. The suspension of his will under a frightening power acts as an inverse image of the subjection of her own will as she mediates his presence. Swift's enemy is certainly the child Lulu, the speaking doll who threatens the petrifaction of the totem, an image of the human subject devoid of all agency.

The play ends with a tortured cry in the voice of Swift repeating Christ's judgement of Judas in the Gospel of Matthew, quoting Job 3:3:

Perish the day on which I was born! (*VPl*, 956)

The figure of Judas from *Calvary* is recalled here, not only calling to mind Swift the rebel banished to Ireland for treachery, but also someone condemned to a fixed course of action from the outset. Discussing the later *Purgatory*, Francis Oppel notes the relevance of Nietzsche's judgement that 'the unhealthy' experienced 'eternal recurrence' as a curse.[35] This rings true for the ghost of Swift as much as the Old Man of *Purgatory* and would appear to lend credence to degeneration readings of *The Words upon the Window-pane* offered by A. S. Knowland and Richard Taylor, in which the nobility of Swift and the age of Grattan's parliament are contrasted with the decrepitude of the contemporary Dublin setting in which his spirit is manifested.[36] For all the contrast intimated between what Yeats identifies in his introduction to the play as the Roman ideal of Swift's generation and the decay of the lodging-house setting, however, it is Swift who is the 'unhealthy' one, living out the collapse of his mind as a perpetual curse.[37] He bears the mark of degeneration as assuredly as those judged his inferiors; for all the Cuchulain-like elevation of his pride, the condition of his spirit is marked by the perpetual stagnation of the Old

---

[35] Frances Oppel, 'Yeats's *Purgatory* and Nietzsche's Eternal Return', *Journal of Australian Language and Literature Association*, 82 (1994), p. 3.

[36] Knowland, *W. B. Yeats*, p. 180. Richard Taylor, *A Reader's Guide to the Plays of W. B. Yeats* (London: Macmillan Press, 1984), pp. 132–9.

[37] Yeats saw that the Protestant aristocracy established in Ireland from the battle of the Boyne brought with it 'the modern world, and something that appeared and perished in its dawn, an instinct for Roman rhetoric, Roman elegance' (*VPl*, 959).

Man trapped by the dried-up well of *At the Hawk's Well*. Yeats ultimately represents the narrative of Swift's private life as a farce.

Swift's inhibition and the somnambulist condition Mrs Henderson assumes in making his spirit present point to the crisis of will at the centre of this play. The 'savage indignation' of the Drapier letters that Yeats admired as the stamp of an independent mind is parodied in its articulation through Henderson, who watches the participants leave their coins with suppressed glee and makes herself a cup of tea when the séance is over. She recalls the figure of Decima from *The Player Queen*, the 'ditch-delivered drab' who, adorning herself with the attire of the Queen, convinces a hostile crowd that she is indeed their leader. Beyond the intellectual power of Swift's will that emerges through the voice of his spirit, beyond the skill of Henderson in assuming his mask and those of his lovers, lies a mechanistic force by which they become as passive instruments, the voice of Lulu its starkest manifestation. The mechanistic determinism that appears to overtake Mrs Henderson in her condition as medium, and Swift's failure of will in the moment with Vanessa, manifest a primitive power subsuming individual agency, the recurrent theme of Toller's Expressionist drama.

Considering the play as the interaction of two dramas, the crisis moment of Swift's life and the performance of the séance itself, it becomes apparent that the primitivist form of this determinism was the representation of a historical process of fetishisation within which human value became reducible to measurable exchange. Both internal and external plays present games within which individual identities become interchangeable, roles more important than the individuals performing them. Undoubtedly derived from Yeats's experience of séances, the members of the gathering appear as types admitted for the conjuring of the appropriate atmosphere: Corbet the youthful, arrogant sceptic; Trench the voice of intellectual defence; MacKenna the acolyte; Mallet the simple-minded enthusiast; Johnson the low-Church evangelical. If Henderson's gift as medium is a capacity to express several personalities not her own, its effect is to render them interchangeable. The voice of Swift, haunting as it is, becomes but one more aspect of the overall performance. Self-invention appears absolute not by virtue of his implacable will but from the possibility of assuming several masks in circumstances where all roles hold equal value within the determining framework of the game. Self-invention finds its expression not in Swift's powerful personality but in Henderson's polyvocalism, obliging her to turn into an automaton.

The Words upon the Window-pane was more than a lament for the civic culture of eighteenth-century Dublin. It addresses the deterministic force of historical process through the antithesis it generated in the form of pure self-invention. Like *The Player Queen*, the tension between will and passivity to which this gave rise carried specific political significance. The numerical names of the players in *The Player Queen* functioned as a reflex of mass culture presented in the image of the crowd, within which individual voices became indistinguishable. The figure of Mrs Henderson was anticipated in Decima's capacity to assume the role of Queen successfully. The medium also finds a precursor in the Prime Minister of *The Player Queen* who mediates between the citizens and the court. He is the modern-day spin-doctor, orchestrating a performance of Noah's ark to placate a public made restless by rumours of the Queen fornicating with a unicorn. The play's conclusion illustrates his awareness of the overarching power of the image. First shocked at the sight of Decima on the throne in the garb of the Queen, he immediately recognises that there is nothing he can do, the crowd being 'mad after her pretty face' (*VPl*, 758).

The crisis of agency in *The Player Queen* is concentrated in the figure of Decima who assumes the mask of the Queen in order that she may die in her place; finding herself adored, she becomes this mask. This subjection of her entire will to a single public image finds its ideological reflex in the crowd who submit to her at the end of the play, in which all is subsumed under a collective will. John Rees Moore notes that, in becoming Queen, Decima has merely exchanged one role for another, observing that it 'is possible to exchange one mask for another; it is not possible to go without one'.[38] The self-conscious theatricality of the play derives from the ease with which roles are exchanged, representing the function of exchange in tribal ritual as the rudimentary form of exchange-value in modern capitalism that Marx described. Yeats touched upon the connection between the freedom of arbitrary self-invention and the flattening of all human value through a universal system of exchange in a comment on the rise of English capitalism in his 1930 diary:

> The capture of a Spanish treasure ship in the time of Elizabeth made England a capitalist nation, a nation of country gentlemen, who were paid more in kind than in money and had traditional uses for their money, were to find themselves in control of free power over labour, a power that could be used anywhere for anything.[39]

By this account, the growth of the British Empire happened more by accident than design. That 'nation of country gentlemen' did not choose

---

[38] Moore, *Masks of Love and Death*, p. 177.
[39] Yeats, *Pages for a Diary*, p. 51.

the absolute power that came their way. As something 'that could be used anywhere for anything', this power would accelerate the equalisation of value by which anything could be exchanged for anything else but nothing could lie outside the system of exchange itself. Whether or not Yeats's statement stood up to historical scrutiny, it was certainly consistent with the historical perspective informing *The Player Queen*.

Rumour of the Queen's copulation with the unicorn that incites the crowd to revolt represents an event outside the system of exchange the play intimates through the interchangeability of roles. In 'Per Amica Silentia Lunae', Yeats remembered someone in Goethe's *Wilhelm Meister* saying that accident was destiny; the old beggar braying like a donkey to signal the bestial act gives expression to the unfolding of events in *The Player Queen* in accordance with this sentiment.[40] Existing outside the structure of exchange in the play, this occult correspondence has no discernible value. It nonetheless encapsulates the historical moment in which all identities become masks, image taking precedence over substance. As if to emphasise the fictionality of the unicorn, the reputed copulation is reported at two removes – the Tapster tells the citizens and countrymen that 'Strolling Michael' told him he had seen it. The occurrence of the event is as hypothetical as the figure of the unicorn itself, yet it provokes the revolutionary stirrings in the play.

The transgressive power of the bestial image in *The Player Queen* lies in its mystical aspect. The Queen is certainly an ascetic, prefiguring Attracta in *The Herne's Egg*, a woman who commits herself to virginity in preparation for mystical sexual union with the Great Herne. Septimus defends the chastity of the unicorn to whom the Queen is devoted, describing it as a beast of utmost purity. However, he is drunk as he speaks, citing from 'The Great Beastery of Paris' in defence of the unicorn's chastity. Yeats clearly had the Paris of the 1890s in mind, of Arthur Symons, MacGregor Mathers, Villiers de l'Isle Adam and Maurice Maeterlinck. Alison Armstrong states that the idea of Attracta's 'dual sexual allegiance' in *The Herne's Egg* was developed from the figures of Decima and the Queen in *The Player Queen*, identifying in Attracta an image of the Virgin Mary, 'nominal wife of Joseph and the actual bride of God – at once married and virginal, impregnated not by man but by the Holy Ghost'.[41] Thus the bestial act seems purely symbolic. However, the observation also calls to mind the 'Proteus' episode of Joyce's *Ulysses*, first published

---

[40] Yeats, 'Per Amica Silentia Lunae', p. 11.
[41] W. B. Yeats, *The Herne's Egg: Manuscript Materials*, ed. Alison Armstrong (Ithaca: Cornell University Press, 1993), p. xviii.

(like *The Player Queen*) in 1922, wherein Stephen Dedalus quotes from Gabriel Jogand-Pages's 1884 *La vie de Jésus* in musing on the possibility that the Virgin's impregnation was as much bestial as sacred.[42] The ambivalence that Joyce satirically introduces here is likewise present in the anxiety evoked by news of the Queen's copulation in *The Player Queen*, news that provokes a farcical response from one of the countrymen: 'I will not have the son of the unicorn to reign over us, although you will tell me he would be no more than half a unicorn' (*VPl*, 724). It is unclear whether the townspeople fear more a leader who is part human, part supernatural, or someone who is part human, part beast. Yeats's sense of a regression to primitive totem worship in modern civilisation was a strong influence here, given the role of fetishes in identifying the human soul with particular animals as described by Frazer in *The Golden Bough*.

A number of the later plays address mystical experience in animal terms. Recalling the Queen of *The Player Queen* and anticipating Attracta in *The Herne's Egg*, the Queen of *A Full Moon in March* is 'cruel as the winter of virginity'. The Swineherd appears of animal–human descent, his own image making him think his origin 'more foul than rag or flesh'. He has 'rolled among the dung of swine and laughed' and he tells of a woman impregnated by the blood in which she bathed, flowing from a severed head she held. The Queen dances in adoration of the swineherd's severed head while the attendants speak of 'desecration and the lover's night' (*VPl*, 981–9). In *The Resurrection*, the Greek's response to the Hebrew's assertion that the Messiah would be born of a woman reverses the basis on which Dedalus's speculation on the Virgin birth in *Ulysses* is judged blasphemous:

To say that a god can be born of a woman, carried in her womb, fed upon her breast, washed as children are washed, is the most terrible blasphemy. (*VPl*, 911)

The Greek's revulsion here is akin to that aroused by rumour of the Queen's copulation with the unicorn in *The Player Queen*: God becomes human as human becomes beast. Thinking of the death of the sage in contemporary European culture, Yeats was reminded of a quotation from Bacon that Wordsworth used for *The White Doe of Rylstone*: 'God puts divinity into a man as a man puts humanity into his dog.'[43] In *The Herne's Egg*, the brutal rape of Attracta by Congal and his henchmen happens at

---

[42] James Joyce, *Ulysses*, Bodley Heud edition (London: Penguin Press, 1992), p. 51. Dona Gifford and Robert J. Seidman, *Ulysses Annotated*, 2nd edn (Berkeley, CA: University of California Press, 1988), pp. 52–3.
[43] Yeats, *Pages from a Diary*, pp. 8–9.

the same moment she experiences mystical union with the Great Herne. And for daring to challenge the power of the Great Herne, Congal is reincarnated as a donkey.

F. A. C. Wilson has traced the mysticism of *The Herne's Egg* to two main sources: Swedenborg and *The Upanishads*, combined in Balzac's esoteric novel of 1835, *Seraphita*. He notes that Yeats was working on a translation of the Upanishads with Shri Purohit Swami as he was composing *The Herne's Egg*, and claims that, during her rape, Attracta is in a condition of *Samadhi*, a state of waking trance in Hindu mystical experience.[44] This idea was nothing new in Yeats and Wilson looks back to figures from his youth for sources to *The Herne's Egg* symbolism–Mohini Chatterjee and Madame Blavatsky. A figure closer to home was George Russell; in his 1938 preface to Swami's *The Ten Principal Upanishads*, Yeats remarked that Russell had quoted passages from the Upanishads to him over the previous forty years, Yeats hoping to discover one day if Russell knew what he was talking about.[45] In Blavatsky's 1880s works *Isis Unveiled* and *The Secret Doctrine*, Indian traditions within which the bird was conceived as a form of divinity are considered, in particular the swan, and the egg or sphere is discussed as the form of all manifest existence, emblem of eternity and infinity. The second volume of *The Secret Doctrine* opens with what Blavatsky claims to be translations from the ancient book of Dzyan, describing the birth of 'the Man-Swan' from the egg of a race descended from the original race of 'Yoga'.[46] The symbolism of *The Herne's Egg* finds its source here, the plot of which centres upon the substitution of *The Herne's Egg* for an ordinary egg at Congal's banquet.

Later in *The Secret Doctrine*, Blavatsky returns to the egg symbol when discussing the myth of Leda, writing of her giving birth to the egg from which the sons of Zeus – Castor and Pollux – are born, and of Leda assuming the aspect of a white swan when uniting herself to the 'Divine Swan'. Leda is described as 'the mythical bird' of traditions particular to the various peoples of the Aryan race.[47] In an early draft of Attracta's

---

[44] Yeats discusses the condition of *Samadhi* extensively in 'The Holy Mountain'. See *Essays and Introductions*, pp. 448, 473. See also his introduction to the collaborative translation of Bhagavan Shri Patanjali's *Aphorisms of Yoga* (London: Faber and Faber, 1938), p. 15. For discussion of the influence of Swami, see Guha, *W. B. Yeats*, pp. 125–31, and Sankaran Ravindran, *W. B. Yeats and Indian Tradition* (Delhi: Konark Publishers, 1990), pp. 81–110.
[45] Shree Purohit Swami and W. B. Yeats, *The Ten Principal Upanishads*, p. 7.
[46] Helena Petrovna Blavatsky, *The Secret Doctrine: The Synthesis of Science, Religion, and Philosophy*, vol. II (Point Lama, CA: The Aryan Theosophical Press, 1925).
[47] *Ibid.*, p. 122.

speech from scene five of *The Herne's Egg*, Yeats returned to 'Leda and the Swan', published almost ten years earlier in the 1928 collection, *The Tower*. Here, Attracta understands her violation as joyful communion with the Godhead; the words directly borrowed from 'Leda and the Swan' are absent in the final version:

> While I remember last nights joy
> I share his knowledge & his power
> And can condemn to some fearful end[48]

First published with *The Cat and the Moon* in 1924 and revised for publication in the 1925 edition of *A Vision*, 'Leda and the Swan' was originally intended as a mythical representation of emergent totalitarianism.[49] In turning to a mythical image of bestial copulation to express the momentous transformation of world politics resulting from the rapid consolidation and spread of the Soviet Union, Yeats was remembering *The Player Queen* as much as *The Secret Doctrine*, for the play explicitly lent the image historical and political import. Set in the context of *A Vision*, 'Leda and the Swan' was intended to express the critical moment at which the gyres had fully interpenetrated, the moment at which a new order arose suddenly from the destruction of the old. As well as emphasising the momentous historical and political significance of this moment, however, *The Player Queen* also infused the bestial image with the quality of farce, an aspect absent from 'Leda and the Swan' but certainly present in *The Herne's Egg*. This is crucial to evaluating what historical meaning attaches to the mystical symbolism of the play, since it links *The Herne's Egg* directly to Expressionism and the Absurdist manner of Pirandello – threatening its symbolic edifice from within.

Aside from *Purgatory*, critics have paid relatively little attention to the grotesque and transgressive aspects of the later plays.[50] Lisabeth Buchelt and F. A. C. Wilson address the matter in terms of mysticism. Buchelt sources the occasions of violation, debasement and sacrilege in the plays to the ancient Egyptian mysticism of Hermes Trismegistus and his doctines of ascent and descent.[51] Wilson looks to *The Upanishads*, seeing *The*

---

[48] Yeats, *The Herne's Egg: Manuscript Materials*, p. 123; compare with the penultimate line of 'Leda and the Swan' (*VP*, 441).
[49] Foster, *W. B. Yeats*, vol. II, p. 243. Vendler, *Yeats's Vision*, p. 108.
[50] Susan Canon Harris's perceptive reading of *The Herne's Egg* is a notable exception. See *Gender and Modern Irish Drama* (Bloomington, IN: Indiana University Press, 2002), pp. 230–4, 248–60.
[51] Lisabeth C. Buchelt, 'Alchemical and Tarot Imagery in Yeats's Later Plays: *The Resurrection* and *A Full Moon in March*', *Cauda Pavonis: Studies in Hermeticism*, 16:1 (1997), 2–6.

Herne's Egg bear out its idea that 'Spirit is the Good in all', however elevated or base.[52] Yet in his preface to Purohit Swami's translations, Yeats writes of a 'Buddhistic hatred of life', echoing Nietzsche's view of Christian doctrine as a denial of life.[53] Mystical interpretations overlook the centrality of farce in understanding violence and sexual transgression in the later plays. Admittedly Wilson has provided the most attentive consideration of the irreverence of *The Herne's Egg*. Acknowledging that the play is 'extremely uninhibited', he rightly points out that its 'tragi-comic levity' was not unique in English drama, pointing to long stretches of *Hamlet* by way of example. Most significant are the comparisons he draws between *The Herne's Egg* and a Picasso painting from the 1930s, 'Minotaur Carrying a Dying Horse', a comparison strengthened by the influence of Cubism on Yeats's staging, Yeats employing cubes as thrones in *The King of the Great Clock Tower* to create an abstract Expressionist effect.[54] This recalls what may well be seen as the Cubist experiment of the 1911–12 versions of *The Hour-Glass*, produced with Gordon Craig's screens and mobile cubes gridded over the entire stage.[55] It also followed from the avant-garde production of *Fighting the Waves* at the Abbey in 1929, in which the atonal score of George Antheil was combined with the masks of Hildo van Krop and the abstract Expressionist dance mode of Ninette de Valois, repeated for the 1934 performance of *The King of the Great Clock Tower*. Yeats regarded this performance as his greatest success in the theatre since *Cathleen ni Houlihan*, telling Olivia Shakespear that everyone was convinced that he had discovered a new form by the combination of dance, speech and music employed. He described his excitement at the dancing of the goddess 'in her abstract almost non-representative mask'.[56]

The ribald aspects of *The Herne's Egg* were far from comic relief. As with Mrs Henderson gleefully eyeing the coins near the end of *The Words upon the Window-pane*, they threaten to expose the entire mystical pattern of the play as a charade. Congal ridicules Attracta's submission to the Great Herne, deriding her belief in its mystical power:

[52] Swami and Yeats, *The Ten Principal Upanishads*, p. 23.
[53] *Ibid.*, p. 9.
[54] Wilson, *W. B. Yeats and Tradition*, p. 115.
[55] For discussion of these productions, see Dorn, *Players*, pp. 17–26.
[56] Yeats to Olivia Shakespear, 24 August 1929. Wade, *The Letters*, p. 768. While emphasising Yeats's reticence at the geometric-based art of the Vorticists, Elizabeth Loizeaux nonetheless acknowledges that Yeats drew comparison between the geometric patterns of *A Vision* and those of the Cubist works of Wyndham Lewis and Constantin Brancusi. Loizeaux, *Yeats and the Visual Arts*, pp. 162–3.

> Refused! Must old campaigners lack
> The one sole dish that takes their fancy,
> My cooks what might have proved their skill,
> Because a woman thinks that she
> Is promised or married to a bird? (*VPl*, 1015–16)

The play is haunted by the possibility that Attracta's desire is bestial rather than sacred, a prospect particularly disturbing given the graphic violation that stands at the centre of this play. Susan Canon Harris writes that her devotion to the Great Herne 'combines spiritual purity and sensual depravity, creating as its object an entity that is both divinely ideal and grossly material'.[57] Reviewing the manuscript materials, Richard Cave notes that the main difficulty Yeats faced when composing the play lay in getting control over shifts in tone between farce and mysticism.[58] This is its great challenge; it takes its audience's credulity in mystical symbolism as far as it can go, holding open the possibility that the entire process is built on delusion. For this reason, the rape of Attracta seems the most disturbing moment in the entire corpus of Yeats's work, perhaps even more disturbing than the murder of the young boy in *Purgatory*, and was the chief reason why the Abbey board rejected it in 1936.[59]

The sense of disturbance in *The Herne's Egg* was accentuated through its use of Expressionist techniques. Ruth Nevo draws attention to the choreographed image of battle at the start of the play in which 'men move rhythmically as if in a dance' and the swords and shields never meet; we encounter the same movement of warriors at the start of Kokoschka's *Murderer, Hope of Women*, a drama prefiguring the violation of Attracta of *The Herne's Egg* in its ritual branding of the Woman (*VPl*, 1012).[60] The 'moon of comic tradition' appears straight out of Brecht, the moon that announces its own artifice.[61] In keeping with the deep ambivalence to mysticism in the play, the techniques constantly challenge the audience's perception that what is happening is real: swords and shields do not touch in battle; the fight at the banquet is carried out with the table legs; a cooking-pot is worn as a helmet and a wooden donkey appears on stage on which eggs are painted. Richard Taylor traces this to classical Indian

---

[57] Harris, *Gender and Modern Irish Drama*, p. 248.
[58] Richard Allen Cave, review of W. B. Yeats, *The Herne's Egg: Manuscript Materials*, ed. Alison Armstrong, *Yeats Annual*, vol. XII, ed. Warwick Gould (London: Macmillan, 1996), p. 291.
[59] Harris, *Gender and Modern Irish Drama*, pp. 230–1.
[60] Ruth Nevo, 'Yeats's Passage to India', *Yeats Annual*, vol. IV, ed. Warwick Gould, (London: Macmillan Press, 1986), p. 15. Kokoshchka, *Murderer, Hope of Women*, p. 22.
[61] In Brecht's 1927 play, *The Elephant Calf*, the Moon appears as Uriah, a character in this play for the foyer of the auditorium. *The Elephant Calf, Brecht: Collected Plays*, vol. II, pp. 80–1.

theatre in which toy animals are introduced on stage but also notes that Brecht exploits the device for *Verfremdungseffekt* in *The Elephant Calf* and *Man Equals Man*.[62] This wooden donkey may anticipate the 'parallelograms of painted wood' used as emblems of Cuchulain's dead enemies in *The Death of Cuchulain* but equally points to the 'wooden' figures of Degas's paintings that the Old Man spits upon in the prologue to Yeats's last play.

These props not only ridicule the action, but they also point to Attracta herself as a 'doll upon a wire' and 'but a puppet under the influence of the Great Herne' (*VPl*, 1021). Moving as if in a trance, she may indeed be as ridiculous or frightening as Mrs Henderson in her automaton state as medium.[63] In any case, it illustrates how central questions of agency are to Yeats's use of farce in *The Herne's Egg*. As with *The Player Queen* and *The Words upon the Window-pane*, the puppet-theatre metaphor operates as the expression of the force of history reducing individuals to submissive passivity. Congal's belief that he could overcome the Great Herne is as wrongheaded as Cuchulain fighting the waves in *On Baile's Strand*: the pattern of destiny cannot be reversed. This historical force shows itself in the form of the fetish in the play: crude objects are scattered around through which the mystical narrative unfolds; the wooden donkey, the table legs, the comic moon, the cauldron lid, pot and cooking-spit with which the Fool fights Congal, and the same cooking-spit with which Congal mortally wounds himself. This motley group of objects not only deflates the image of Congal as proud warrior, it parodies that purity to which Attracta submits herself through communion with the Great Herne, suggesting that this finally amounts to nothing more than bestial copulation. They also show how the improvisational mode of the play itself works against its own mythical narrative. They are stage props, items ready to hand from which the esoteric power of the play emerges. Yeats's representation of the force of historical necessity through the contingent and situational in *Calvary* and *The Death of Cuchulain* is once more in evidence.

Through this use of stage props, Attracta's complete submission to a mystical power becomes connoted with a historical process of instrumentalisation. Immediately following Congal's death before the end of the play, she commands Corney to have sex with her in order to save Congal

---

[62] Taylor, *The Drama of W. B. Yeats*, p. 180.
[63] Nevo, 'Yeats's Passage to India', p. 19.

from reincarnation as a lower beast. She tells Corney to forget his fear of the Great Herne:

> Lie and beget.
> If you are afraid of the Great Herne,
> Put that away, for if I do his will,
> You are his instrument or himself. (*VPl*, 1039)

Her command that he become an instrument of an invisible power is consistent with her own submission. The attempt fails; the donkeys copulate immediately, leaving Attracta no time for sex with Corney.[64] The donkey at the play's end is simply the final image of all those farcical elements scattered throughout. Rather than redemption through complete submission to an invisible power, the clumsy attempt at sexual intercourse between Attracta and Corney sums up a situation in which human value has become distorted through commerce. Attracta's deadening virginity descends to this crude level; the birth of a donkey is its most appropriate image. The play's conclusion bears witness not to the power of the Great Herne but to the fetishism of the commodity, the hollowness at the heart of which is expressed in the nihilistic laughter of Corney as he delivers the play's concluding lines:

> All that trouble and nothing to show for it,
> Nothing but just another donkey. (*VPl*, 1040)

Just as the Herne's egg may simply be an egg, this donkey may simply be another donkey. The farcical quality of *The Herne's Egg* subverts its mystical vision from within, a late reminder of the self-undoing ritual of *On Baile's Strand*.

The Player Queen, *The Words upon the Window-pane* and *The Herne's Egg* are infused with Yeats's long engagement with esoteric mysticism of various kinds. But they also carry a subversive current that derides the transcendental portentousness of the symbolism they draw upon. Particularly in *The Player Queen* and *The Words upon the Window-pane*, this draws Yeats's drama close to the nightmarish political vision of Toller and Pirandello's existential farces. And in plays as obscure as *A Full Moon in March* and *The Herne's Egg*, consonance with *Verfremdungseffekt* was striking, inducing a critical distance consonant with that effect on audiences Brecht sought, even as he brought a very different set of values to

---

[64] Francisco Torres Ribelles suggests that the conclusion is an ironic swipe at the doctrine of metempychosis; Congal reincarnated as a donkey is a mocking image of the entire idea. 'Predetermination and Nihilism', p. 146.

the theatre.⁶⁵ Human agency emerges as the crucial question of these plays. In the allegorical rigidity of *The Player Queen*, the automaton state of the medium in *The Words upon the Window-pane*, George Antheil's searing atonal score for *Fighting the Waves*, and that image of Attracta as 'a doll upon the wire', the fetishism of a commercialised culture is manifested with the paralysing allure of the primitive totem.⁶⁶ The tautened mode by which an impersonal super-agent appears to reduce the protagonists of these plays to puppets demonstrates the extent to which they were developed in response to totalitarianism. All this is mediated, however, through forbidding mystical symbolism or the peculiar setting of the séance. Turning from the esoteric to the historical in his penultimate play *Purgatory*, the full extent of Yeats's historical consciousness and his understanding of modernity comes into view.

---

[65] Cave suggests that the farcical nature of *The Herne's Egg* serves to keep the audience 'detached and critical of the characters' conceptions of themselves'. That sense of critical distance was central to Brecht's idea of theatre. *Yeats's Late Plays*, p. 305.

[66] In April 1929, Yeats described Antheil's score to Gregory as the only dramatic music he ever heard – 'something heroic and barbaric and strange'. Yeats to Gregory, 10 April 1929. Wade, *The Letters*, pp. 761–2.

CHAPTER 8

History inside out: Purgatory

On 5 August 1938, Samuel Beckett wrote to his friend George Reavey that he hoped to remain in Dublin beyond the following Wednesday in order to attend the opening of Yeats's new play *Purgatory*.[1] The play was premiered with a revival of *On Baile's Strand* at the Abbey on 10 August. The impact of that night's performance on the thirty-two year old is evident in several of Beckett's greatest theatrical achievements after the war. There's a faint image of the symbolic tree of *Purgatory* in the bare tree of *Waiting for Godot*. The strange boy who appears as Mr Godot's messenger recalls the Young Man who comes from the sea in *On Baile's Strand*, and the boy who is murdered in *Purgatory*. The Old Man's intention to kill his son in *Purgatory* to end his family line resonates in Hamm's horror in *Endgame* at Clov's claim that he had seen a boy alive outside, and Hamm's taunt against Nagg, 'Accursed progenitor'.[2] The Oedipal trauma of both Yeats's plays performed that night in 1938 and the tautened mode of their theatrical representation are discernible in the haunting, claustrophobic atmosphere of *Footfalls* and *Play*.[3] The sense of relentless circularity, enclosure and cruelty that characterises *Purgatory* become trademarks of Beckett's drama. Lynn Haims suggests that the ruined house in Yeats's play symbolises the interior landscape of the mind in which an intense Oedipal struggle is fought, reminding us of Hugh Kenner's description of the stage of *Endgame* as the inside of a skull.[4] The influence of Yeats was directly acknowledged in Beckett's 1977 television play '... but the

[1] Beckett to George Reavey, 5 August 1938. Martha Dow Fehsenfeld and Lois More Overbeck eds., *The Letters of Samuel Beckett*, vol. I, *1929–1940* (Cambridge University Press, 2009), pp. 639–40.
[2] Samuel Beckett, *The Complete Dramatic Works* (London: Faber, 1986), p. 96.
[3] Worth believes that the influence is particularly marked in *Play*. *The Irish Drama of Europe*, p. 183.
[4] Lynn Haims, 'Apocalyptic Vision in Three Late Plays by Yeats', *Southern Review*, 14 (1978), 61. Hugh Kenner, *Samuel Beckett: A Critical Study* (Berkeley, CA: University of California Press, 1968), p. 155.

clouds …', taking its title from the concluding lines of 'The Tower', and Katharine Worth gives an illuminating comparative reading of this play against *The Words upon the Window-pane*.[5] Worth also notes how the Blind Man and Lame Man of *The Cat and the Moon* anticipate the debilitated and interdependent pairs of Beckett's drama, a play that Richard Taylor perceptively describes as a 'structured happening', a phrase appropriate to several of Beckett's later minimalist pieces.[6] In its immediacy and intensity, however, no Yeats play quite anticipates the vision of Beckett so effectively as *Purgatory*.

This chapter considers the precedent *Purgatory* created in its Expressionist aspect for Beckett's post-war drama, evident in the significance of Strindberg's *The Ghost Sonata* to both *Purgatory* and *Waiting for Godot*. In so doing, I reconsider the political meaning of Yeats's play. William Morris's importance to Yeats remained throughout his life and in *On the Boiler*, the controversial pamphlet with which *Purgatory* was first published, Yeats turned to the towering figure of John Ruskin. Ruskin's *The Stones of Venice* (1851–3) had been a formative influence on Morris, for both its ideas on art and its attack on the social division of labour. With the notable exception of W. J. McCormack's urgent reading of *Purgatory*, discussion of Yeats's politics in the 1930s has taken no account of its experimental form.[7] Ruskin was a vital figure in this regard, a presence not only in Yeats's vision of society in the 1930s but also in the philosophy of perception behind the experimental nature of *Purgatory*.

Ruskin's influence provides a social and political context to the specifically theatrical influence on *Purgatory* of *The Ghost Sonata*, the earliest piece of Expressionist theatre. As shown in Chapter 1, *The Land of Heart's Desire* – Yeats's first publicly performed play – had anticipated key aspects of Strindberg's 1907 work. Yeats had come to admire Strindberg immensely in the 1920s, comparing *The Ghost Sonata* to *King Lear* in 1926. Strindberg was a favourite with the Dublin Drama League; five of his works were performed at the Abbey in the 1920s. Against a mounting tide of public pressure to introduce more rigorous censorship in the Irish Free State that led to the creation of the Committee on Evil Literature in February 1926, Yeats issued a strident defence of artistic experiment in the

---

[5] Worth, '*The Words upon the Window-pane*', pp. 138–41. See also Terence Brown, *The Life of W. B. Yeats*, p. 382.

[6] Worth, *The Irish Drama of Europe*, p. 182; Taylor, *The Drama of W. B. Yeats*, p. 148. See also Moore, *Masks of Love and Death*, p. 246.

[7] W. J. McCormack, *From Burke to Beckett: Ascendancy, Tradition, and Betrayal in Literary History*, 2nd edn (Cork University Press, 1994), pp. 354–8.

course of which Strindberg was cited as a great innovator whose vision was yet consistent with Christian mysticism. When he wrote that Lennox Robinson had created a vision of life that Tertullian could have accepted, Yeats had in mind Robinson's performance of the Student in the Drama League's production of *The Ghost Sonata* the previous April.[8] Yeats identified for Strindberg's well-publicised mysogny a precedent in Tertullian, the early Church Father notorious for his image of woman as 'she-devil'. This explains the Old Man's instruction to the Boy to 'fetch Tertullian' in *Purgatory*, the most obscure reference in the play, testifying Strindberg's influence (*VPl*, 1046). This acquires added significance in view of the fact that Beckett first offered *Waiting For Godot* to Roger Blin at the end of 1949 after he had twice seen Blin's production of *The Ghost Sonata* at the Gaîté-Montparnasse theatre.[9] Although *Waiting For Godot* was composed before this between October 1948 and January 1949, Beckett's decision suggests that he sought a production along the lines of the kind of *stationdramen* Expressionism we encounter in *The Ghost Sonata*.[10] Given its influence on Yeats's penultimate play, Beckett may well have recollected the 1938 performance of *Purgatory* when attending the Paris productions of Strindberg's play in 1949.

Purgatory bears the influence of *The Ghost Sonata* in several thematic aspects, including madness, ancestral degeneration, petrifaction and the supernatural. Each of these is related through a preoccupation with perception. The Old Man Hummel, wheelchair-bound, hears the Student speaking to someone but cannot see who it is; he wonders if the Student is mad.[11] The milkmaid is the supernatural figure the Old Man cannot see – he is filled with terror on realising her presence. In *Purgatory*, a window in the ruined house lights up to show the figure of a young girl; the Old Man points to it but the Boy cannot see anything, declaring the Old Man mad (*VPl*, 1045). The Old Man describes the events in the household on the night of his conception as if they were happening again and when the window lights up a second time, the Boy sees in horror the outline of a presence (*VPl*, 1048). The Old Man and his son stand before the ruined house and observe the ghostly re-enactment of the night of the Old Man's conception as an audience watching a dumb show. In like manner, the Old Man Hummel tells the Student to observe the house before them

---

[8] Yeats, 'The Need for Audacity of Thought', p. 201; Clarke and Ferrar, *The Dublin Drama League*, p. 29.
[9] Beckett, *Samuel Beckett: An Exhibition*, Reading University Library, May–July, 1971 (London: Turret Books, 1971), p. 63.
[10] Knowlson, *Damned to Fame*, p. 378.   [11] Strindberg, *The Ghost Sonata*, p. 158.

in *The Ghost Sonata*. They look upon its occupants standing or moving in silence, Hummel describing each character as the Old Man describes events being enacted in *Purgatory*.[12]

Yeats had employed a similar technique in *The Words upon the Window-pane*, those present at the séance observing the medium, Mrs Henderson, enact Swift's encounter with Stella and the strange child Lulu, wondering if what they were witnessing was real or delusional. Significantly, the Student has been chosen as a medium in *The Ghost Sonata* and tells Hummel of rescuing a child from a collapsing house the previous day only for her to vanish in his arms.[13] The treatment of perception in *The Ghost Sonata* and *Purgatory* was strongly indebted to the influence of Swedenborg on both playwrights but it also bore a vital relation to changes in human understanding opened up by the advent of the new physics in the early years of the twentieth century. The political meaning of *Purgatory* lies within this context, given the place of Ruskin in Yeats's response to Einsteinian physics in the 1920s. The later Ruskin was significant to Yeats not only as the advocate of familial traditions brought under pressure by the rise of science and democracy in the Victorian age, but also as an emblematic figure in Yeats's resistance to the authority of 'common sense'. This was evident in his dispute with Thomas Sturge Moore in early 1926, soon after completing the first volume of *A Vision*. Yeats engaged analytic philosophy at this time in the hope that, by bringing nineteenth-century utilitarianism and materialism to an end, it might offer grounds for the tenability of paranormal experience. Encountering Einstein's special theory of relativity through Bertrand Russell's *ABC of Relativity*, Yeats identified an opportunity for spiritualism to gain intellectual credibility following the demise of mechanistic philosophy and its Victorian progeny.[14] The aspiration was misplaced as Moore's thorough and sometimes impatient refutation of Yeats's insistent assertions showed. At issue here was something more than tenability of claims to paranormal experience, however; of greater significance were the conflicting modes of understanding perception that divided Yeats and Moore.

The example of 'Ruskin's cat' that Yeats introduced was far from arbitrary, carrying as it did a whole panoply of values implicit in Ruskin's vision of human culture in the Victorian era. In a letter to Moore of January 1926, Yeats described the incident in which, during a conversation

---

[12] *Ibid.*, pp. 162–7.   [13] *Ibid.*, p. 163.
[14] See Yeats to T. Sturge Moore, 8 December 1925 and 5 January 1926. Bridges, *W. B. Yeats and T. Sturge Moore*, pp. 58–61.

with Frank Harris, Ruskin threw a cat out of the window, claiming it to be a demon in animal form.[15] Yeats had identified in Bertrand Russell's argument that sense-data ought not to be confused with physical objects, an opportunity for reinstating George Berkeley's spiritualist theory of perception in modern philosophy.[16] He proposed that the cat Ruskin saw was a perception of something real, because it was as much sense-data as any other perception, a position Moore rejected.[17] The preoccupation with perception in his last plays, particularly *The Resurrection*, *Purgatory* and *The Death of Cuchulain*, derived in significant measure from this attempt to accommodate new developments in scientific understanding to supernatural belief.

The importance of these exchanges to Yeats's political attitudes lay in the recourse Moore took to common sense and probability in addressing ambiguities surrounding the status of perception that Bertrand Russell's view of sense-data introduced, following Einstein's displacement of Newtonian physics. Moore's difficulty was that, despite flagrant inconsistencies in Yeats's propositions, Russell's account of sense-data did not provide a basis for a categorical denial of Ruskin's hallucinatory perception. Consequently, he turned to notions of common sense, probability and verification in refuting Yeats's exaggerated claims.[18] Yeats identified Russell behind this, disdainfully remarking in response that the 'reality' of Ruskin's cat grew 'with the number who hear it mew'.[19] Objecting to common sense as a basis upon which a perception might be judged real or fanciful, Yeats rejected what he saw as the democratisation of understanding, accusing Russell of philosophising like a politician, despite his power as mathematician. Through the course of this eccentric argument over 'Ruskin's cat', Yeats denied the authority of common sense to dictate judgements of perceptions as real or hallucinatory. In this way, he was not only making a case for the tenability of paranormal experience, but defending Ruskin against the widespread view that he had become deranged in his last years.

This question of Ruskin's sanity in Yeats's 1926 correspondence with Moore projects the dispute forward to *On the Boiler* as Yeats's *Fors Clavigera* and a demented Jonathan Swift as a presence in the essay. Equally, it opens up the connection between the Old Man's psychological

[15] Yeats to T. Sturge Moore, 16 January 1926. *Ibid.*, p. 63.
[16] Yeats to T. Sturge Moore, 5 and 26 January 1926. *Ibid.*, pp. 60, 66.
[17] Yeats to T. Sturge Moore, 18 June 1926. *Ibid.*, pp. 95–6.
[18] Yeats to T. Sturge Moore, 16 Jan 1926. *Ibid.*, p. 65.
[19] Yeats to T. Sturge Moore, 26 Jan 1926. *Ibid.*, p. 67.

condition and the problem of representation in *Purgatory*. Eccentric as it was, the dispute with Moore underlined the centrality of the play to modernism, dealing as it did with the questions of perception thrown up by Bertrand Russell's reading of the special theory of relativity, anticipating Beckett's later obsession with questions of perception in the theatre. Barton Friedman finds an echo of the dispute over 'Ruskin's cat' in the thought experiment that Erwin Schrödinger – winner of the 1933 Nobel prize for physics – used in 1935 to explain the undecidable condition of atoms in quantum mechanics, an experiment, curiously enough, that involved another unfortunate cat. Placed in a box with a vial of poison released if a detector recorded a radioactive event, Schrödinger pointed out that it would be impossible to know if the cat was dead or alive for the duration of the experiment.[20] Yeats's dispute with Moore was somewhat less far-fetched in this light, Schrödinger's thought-experiment being influenced by his interest in Hindu mysticism. Though lacking anything of Schrödinger's mathematical rigour, Wallace's *Cosmic Anatomy* of 1921 – an important precedent for the 1925 edition of *A Vision* – anticipated Schrödinger in drawing together Hindu mysticism and the new physics. Wallace identified *Laya*, the point of mergence of *Purusha* and *Pradhana* or 'self' and 'anti-self' in Hindu mysticism, as 'the condition of interference between two wave-systems'.[21]

In his 1926 dispute with Moore, Yeats attempted to place Irish intellectual culture at the heart of advanced scientific understanding through the connection he drew between Einstein's theory of relativity, as outlined by Bertrand Russell, and Kilkenny Bishop Berkeley's theory of perception. Schrödinger's move to Ireland at the outbreak of the Second World War, where he joined De Valera's new Institute for Advanced Study, suggests that Yeats's sense of Ireland's contribution to scientific and philosophical knowledge at this time was not entirely wayward.[22] Berkeley was to carry equal importance for Beckett, his 1963 *Film* being a meditation on the famous phrase of his eighteenth-century Irish Protestant predecessor, 'esse est percipi'.[23] Obviously couched in Yeats's supernatural beliefs, the spectral scene in *Purgatory* that the Old Man and the Boy witness nonetheless shares something with Schrödinger's experiment of 1935. Manifestation of

---

[20] Friedman discusses the relevance of this problem in perception to *The Resurrection*, considering the play as a clash of diametrically different perceptions of the same event and pointing to the irrational nature of micro and macrocosm, following relativity and quantum theory. 'Yeatsian (Meta)physics: *The Resurrection* and the Irrational', pp. 148–9.
[21] Oxon, *Cosmic Anatomy*, p. 60.   [22] Wills, *That Neutral Island*, p. 281.
[23] Beckett, *The Complete Dramatic Works*, p. 323.

'life-in-death and death-in life' heralded in 'Byzantium', the figures of the Old Man's parents on the night of his conception are, like Schrödinger's cat, neither dead nor alive.

The treatment of perception in *Purgatory* was a response not only to radical changes in scientific understanding but also to the emergence of mass culture and its commercialisation from the end of the nineteenth century. The Old Man's madness links the play directly to *On the Boiler*, in the first instance through the influence of Swift on the composition of this pamphlet. *The Words upon the Window-pane* and Yeats's extended introduction to the 1931 publication of the play presents Swift not only as a prophet 'of the ruin to come' but also of a man 'who dreaded transmitting madness' (*VPl*, 960, 965). Many of the eugenicist ideas proposed in *On the Boiler* owe their influence to the *Drapier Letters* and its revolt against 'the tyranny of the Many' (*VPl*, 961). Above all, the scientific evidence that Yeats invokes, drawing on the work of the eugenicist Raymond Cattell, owes much to the rhetoric of Swift's *A Modest Proposal*.[24] At the same time, the pamphlet admires Swift for the rage with which he confronted the materialist mindset of his day.[25] Yeats may have been partly drawn to the double-edged nature of Swift's satirical address, with its predilection for statistics from which extreme conclusions were drawn, in which the poor were, quite literally, to be treated like animals.[26] Admiring Swift's revulsion for 'Whiggish materialism' that had led to humanity being replaced by 'something that can be chopped and measured like a piece of cheese', we yet encounter a citation of statistics in *On the Boiler* that is rare in Yeats's writing.[27]

This flagrant contradiction suggests the extent to which *On the Boiler* was as much a reflection on Swift's descent into insanity as it was testimony to Yeats's belief that contemporary European civilisation was degenerating. *On the Boiler* takes its title from an eccentric local character Yeats remembered from his childhood in Sligo. The Old Man's determination in *Purgatory* not to 'pass pollution on' attends as much to the figure of a deranged Swift suggested in this character as it does to the eugenicist ideas that interested Yeats in the 1930s. The voice of Swift utters the following

---

[24] Yeats, *On the Boiler*, p. 17. For discussion of Cattell's influence see Howes, *Yeats's Nations*, pp. 161–70; David Bradshaw, 'British Writers and Anti-Fascism in the 1930s: II, Under the Hawk's Wing', *Woolf Studies Annual*, 4 (1998), 41–66; McCormack, *Blood Kindred*, p. 264.

[25] Yeats, *On the Boiler*, p. 26.

[26] Jonathan Swift, *A Modest Proposal for Preventing the Children of Poor People from being a Burthen to their Parents or the Country, And for making them Beneficial to the Publick*, 3rd edn (London: Weaver Bickerton, 1730), pp. 8–23.

[27] Yeats, *On the Boiler*, p. 26.

in *The Words upon the Window-pane*: 'I have something in my blood that no child must inherit' (*VPl*, 949). In the disgust he shows towards his own son, the Old Man of *Purgatory* recalls Swift's panic before the child Lulu in the earlier play. This suggests how Yeats might have intended us to read the influence of Swift on *On the Boiler*; expressing a horror of the future, it also points to a derangement of the mind. Considering the essay in this way, the line between a degenerating mind and a diagnosis of cultural degeneration appears very thin indeed.[28]

McCormack rightly observes that Swift's influence on Yeats in the 1930s, no matter how large, was not unmediated, taking issue with Joseph Hassett's study of Yeats's politics on this basis.[29] Mediating voices are many, but McCormack pays little attention to the figure Yeats identifies most clearly for *On the Boiler* – John Ruskin. Yeats's characterisation of the essay as his *Fors Clavigera* was notably insistent in late 1937: twice in letters to Wellesley and once to Mannin.[30] Ruskin's *Unto this Last* was cited in what at first seems an offhand reference (Yeats's admitting to having no recollection of a single word of the text) but one which turns out to be a revealing moment in *On the Boiler* for understanding its relation to *Purgatory*. On the face of it, the Christian communism of Ruskin's St George's Company discussed in the letters of *Fors Clavigera* appears far from the sentiment of Yeats's essay, in which the separation of classes is so pronounced. Nevertheless, the precedent of Ruskin was not chosen lightly: some of the most unpalatable sentiments of Yeats's essay, discreet or pronounced, are traceable to him. Ruskin's sustained attack on commerce and the corruption of moral life in England had its anti-semitic aspect in the particular invective he saves for usurers going to Synagogue on Sunday.[31] Anti-Republicanism and belief in the inferiority of black peoples were also in evidence.[32] Ruskin founded his St George's Company from a belief in the degeneracy of contemporary English society and the imminence of major natural calamities, born out of a pervasive indifference to the natural world he judged perverse. He did not rule out the use of violence in the imposition of the anti-capitalist

---

[28] Sandra F. Siegel observes that as Yeats redrafted *Purgatory*, the Old Man loses his self-knowledge while continuing his preoccupation with purification, becoming 'increasingly ignorant that he is the pollution'. *Purgatory: Manuscript Materials*, p. 13.
[29] McCormack, *Blood Kindred*, p. 50. Joseph Hassett, *Yeats and the Poetics of Hate* (Dublin: Gill & Macmillan, 1986).
[30] Yeats to Dorothea Wellesley, 11 November 1937; 17 December 1937; Yeats to Ethel Mannin, 17 December 1937. Wade, *The Letters*, pp. 900, 902, 903.
[31] Ruskin, *Fors Clavigera*, vol. VI, p. 47.
[32] *Ibid.*, pp. 92, 109.

vision of St George's Company and he was menacingly discreet on what actions might be taken to overturn the existing state of things.[33] While an early nod in the direction of anarcho-syndicalism might be detected here, Ruskin's case for necessary violence elsewhere carried no such ambiguity: 'Moral education begins in making the creature to be educated, clean, and obedient. This must be done thoroughly, and at any cost, and with any kind of compulsion rendered necessary by the nature of the animal, be it dog, child, or man.'[34] These illustrate a reactionary strain in Ruskin's social criticism, even as the letters retain a radical anti-capitalist outlook. He was also significant to Yeats through the way in which his growing sense of contemporary English society as 'a loathsome insanity' had disturbed his own mental equilibrium in his last years.[35] Swift finds his late-Victorian successor here – a communion of spirits that unsettles the Ruskinian framework for *On the Boiler* as it does the Swiftian voice it inflected.

Yeats's emphasis upon race in his later years expressed something more complex than a thesis of Anglo-Irish decline. It is true that contained within it was a lament for the demise of Big House culture in Ireland and with it those values Yeats held with increasing reverence as the years advanced: custom, tradition and ceremony. The cultivation of nobility and the protection of old Ascendancy families in Ireland during a period of immense political turmoil were very much part of that emphasis. Yet whatever might be said of the class affiliations this disposition entailed, Yeats's ideas on race were, like Ruskin's ideas on class, part of a larger response to the historical forces shaping modern European society. The intellectual trajectory Yeats outlined in his notes for a race philosophy point to how profoundly he regarded his ideas on race to be the outcome of a long struggle between materialist and idealist accounts of dialectics. Taking the Hegelian dialectic schematically, he set dialectical materialism against Vico and Italian philosophy, regarding Fascism as the outcome of the latter. His schematic race philosophy developed from the view that these antinomies could never be resolved, leaving a perpetually deferred synthesis of the dialectic.[36] While undoubtedly influenced by Darwinian ideas of perpetual struggle, the 'Genealogical Tree of Revolution' refused the completion offered by the utopian Socialist or the organic Fascist state.

[33] *Ibid.*, pp. 174, 209.   [34] *Ibid.*, p. 225.   [35] *Ibid.*, p. 174.
[36] Yeats, 'Genealogical Tree of Revolution', *W. B. Yeats: Man and Poet*, 2nd edn, ed. Norman Jeffares (London: Routledge & Kegan Paul, 1962), pp. 351–2. For discussion of this, see Cullingford, *Yeats, Ireland and Fascism* (London: Macmillan Press, 1981), p. 216.

Marjorie Howes argues that the 'Genealogical Tree of Revolution' was practically useless as a guide to political decisions, presenting human experience instead as driven by impersonal historical processes.[37] In fact, Yeats identified the function of government as enabling creative families and individuals to flourish in the struggle of the individual with the family, into which the government had no authority to intervene. At the same time, individuals and families judged creative had no right to an unlimited acquisition of power; at issue in deciding at what point a limit should be set was the quality of culture achieved and to be sustained.[38] This is in keeping with a sentiment he proposes early in *On the Boiler*: 'If ever Ireland again seems molten wax, reverse the process of revolution. Do not try to pour Ireland into any political system. Think first how many able men with public minds the country has, how many it can hope to have in the near future, and mould your system upon those men.'[39] Howes points out that his notions of individual greatness and family strength presumed the acquiescence of women in a regulated reproductive process, witheld in *Purgatory* to catastrophic effect.[40] Nevertheless, not only did Yeats subordinate the authority of government to the individual and family, he declared no preference towards any particular system of governance. In principle at least, 'The Genealogical Tree' allowed for the possibility of rebellion against government in circumstances where it exceeded the role Yeats accorded to it.[41]

At issue here was that tension between will and passivity in contemporary politics that drew Yeats to the Expressionist forms we encounter in Toller. A passage from his 1934 essay 'The Holy Mountain' brings out the political ambivalence of the perspective on dialectics in 'The Genealogical Tree':

The Spirit, the Self that is in all selves, the pure mirror, is the source of intelligence, but Matter is the source of all energy, all creative power, all that separates one thing from another, not Matter as understood by Hobbes and his Mechanists, Matter as understood in Russia, where the Government has silenced the Mechanist, but interpreted with profound logic almost what Schopenhauer understood by Will.[42]

---

[37] Howes, *Yeats's Nations*, pp. 162–3.
[38] Yeats, 'Genealogical Tree of Revolution', p. 352.
[39] Yeats, *On the Boiler*, p. 13.   [40] Howes, *Yeats's Nations*, p. 176.
[41] Paul Scott Stanfield's claim that *On the Boiler* is an argument for aristocratic government is open to challenge and certainly not supported by the evidence of 'The Genealogical Tree of Revolution', *Yeats and Politics of the 1930s*.
[42] Yeats, 'The Holy Mountain', *Essays and Introductions*, p. 461.

One of those essays written in the 1930s out of the renewed interest in Indian mysticism inspired by Yeats's friendship with Shree Purohit Swami, 'The Holy Mountain', draws upon the doctrines of *The Upanishads* in its understanding of contemporary historical developments. Even more striking, it draws attention in this passage to what would seem the historical development least amenable to Hindu mysticism, the advent of the Soviet Union. Yeats's ambivalence towards dialectical materialism here is at odds with the strident warnings he expressed in 1919 following the Russian Revolution in 'If I Were Four and Twenty'. In comparing official Soviet ideology to Schopenhauer's idea of Will, Yeats was certainly configuring dialectical materialism in mystical terms.[43] But he is also taken with the manner in which both the Marxist idea of history and the compulsion of Schopenhauer's Will describe a force anterior to human agents propelling them forward in time, a force over which they could exercise little rational control. This was precisely the preoccupation of Toller's *Masses and Man*. Many years earlier, in an early draft of his autobiographical essay 'Ireland after Parnell', Yeats had wondered whether modern civilisation was 'a conspiracy of the subconscious' motivated by a hidden power: 'Even when no facts of experience were denied, might not what had seemed logical proof be but a mechanism of change, an automatic impulse?'[44]

For all its association with the cultivation of Anglo-Irish ascendancy, Yeats's idea of race was heavily invested with totemistic connotations in *Purgatory*. Something automatic, machine-like, a kind of inexorable necessity, it evoked that mesmerising power paralysing characters, reducing them to somnambulism in so many Yeats plays. Taken together, *On the Boiler* and *Purgatory* create the impression of race as the unhuman element within the human subject. It is no surprise, therefore, that kindred was so intimately bound to hatred in the tone and sentiment of pamphlet and play, for hatred was symptomatic in Yeats's work of that against which it was directed – the congealment of human subjects under the power of historical processes manifested in the commercialisation of daily life. This was evident in a definition of hatred as 'passive suffering' Yeats offered to Wellesley in December 1936, a phrase evoking the automaton strain coursing through Yeats's drama right back to the crucifix of *The Land of Heart's Desire*, the 'tortured thing'.[45] The Old Man's

---

[43] Quoting the passage as evidence of Yeats's expression of Schopenhauerian duality through Indian mysticism, it is telling that Ruth Nevo omits entirely his reference to the Soviet Union. Nevo, 'Yeats and Schopenhauer', p. 16.
[44] Ts. 'Ireland after Parnell', W. B. Yeats Collection, ms. 600, Emory.
[45] Yeats to Dorothy Wellesley, 23 December 1936. Wade, *The Letters*, p. 876.

revulsion in both *Purgatory* and *The Death of Cuchulain* has the relentless process of reification in modern life as its object, 'in which everything can be chopped and measured like a piece of cheese', but his fanaticism turns into the very dogmatism against which it reacts. Howes notes that kindred relations in *Purgatory* were those of 'violence, discontinuity and death'.[46] This expressed more than a conflict of aristocratic ideals with contemporary realities, it identified a crisis within the institution of the family itself arising from the entanglement of race, as biological determinism, with the petrifaction of the fetish, a dominant theme in Marx, Freud and Victorian ethnology.

At the start of the section entitled 'Tomorrow's Revolution' in *On the Boiler*, Yeats recalled an incident that directly connects the subject of *Purgatory* to his own family experience. Here he describes a moment from his early twenties when his father encountered him reading Ruskin's *Unto This Last*. A devotee of Mill, John Butler Yeats began an argument between them, during which he banged the young Yeats's head against a picture.[47] A liberal agnostic, Yeats's father personified the antithesis of much contained in *On the Boiler*. Mentioning this incident, Yeats insinuated the great intellectual conflicts shaping Victorian society through the private tensions of family life. The clash of Mill's democratic liberalism and Ruskin's feudal communism was dramatised as a bitter argument between father and son, providing a biographical context to the reversal of the Oedipal struggle in *Purgatory*, where the father kills the son.

Following David Bradshaw's discussion of the first draft for *On the Boiler*, McCormack identifies in the incident a crucial moment in the formation of Yeats's project of artistic self-begetting, laying particular stress on references to Mill in the draft.[48] Of equal importance was the reference to Ruskin that survives in the published version of the essay, for this directly addressed the problem of historical representation that *Purgatory* poses. In this argument with his father, Yeats's position was subject to a double contradiction. In allegiance to Ruskin, he was defending not just belief in supernatural vision against the utilitarianism of Mill, but also those traditions Ruskin upheld, including the organic bonds of kindred. Yeats was, in other words, breaking from his father's authority in defending those traditions utilitarianism threw into crisis during the nineteenth century. McCormack is sharp in detecting the symbolic elimination of the progenitor in the pursuit of self-begetting here. However, in defending

---

[46] Howes, *Yeats's Nations*, p. 184.   [47] Yeats, *On the Boiler*, p. 14.
[48] McCormack, *Blood Kindred*, p. 266.

Ruskin's values against the secular liberalism of Mill, Yeats was also defending paternal authority. In the incident described, John Butler Yeats exercised this authority with force, but precisely in defence of a liberalism that broke with the traditions Ruskin was keen to sustain. The moment of the Old Man stabbing the Boy in *Purgatory* is captured here in a way that shows the weight of historical significance attached to the gesture.

The irony of the incident recalls Yeats's early plays in which the young embrace traditional customs in rebellion against the modern-day common sense of their parents. *Purgatory* returns to the Naturalism of *The Land of Heart's Desire* and *Cathleen ni Houlihan* – the ruined house, after all, was clearly an Ascendancy Big House and its former glory of the eighteenth century, another link to those earlier plays, set as they were in the late eighteenth century. Roles within the family were reversed in those earlier plays; the elder generation embodying middle-class values of financial prudence and civic rectitude, the younger generation breaking from these through the lure of ancient myths their elders had discarded. John Butler Yeats could never have been accused of financial prudence but his subscription to Mill acknowledged the precedence of science over religion, and liberal democracy as the supreme mode of political organisation. Of course, the parents in both of those early Yeats plays remain steeped in religious piety but the principles of John Butler Yeats identified a general cultural framework within which their accommodation of religion to financial imperatives became plausible. It was against this compromise that the young react in *The Land of Heart's Desire* and *Cathleen ni Houlihan*. As a play that carried the memory of this ambivalence between revolution and return, *Purgatory* was Yeats's last turn back to the excitement of the Symbolist revolution in the 1890s, a movement that looked back to the medieval in moving beyond Naturalism. The decision to produce the play at the Abbey in 1938 with *On Baile's Strand* was entirely appropriate for history was represented in an Oedipal frame in the 1903 play.[49] David Vanderwerken points out that the myth of ritual sacrifice in both plays is displaced: unlike the sacrifice of Abraham, the killing of the Boy proves of no redeeming purpose.[50]

---

[49] John D'Ambrosio suggests that Yeats's role in the psychoanalytic relation shifted from that of patient in *On Baile's Strand* to father–psychoanalyst in *Purgatory*, the sexual union of the parents remaining hidden in the first play, put on view in the later. 'William Butler Yeats's Evolving Drama of Self-Analysis: The Psychoanalytic Process of *On Baile's Strand* and *Purgatory*', *Literature and Psychology*, 39:1–2 (1993), 49–50.

[50] David L. Vanderwerken, '*Purgatory*: Yeats's Modern Tragedy', *Colby Library Quarterly*, 10: 5 (1974), 266–7. For further discussion of the inversion of *On Baile's Strand* in *Purgatory* see Taylor, *The Drama of W. B. Yeats*, p. 195.

The marks of those great changes in nineteenth-century European society are inscribed in the interior landscape of *Purgatory*. As with many of the later plays, *Purgatory* is characterised by a subtle interaction of commentary, retreat and consequence. In its esoteric form, it offers judgement upon the rise of mass culture while retreating from it; in its violent self-implosion, it appears consequent upon that historical development. *Purgatory* is distinguished from all Yeats plays after *Cathleen ni Houlihan* in the collapse of its mythic narrative structure.[51] This has contributed in significant measure to the positive critical reception this play has received by contrast to the rest of Yeats's drama. It was consistent with the determination Yeats expressed to Ethel Mannin to give voice to 'the barbarism of truth' in *On the Boiler*.[52] Barbarism intimated not simply the Old Man's views, his murderous action or the decline into which the great house has sunk in *Purgatory*, but it also points up the vulgarity of staging before him the sexual act in which he was conceived. The mythic frame served to deflect this in *On Baile's Strand*; abandoning it in *Purgatory*, Yeats brought before his audience the vision of reality we encounter at the end of *The Death of Cuchulain* without any heroic sentiment, lending credence to Francisco Ribelles's sense of the play's hopelessness and absurdity.[53] This is perhaps the most striking manner in which the play anticipates the drama of Beckett, enclosing birth and death together in the family circle. In character and action, the Old Man embodies the sentiment opening Beckett's 1979 work, *A Piece of Monologue*: 'Birth was the death of him.'[54] The achievement of *Purgatory* that paved the way for Beckett was in managing to create the sense of historical trauma through the transgression of a primary Oedipal taboo prerequisite to conventional forms of representation. In this way, the play resonated the tone of Strindberg, Kokoschka and Toller.

This crisis of perception, a sign both of Strindberg's influence and Yeats's response to the new physics, was central to *Purgatory* because historical pressures weigh so heavily on the play. All is laid bare; the audience exposed to the most unpalatable elements, the Old Man killing his own son at the same moment he witnesses the moment of his own conception. None of this was cloaked in myth – he stabs the Boy without any pretence

---

[51] Anthony Bradley has identified its effectiveness in the fact that the characters are human rather than mythic. *William Butler Yeats*, p. 235.
[52] Yeats to Ethel Mannin, 17 December 1937. Wade, *The Letters*, p. 903.
[53] Torres Ribelles, 'Predetermination and Nihilism', p. 147. See also Gutierrez, 'Ghosts Benefic and Malign', p. 47.
[54] Beckett, *The Complete Dramatic Works*, p. 425.

of ceremony and sees himself a murderer. The Oedipal frame for the Old Man's violence encourages the Boy's view that he was indeed mad, one of the reasons no doubt why Yeats distanced himself from identification with him as the revised drafts of the play indicate.[55] Yet the conditions under which the Boy's judgement is made are altered so as to bring it into question as we move from the first prose scenario to the final draft version of the play. In the original version, the Old Man gives a coherent version of the history attached to the house; the figures he identifies as the ghosts of his parents seem characteristic of nineteenth-century gothic literature, spirits returned from the past. In the final verse draft, however, this historical contextualisation is greatly reduced. It is less certain whether the audience is exposed to the deranged perspective of the Old Man, a representation of particular historical events, or a mediated representation of the latter through the former. In the prose version, for example, we learn early on that the Old Man and the Boy are pedlars; the Old Man's present status is only fleetingly alluded to in the final version, in which the emphasis is much more assuredly focused on his lament for former glories lost.[56] Additionally, the Old Man accuses the Boy of stealing his money in the prose draft, a claim absent in the final version.[57] These aspects colour the Old Man in the hues of the stable-man father he has killed rather than the aristocratic mother he laments. Any claim that we encounter the voice of Yeats himself in the figure of the Old Man needs to take into account the distance of his characterisation in the original version from those figures celebrated as Irish nobility in *On the Boiler*.

Critics have commented upon the dramatic effectiveness of the play's temporal structure, the intensity achieved from bringing everything to a single location in a single instant, amplified by the circular pattern of repetition.[58] This is nothing new in Yeats's drama – *Deirdre*, *At the Hawk's Well*, *The Dreaming of the Bones* and *Calvary* all concentrate upon a single instant. What is striking about *Purgatory* is its refusal to accord any transformative power to the intensity of the single moment, utterly unlike the suicide of *Deirdre*, for example. Related to this is the nakedly pathological aspect to repetition in the play. Patrick Keane attributes this

---

[55] Sandra F. Siegel notes that in the process of revising his character, Yeats created a figure who becomes more and more self-deluded, one who is, unlike his creator, 'wholly ignorant of himself'. *Purgatory: Manuscript Materials*, p. 25. See also Howes, *Yeats's Nations*, p. 181.
[56] Yeats, *Purgatory: Manuscript Materials*, p. 37.
[57] *Ibid.*, p. 49.
[58] See, for example, Bradley, *William Butler Yeats*, p. 236; Ure, *Yeats the Playwright*, p. 111. Oppel, 'Yeats's *Purgatory*', p. 14.

to the negative underside of Nietzsche's idea of eternal recurrence, the dread of perpetual entrapment in a cyclical pattern that was the lot of 'the lower orders'.⁵⁹ This, however, is to deny the play any effective historicity. Whatever significance attaches to cyclical pattern in the play, it can only have meaning with reference to a linear historical pattern of aristocratic decline and growth in middle-class influence. Indeed, it is not entirely beyond the bounds of possibility to detect behind the Old Man's eccentricity the banalities of a thwarted middle-class aspiration to upper-class grandeur and determination to rid himself of lower-class associations. In any case, an irreversible historical shift has taken place, bearing obvious relation to 1930s Ireland. The Old Man's pathology derives from his inability to come to terms with this altered landscape, leaving him perpetually entrapped in the sordid moment of his begetting. Frances Oppel accurately discerns a pattern of repetition and reduction governing the play in which the house 'is reduced to a ruin, the tree to a stick, the hero to a tattered peddler, his son to a thief' and in which the Old Man returns to the scene of his begetting as do the spirits of his parents.⁶⁰ This pattern of reduction, however, moves *against* that of repetition – one points to a historical process of degeneration, the other to a suspension of chronology. The effect is one of distortion within which the very denial of historical process on the part of the Old Man becomes a symptom of the historical process he seeks to arrest through the murder of his son. Here again Yeats anticipates Beckett in an important aspect – the combination of stasis and slow decay in *Waiting For Godot*.

Even in the brief space of time the play affords us and despite the darkness of its mood, nothing prepares the audience for the murderous act in *Purgatory*. Like the Blind Man stabbing Cuchulain in Yeats's final play, it is interventionist rather than culminatory. That Yeats wished to achieve a shock-effect was evidenced in the fact that he moved from an original intention to have the Old Man strangle the Boy after the Boy approaches him slowly to have him instead stab the Boy with an old jack-knife without any warning.⁶¹ Yeats employs the same strategy again in *The Death of Cuchulain* – instead of Emer inflicting a final blow on the wounded warrior, the Blind Man suddenly appears on stage to do the dirty deed. The Old Man's action appears mechanical and automated, as if in a trance. This is reinforced by the child-like lullaby into which he breaks immediately following the murder, an echo back to the uncanny voice of the

---

⁵⁹ Keane, *Yeats's Interactions*, p. 161. ⁶⁰ Oppel, 'Yeats's *Purgatory*', p. 16.
⁶¹ Yeats, *Purgatory: Manuscript Materials*, p. 53, 198.

child Lulu from *The Words upon the Window-pane*, itself recollecting the baby voice of the colonel's demented wife in Strindberg's *The Ghost Sonata* (*VPl*, 1048). The murder is the most dramatic instance in Yeats's drama of 'the murderous innocence of the sea' of which he writes in 'The Second Coming'. A symptom of the automatisation of human beings in modern industrial society, it expresses the crisis of modernity as the sudden interruption of a primitive barbarism that can yet never recuperate the condition of primitive innocence. It enacts a critical genealogical rupture in the very attempt to sustain the integrity of family. Howes states that *Purgatory* represents the culmination of Yeats's eugenicist theory of nationality as kindred.[62] In fact, the pathology of *Purgatory* is driven by the sustained ambivalence between totemism and commodity fetishism haunting Yeats's drama from its inception and determining its configuration of modernity. As the façade of an impervious historical process, kindred is weighted with the cold automatism of a mechanised humanity that can only lead to the murder we encounter in *Purgatory*; as the re-emergence of totemistic power in the modern era, this automatism remains a subject of fascination for Yeats throughout.

The power of *Purgatory* derives from the cluster of influences it manages to sustain in such a brief space. Political, biographical, scientific and philosophical considerations are harnessed into a single moment of violent transgression. Each of these aspects is interrelated – occult questions of perception, for example, are given new relevance in the understanding of Einstein's theory that Yeats garnered through Bertrand Russell in the 1920s. Most importantly, the political meaning of *Purgatory* links back to the radicalism of the early Yeats, given the extent to which the reactionary elements of *On the Boiler* owe their influence to Ruskin's *Fors Clavigera*, a work at once radical and reactionary that was greatly significant to William Morris, one of the most formative influences on the young Yeats. In those Expressionist aspects Yeats found in Strindberg and Toller, and in the ground it laid for Beckett's extraordinary achievements after the war, *Purgatory* was, along with *The Death of Cuchulain*, Yeats's final representation of contemporary history as farce. The Old Man's folly in attempting to reverse a process of degenerative commercialism through a sacrificial act appears a parody of sacrificial redemption, like the Blind Man stabbing Cuchulain in Yeats's last play. Its estranging effect in the theatre was Yeats's final contribution to a revolution that began in the 1890s with the contest of Naturalism and Symbolism.

[62] Howes, *Yeats's Nations*, p. 176.

Conclusion

Whatever their shortcomings for theatre-goers today, Yeats's plays contributed significantly to the major developments in European theatre between 1890 and 1939, including Naturalism, Symbolism, Expressionism and Surrealism. Constantly experimenting with new forms, he was attentive to the evolution of theatre as a medium through which the forces shaping European society of his time could be represented in ways that did not compromise its artistic values. The treatment of perception in *Purgatory* is strongly indebted to the drama of Strindberg and Maeterlinck in its preoccupation with blindness and vision. His themes of will and passivity in several of the later plays developed in line with Expressionism as the evolution of two competing forces within the drama of Ibsen – revolutionary collectivism and revolutionary individualism. The elements of farce that become pronounced after *The Green Helmet* owe much to an interest in medieval grotesque Yeats shared with Jarry, and the Automatic Writing experiment that produced plays such as *The Only Jealousy of Emer* and *Calvary* aligned Yeats in significant ways with French Surrealism.

These influences and interactions were mediated through Yeats's esotericism. Rather than isolating his drama from patterns of social change, however, his absorption in the writings of Swedenborg, Blake and the Upanishads enabled a theatre of estrangement reflecting in unique ways structures of power and forms of collective energy represented more directly elsewhere. James Longenbach comments that poems such as 'The Second Coming' 'have seemed to several generations of readers to be completely idiosyncratic, bound up with Yeats's occult vision of the afterlife, and at the same time an expression of horror in which an entire culture could participate'.[1] The same could be said of Yeats's later plays, testifying how effectively he shaped esoteric symbolism in both his poetry

---

[1] James Longenbach, 'Modern Poetry', *The Cambridge Companion to Modernism*, ed. Michael Levenson (Cambridge University Press, 1999), p. 111.

and drama, creating moods of estrangement and a sense of disturbance that captured the turmoil of European society since 1914 in a very peculiar way. As Fredric Jameson, Franco Morretti and Marshall Berman have argued, the adequacy of realism to historical representation was straining as this turmoil deepened.[2] Yeats's theatre of ritual from the 1900s – laying the foundations for his radical Noh experiments in subsequent decades – was a progressively more determined attempt to develop forms of theatre that might give symbolic expression to the historical forces defining the age. This did not involve outright repudiation of the Naturalist revolution but its incorporation into a more far-reaching Symbolist project in which the medium of theatre itself became subject to the kinds of disturbance Ibsen had directed against the social order in his day.

Yeats's criticism of international art was sincerely held, believing as he did that literary expression divorced from locality would struggle to find perspective on the underlying patterns of contemporary historical experience, and instead become absorbed in its ephemeral surface moments. This, however, did not disguise the extent to which, as playwright at least, he worked in constant dialogue with new developments in London, Paris and throughout the European continent. Rather than regard in his artistic commitment to Irish popular and heroic literary traditions a determination to withstand the 'filthy, modern tide', the experimental forms he adopted on stage in giving these traditions new life indicate a desire for Ireland's prominence within European modernism, the necessity of engaging new thought, speculation and experiment if its claims to nationhood were to find artistic justification. This was clear from his response to the clamour for censorship that pressurised Free State minister Kevin O'Higgins into creating the Committee For Evil Literature in 1926:

> To some extent Ireland but shows in acute form the European problem, and must seek a remedy where the best minds of Europe seek it – in audacity of speculation and creation. We must consider anew the foundations of existence, bring to the discussion – diplomacies and prudences put away – all relevant thought.[3]

---

[2] See Fredric Jameson, 'Beyond the Cave: Demystifying the Ideology of Modernism', *The Ideologies of Theory: Essays 1971–1986*, vol. II (London: Routledge Press, 1989), pp. 115–32; Franco Morretti, 'The Long Goodbye: *Ulysses* and the End of Liberal Capitalism', *Signs Taken for Wonders: Essays in the Sociology of Literary Forms*, trans. Susan Fischer, David Forgacs and David Miller (London: Verso, 1983), pp. 182–208. Berman sees avant-garde modernism as 'realism' for the historical circumstances in which it emerged. *All That is Solid Melts into Air: The Experience of Modernity*, 2nd edn (London: Verso, 1983), pp. 87–129.

[3] Yeats, 'The Need for Audacity of Thought', p. 201.

This 'European problem' included the expansion of the Soviet Union and Mussolini's accession to power in 1922 but Yeats had in mind here a deeper pattern of which these major political developments were symptomatic – the suppression of free thought and decline of imaginative vitality as the modern idea of the state subject became entrenched through the instruments of the state itself, the press and, in certain countries, the church. Yeats held some sympathy for the state suspension of individual liberties in the Soviet Union and Fascist Italy in breaking up liberal democracy, yet lamented the prospect that the worst element of democracy might expand rather than diminish – the culture of uniformity it created in the name of freedom.

Yeats's tragedies and the tension between tragedy and farce in his later plays exemplified those tensions between nationhood and modernity in several peripheries of metropolitan Europe at the end of the nineteenth century, including Ireland, Scandinavia and Hungary. Modern tragedy being, in Terry Eagleton's view, an essentially transitional literary form, Yeats's tragedies, and the complex nature of their staging, marked the social disjunctions effected by a rapidly expanded industrial economy on agricultural and maritime communities at the start of the last century.[4] If this suggests a drama of the periphery for which the obscurity of the occult seemed appropriate, it also anticipates a later and alternative internationalism in which the Enlightenment rationalist assurance of modern Europe would be challenged by 'Asiatic immensities', vast, ancient civilisations impressing themselves more directly upon the European mind as commerce became more thoroughly global through the tentacles of Empire. Those cultural interchanges of Irish, Greek, Arabian, Indian, Tibetan and Japanese traditions evident in the varieties of experiment Yeats adopted in the plays were more than exotic embellishments; not only a means of sharpening a consciousness of human alienation engendered through commerce and state regulation, they also suggested new forms of religious and cultural expression that might reinvigorate Christian traditions grown lethargic in Europe.

The attitudes to race informing some of the later plays, particularly *Purgatory*, suggest deeply conservative political instincts. Yeats's interest in eugenicism and some of the views expressed in *On the Boiler* appear to confirm this, pointing to a strong leaning in the direction of Fascism.

---

[4] Terry Eagleton, *Sweet Violence: The Idea of the Tragic* (Oxford: Blackwell Press, 2003), p. 145. As John Orr notes, the struggle between individual and family preoccupied several of the major playwrights native to these regions, including Ibsen, Chekhov, Synge and Yeats himself. *Tragic Drama and Modern Society* (London: Palgrave-Macmillan, 1981), p. xvii.

The emergence of the Blueshirts in Ireland certainly awakened his enthusiasm. In August 1933, he wrote to Edmund Dulac that Ireland was 'in the excitement of "the blue shirts". Fashist ideas started up in the country some two or three months ago & now they cannot make the shirts fast enough.'[5] Earlier that year he wrote to Olivia Shakespear of politics 'growing heroic' in Ireland, with the coming to power of de Valera forcing political thought to face the most fundamental issues. His case for 'despotic rule of the educated classes as the only end of our troubles', the argument of *On the Boiler*, is made here but under request that it be kept secret.[6] In January 1931, Thomas Sturge Moore reported Wyndham Lewis's impressions of the Nazis to Yeats, commenting on their 'unbelievable' enthusiasm, noting their intention to denounce the Versailles Treaty and legislate against Jews, seeming to Moore 'a refreshing crowd'.[7] Despite the overstated case for anti-semitism in Yeats that W. J. McCormack sets out in *Blood Kindred*, he is correct in countering R. F. Foster's claim that there was no evidence for it. McCormack himself overlooks one glaring instance, a letter to Olivia Shakespear of August 1931 in which he considers H. S. Ede's *Savage Messiah* as typical of the generation of Henri Bergson: 'I am full of admiration and respect, but I hate the Jewish element in Bergson, the deification of the moment, that for minds less hard and masculine than Gaudier's turned the world into fruit-salad.'[8]

How deep this sentiment ran is a matter of debate – unlike many other thinkers of his era, Yeats never denounced usury in his criticism of the commercialisation of modern life. His initial support for Franco was motivated largely by his deep aversion to British Imperial policies in the 1930s, particularly in regard to India. In a letter to Ethel Mannin, he hinted that his 'Fenian' leanings would support Franco's victory because it might weaken the Empire, forcing Britain to grant India independence. All this was 'mere instinct', however, upon which he had no intention to act; Yeats expressed his horror at modern politics – 'nothing but the manipulation of popular enthusiasm by false news' – a horror deepened by revelations of what had seemed British government subterfuge in Joseph Maloney's *The Forged Diaries of Roger Casement*.[9] With its claim of forgery, the book

---

[5] W. B. Yeats Collection, HRHRC.
[6] Yeats to Olivia Shakespear, 13 July 1933. Wade, *The Letters*, p. 812.
[7] Moore to Yeats, 11 January 1931. Bridges, *W. B. Yeats and T. Sturge Moore*, p. 167.
[8] Yeats to Olivia Shakespear, 2 August 1931. Wade, *The Letters*, p. 782. Foster denies any anti-semitic or pro-Nazi undertone to *On the Boiler*. *W. B. Yeats*, vol. II, p. 631.
[9] Yeats to Mannin, Riversdale, 11 February 1937. Wade, *The Letters*, p. 881. Cullingford argues that the letter shows how what seems pro-Fascist was, in fact, anti-English, refuting O'Brien's claim

prompted Yeats's poem on Casement which appeared in February 1937 in de Valera's *Irish Press*.[10]

In a 1935 Radio Eireann broadcast, Yeats remembered the Dublin from which the Irish Revival started out as 'a vile hole' where 'Unionist Ireland was a shabby and pretentious England' and 'Nationalist Ireland was torn with every kind of political passion and prejudice'. He went on to describe the new Dublin as 'an Irish Capital with vigorous thought of a Capital city, to some extent a European Capital'.[11] In significant measure, the tone of invective he directed against political democracy in *On the Boiler* was consistent with this: for all its shortcomings, Yeats still felt Irish culture of the 1930s was in a better state than that of England. In the pamphlet he contrasts with derision the oratorical skills of Lloyd George against those of the ancient Greeks, symptomatic of a prevailing degeneracy he observed in British society.[12] At the same time, Yeats became terrified of the consequences for political and cultural life in Ireland should the Blueshirts return victorious from Spain. He wrote to Mannin in March 1937 of his trepidation at the rise of the Catholic Front, their demand that de Valera recognise the legitimate authority of Franco immediately, and their characterisation of the Abbey as a pagan institution: 'A friar or monk has already threatened us with mob violence.'[13]

This study of the plays shows the extent to which Yeats's later race attitudes, however unpalatable, were rooted in an early radicalism. His theatrical experiments represent through the states of trance into which characters enter the petrifaction of human experience in a European society increasingly saturated by commodities and dominated by industrial production. Yeats's idea of race as instinctive automatism encapsulated his response to the mechanisation of human society as the manifestation of a primeval worship of the fetish. Under the influence of Morris's socialism and engaging the Symbolist techniques of Maeterlinck and Villiers de l'Isle Adam, he shifted the focus of Ibsen's criticism of modern values from urban to rural settings. In so doing, he sought a way of representing a discreet process driving the commercialisation of modern culture while

---

that Yeats would have supported Germany in the war had he lived. *Yeats, Ireland and Fascism*, p. 219.

[10] For further discussion of Yeats's response to Maloney's claim, see McCormack, *Blood Kindred*, pp. 173–81; Foster, *W. B. Yeats*, vol. II, pp. 571–5.

[11] W. B. Yeats, 'The Irish Literary Movement'. Radio Eireann Broadcast, 12 October 1935. *Collected Works of W. B. Yeats*, vol. x, ed. Colton Johnson (New York: Scribner, 2000), pp. 254–8.

[12] Yeats, *On the Boiler*, p. 18.

[13] Yeats to Ethel Mannin, 1 March 1937. Wade, *The Letters*, p. 885.

also developing forms of theatrical space in opposition to a general state and commercial regulation of social space.

However much at odds with nineteenth-century materialism, Yeats's work in the theatre bore testimony to the legacy of Marx and elements of Freud's theory of the unconscious, particularly in regard to fetishism and childhood. This was evident right into the later phase of his career. In his 1931 essay on Swift, Yeats saw in Marx and Sorel the argument for 'a return to a primeval state, a beating down of all into a single class' (*VPl*, 962). As alluded to previously in Chapter 4, in late 1917 he and his wife wondered whether the terms coming through the Automatic Script shared a correspondence with Freud's theory of the subconscious. Yeats's ideas on race, and the reactionary undercurrent they undoubtedly carried, emerged out of this radical critique. In taking as its point of departure a report in *The Irish Times* that the Galway Library Committee suggested burning the works of George Bernard Shaw on the grounds that nobody would read them, *On the Boiler* identified a radical political origin from which the reactionary eugenicist aspects of the essay had evolved.[14] Whatever the truth of the report, it conjured an image of the Nazi book burnings of 1933, particularly resonant given Shaw's long commitment to Fabian socialism. Less dramatically but perhaps more despairingly in an Irish context, it bespoke the failure to achieve the revolutionary nationalist goal of an Ireland at once artistically creative, culturally vibrant and politically liberated that drove Yeats in the early 1900s.

Given Yeats's openness to experiments on stage, his full participation in debates on theatrical reform in the pages of *The Dome* and *The New Age*, and his persistent willingness to engage the traditions of other cultures, the significance of his achievement in the theatre deserves greater acknowledgement, notwithstanding his experimental failures. Considered in the context of the years in which they were written and first performed, they tell us much about the complex nature of Yeats's political thought and the sophisticated nature of his critique of modern European civilisation hidden within the arcana of his esoteric symbolism. Differences in degree of political allegiance notwithstanding, his drama partook of the profound attack on modern values evident in the Expressionism of Strindberg, Kokoschka and Toller, the Surrealism of Jarry, and the Absurdism of Pirandello. The nature of Yeats's relation to Irish nationalism expressed in *The Countess Cathleen*, *Cathleen ni Houlihan* and *The King's Threshold*, as well as his later ideas on race in *Purgatory*, were particular articulations of

---

[14] Yeats, *On the Boiler*, pp. 10–11.

this more general critique. His hostility to liberal democracy and its influence upon artistic practices was certainly reactionary in later years, but derived from a critical response to commodity fetishism driving much of his mystical interests, a position that brought him close to Marx's thought in his early years, *via* Morris, as well as to the anarchism of Kropotkin. Yeats's sense of the commercialisation of modern civilisation as primitive totemism reawakened continued to inform his creative work in later years but in circumstances in which it was more difficult to voice this sense through any doctrine of political emancipation that would not quickly sound like the propagandist rhetoric he abhorred. In their experiments with voice, mask, dance and space, the late plays showed, among other things, Yeats's hatred of the violation of language he saw in political propaganda, in large measure for its dissembling transparency. The violence of *Purgatory* and the anti-representational nature of its theatrical form was a final expression of this sentiment as a Europe riven by Fascism, Stalinism and a pusillanimous liberalism descended once more into all-out war.

Bibliography

Adams, Hazard, 'Yeats and Antithetical Nationalism', *Literature and Nationalism* (Liverpool University Press, 1991).
Adorno, Theodor W., *Aesthetic Theory*, ed. Gretel Adorno and Rolf Tiedemann, trans. Robert Hullot-Kentor (London: The Athlone Press, 1997).
   Quasi una Fantasia: Essays on Modern Music, 2nd edn, trans. Rodney Livingstone (London: Verso, 1998).
   'Theses Against Occultism', *The Stars Down to Earth and other Essays on the Irrational in Culture*, ed. Stephen Crook (London: Routledge Press, 1994).
Adorno, Theodor W. and Max Horkheimer, 'The Concept of Enlightenment', *Dialectic of Enlightenment* (London: Allen Lane, 1973).
A.E. (George Russell), *The National Being: Some Thoughts on Irish Polity* (Dublin: Maunsel, 1916).
Albright, Daniel, *Myth Against Myth: A Study of Yeats's Imagination in Old Age* (Oxford University Press, 1972).
   'The Fool by the Pool', *Yeats Annual*, vol. VII, ed. Warwick Gould (London: Macmillan Press, 1990).
   Untwisting the Serpent: Modernism in Music, Literature, and Other Arts (The University of Chicago Press, 2000).
Anderson, Perry, 'Modernism and Revolution', *The New Left Review*, 144 (1984).
Bachelard, Gaston, *The Poetics of Space*, trans. Maria Jolas (Boston: Beacon Press, 1969).
Bacigalupo, Massimo, 'Yeats and the "Quarrel over Ruskin"', *Ruskin and the Twentieth Century: The Modernity of Ruskinism*, ed. Toni Cerutti (Vercelli: Edizioni Mercurio, 2000).
Badiou, Alain, *Ethics: An Essay on the Understanding of Evil*, trans. Peter Hallward (London: Verso, 2001).
Bair, Deirdre, *Samuel Beckett: A Biography* (London: Jonathan Cape, 1978).
Bakhtin, Mikhail, *Rabelais and His World*, trans. Helene Iswolsky (Cambridge, MA: MIT Press, 1968).
Balakian, Anna, *The Symbolist Movement: A Critical Appraisal* (New York University Press, 1977).
Barta, Szilvia, 'The Comedy of the Tragic: Anticipations of the Theatre of the Absurd in William Butler Yeats's *The Death of Cuchulain*', *Anachronist* (1999).

Baudrillard, Jean, *For a Critique of the Political Economy of the Sign*, trans. Charles Levin (St Louis: Telos Press, 1981).
Symbolic Exchange and Death, trans. Iain Hamilton Grant (London: Sage Publications, 1993).
The System of Objects, trans. James Benedict (London: Verso, 1996).
Beckett, Samuel, *An Exhibition*, Reading University Library, May–July, 1971 (London: Turret Books, 1971).
Molloy, Malone Dies, the Unnamable, 2nd edn (London: Calder Publications, 1994).
Selection from Samuel Beckett's Work, ed. Richard W. Seaver (New York: Grove Weidenfeld, 1976).
The Complete Dramatic Works (London: Faber, 1986).
Beerbohm, Max, 'The Irish Players', *W.B. Yeats: The Critical Heritage*, ed. Norman Jeffares (London: Routledge Press, 1977).
Benjamin, Walter, 'On Language as Such and on the Language of Man', *One-Way Street and Other Writings*, trans. Edmund Jephcott and Kingsley Shorter (London: Verso, 1985).
'Surrealism', *One-Way Street and Other Writings*, trans. Edmund Jephcott and Kinglsey Shorter (London: New Left Books, 1979).
'Theses on the Philosophy of History', *Illuminations*, ed. Hannah Arendt, trans. Harry Zorn (London: Pimlico Press, 1999).
'The Work of Art in the Age of Mechanical Reproduction', *Illuminations*, ed. Hannah Arendt, trans. Harry Zorn (London: Pimlico Press, 1999).
Bentley, Eric, *In Search of Theater* (New York: Vintage, 1947).
Bergmann Loizeaux, Elizabeth, *Yeats and the Visual Arts* (New York: Syracuse University Press, 2003).
Berman, Marshall, *All That is Solid Melts into Air: The Experience of Modernity*, 2nd edn (London: Verso, 1983)
Binyon, Laurence, 'Mr Bridges' "Prometheus" and Poetic Drama', *The Dome*, 2 (1899).
Bjersby, Birgit, *The Interpretation of the Cuchulain Legend in the Works of W.B. Yeats*, (Dublin: Hodges Figgis, 1950).
Blavatsky, Helena Petrovna, *The Secret Doctrine: The Synthesis of Science, Religion, and Philosophy*, vol. II (Point Lama, CA: The Aryan Theosophical Press, 1925).
Block, Haskell M., 'Symbolist Drama: Villiers de l'Isle-Adam, Strindberg, and Yeats', *New York Literary Forum*, 4 (1980).
Bohlmann, Otto, *Yeats and Nietzsche: An Exploration of Major Nietzschean Echoes in the Writings of W.B. Yeats* (London: Macmillan Press, 1982).
Bonafous-Murat, Carle, 'The Reception of W.B. Yeats in France', *The Reception of W.B. Yeats in Europe*, ed. Klaus Peter Jochum (London: Continuum Press, 2006).
Boyce, D.G., *Nationalism in Ireland*, 3rd edn (London: Routledge, 1995).
Bradley, Anthony, *William Butler Yeats* (New York: Ungar Press, 1979).
Bradshaw, David, 'British Writers and Anti-Fascism in the 1930s: II, Under the Hawk's Wing', *Woolf Studies Annual*, 4 (1998).

Brearton, Fran, *The Great War in Irish Poetry: From W. B. Yeats to Michael Longley* (Oxford University Press, 2000).
Brecht, Bertolt, *Brecht on Theatre: The Development of an Aesthetic*, ed. and trans. John Willet (London: Methuen Press, 1964).
  Collected Plays, vol. II, ed. John Willett and Ralph Mannheim (London: Methuen Press, 1994).
Bridges, Ursula, *W. B. Yeats and T. Sturge Moore: Their Correspondence, 1901–1937* (London: Routledge and Kegan Paul, 1953).
Bronfen, Elisabeth, *Over Her Dead Body* (Manchester University Press, 1992).
Brook, Peter, *The Empty Space* (London: Penguin Press, 1990).
Brown, Terence, *The Life of W. B. Yeats: A Critical Biography* (Dublin: Gill & Macmillan, 1999).
Buchelt, Lisabeth C., 'Alchemical and Tarot Imagery in Yeats's Later Plays: *The Resurrection* and *A Full Moon in March*', *Cauda Pavonis: Studies in Hermeticism*, 16:1 (1997).
Buck-Morss, Susan, *The Dialectics of Seeing* (Cambridge, MA: MIT, 1990).
Bushrui, Suheil, '*The King's Threshold*: A Defence of Poetry', *Review of English Literature*, 4:3 (1963).
  'Yeats: The Poet as Hero', *Essays & Studies 1982: The Poet's Power* (London: Murray, 1982).
Cairns, David and Shaun Richards, *Writing Ireland: Colonialism, Nationalism and Culture* (Manchester University Press, 1988).
Caldwell, Helen, *Michio Ito: The Dancer and His Dances* (Berkeley CA: University of California Press, 1977).
Cardew, A. L., 'Symbolist Drama and the Problem of Symbolism', unpublished PhD thesis, Essex University (1980).
Cave, Richard Allen, Review of W. B. Yeats, *The Herne's Egg: Manuscript Materials*, ed. Alison Armstrong, *Yeats Annual*, vol. XII, ed. Warwick Gould (London: Macmillan, 1996).
  'Staging *The King's Threshold*', *Yeats Annual*, vol. XIII, ed. Warwick Gould (London: Macmillan, 1998).
  Yeats's Late Plays: 'A High Grave Dignity and Strangeness' (London: The British Academy, 1983).
Chekhov, Anton, *The Cherry Orchard*, trans. Michael Frayn (London: Methuen, 1978).
  Three Sisters, Anton Chekhov: Five Plays, trans. Ronald Hingley (Oxford University Press, 1998).
Chesterton, G. K., 'The Hieroglyphics of Innocence', *To-Day*, ed. Holbrook Jackson, 1:2 (1917).
Clark, David R. and Rosalind Clark, *W. B. Yeats and the Theatre of Desolate Reality*, rev. edn (Washington: Catholic University of America Press, 1993).
Clark, Rosalind E., 'Yeats's *The Only Jealousy of Emer* and the Old Irish *Serglige Con Culainn*', *Yeats: An Annual of Critical and Textual Studies*, 8 (1990).
Clarke, Austin, *The Celtic Twilight and the Nineties* (Dublin: the Dolmen Press, 1969).

Clarke, Brenna Katz and Harold Ferrar, *The Dublin Drama League, 1919–1941* (Dublin: The Dolmen Press, 1979).
Clarke, Norma, 'Strenuous Idleness: Thomas Carlyle and the Man of Letters as Hero', *Manful Assertions: Masculinities in Britain since 1800*, ed. Michael Roper and John Tosh (London: Routledge Press, 1991).
Clinton, Alan Ramon, *Mechancial Occult: Automatism, Modernism, and the Specter of Politics* (New York: Peter Lang, 2004).
Connolly, James, 'National Drama', *The United Irishman*, 10:243 (1903).
Cornillier, Pierre Émile, *The Survival of the Soul, and Its Evolution after Death* (London: Kegan Paul, 1922).
Coxhead, Elizabeth, *Lady Gregory: A Literary Portrait* (London: Macmillan Press, 1961).
Craig, Edward Gordon, 'Foreword', *A Living Theatre: The Gordon Craig School: The Arena: Goldoni: The Mask* (Florence: Edward Gordon Craig, 1913).
  'Realism and the Actor', *On the Art of the Theatre* (London: Heinemann, 1911).
  'The Actor and the Über-marionette', *On the Art of the Theatre* (London: Heinemann, 1911).
  Towards a New Theatre: Forty Designs for Stage Scenes with Critical Notes (London: J. M. Dent & Sons, 1913).
Crohn Schmitt, Natalie, 'Ecstasy and Peak Experience: W. B. Yeats, Marghanita Laski, and Abraham Maslow', *Comparative Drama*, 28:2 (1994).
  '"Haunted by Places": Landscape in Three Plays by W. B. Yeats', *Comparative Drama*, 31:3 (1997).
  '"Separating Strangeness" and "Intimacy" in W. B. Yeats's Drama,' *Journal of Dramatic Theory and Criticism*, 15:2 (2001).
Cullingford, Elizabeth Butler, *Yeats, Ireland and Fascism* (London: Macmillan Press, 1981).
D'Ambrosio, John, 'William Butler Yeats's Evolving Drama of Self-Analysis: The Psychoanalytic Process of *On Baile's Strand* and *Purgatory*', *Literature and Psychology*, 39:1–2 (1993).
Daruwala, Maneck H., 'Yeats and the Mask of Deirdre: "That love is all we need"', *Colby Quarterly*, 37:3 (2001).
Dearmer, Nancy, *The Fellowship of the Picture*, ed. Percy Dearmer (London: Nisbet, 1921).
Deleuze, Gilles and Félix Guattari, *Anti-Oedipus: Capitalism and Schizophrenia*, trans. Robert Hurley, Mark Seem and Helen R. Lane (London: Athlone Press, 1984).
De Man, Paul, *Allegories of Reading: Figural Language in Rousseau, Nietzsche, Rilke and Proust* (New Haven: Yale University Press, 1979).
  The Rhetoric of Romanticism (New York: Columbia University Press, 1984).
Derrida, Jacques, *Of Grammatology*, trans. Gayatri Spivak (Baltimore: Johns Hopkins University Press, 1976).
  Specters of Marx, trans. Peggy Kamuf (London: Routledge Press, 1994).
  'Structure, Sign, and Play in the Discourse of the Human Sciences', *The Languages of Criticism and the Sciences of Man*, ed. Richard Macksey and Eugenio Donato (Baltimore: The Johns Hopkins University Press, 1970).

The Post Card: From Socrates to Freud and Beyond, trans. Alan Bass (University of Chicago Press, 1987).
De Saussure, Ferdinand, *Course in General Linguistics*, trans. Roy Harris (London: Duckworth Press, 1983).
Diggory, Terence, 'De Man and Yeats', *Yeats Annual of Critical and Textual Studies*, 8 (1990).
Donoghue, Denis, *The Third Voice: Modern British and American Verse Drama* (London: Oxford University Press, 1959).
'Yeats: The Question of Symbolism', *Myth and Reality*, ed. Joseph Ronsley (Ontario: Wilrid Laurier University Press, 1977).
Doody, Noreen, 'An Echo of Some One Else's Music: The Influence of Oscar Wilde on W. B. Yeats', *The Importance of Reinventing Oscar: Versions of Wilde during the Last 100 Years*, ed. Uive Böker, Richard Corballis and Julie A. Hibbard (Amsterdam: Rodopi, 2002).
'An Influential Involvement: Wilde, Yeats and the French Symbolists', *Critical Ireland*, ed. Aaron Kelly and Alan Gillis (Dublin: Four Courts Press, 2001).
Dorn, Karen, 'Dialogue into Movement: W. B. Yeats's Collaboration with Gordon Craig', *Yeats and the Theatre*, ed. Robert O'Driscoll and Lorna Reynolds (London: Macmillan Press, 1975).
Players and Painted Stage: The Theatre of W. B. Yeats (Sussex: Harvester, 1984).
Dukes, Ashley, 'Modern Dramatists 1 – Bjornson', *The New Age*, 7:21 (1910).
'Modern Dramatists 2 – Strindberg', *The New Age*, 7:22 (1910).
'Modern Dramatists 5 – Arthus Schnitzler', *The New Age*, 7:26 (1910).
Eagleton, Terry, *Crazy John and the Bishop* (Cork University Press in association with Field Day, 1998).
Heathcliff and the Great Hunger: Studies in Irish Culture (London: Verso, 1995).
'Marxism and the Past', *Salmagundi*, Fall–Winter (1985–6).
Sweet Violence: The Idea of the Tragic (Oxford: Blackwell Press, 2003).
Eaves, Gregory N., 'The Anti-Theatre and its Double', *Yeats Annual*, vol. XIII, ed. Warwick Gould (London: Macmillan Press, 1998).
Edwards, Phillip, *Threshold of a Nation* (Cambridge University Press, 1979).
Ellis, Steve, 'Chaucer, Yeats and the Living Voice', *Yeats Annual*, vol. XI, ed. Warwick Gould (London: Macmillan Press, 1995).
Ellis, Sylvia, *The Plays of W. B. Yeats: Yeats and the Dancer* (London: Palgrave-Macmillan, 1994).
Ellmann, Richard, *Yeats: The Man and the Masks*, 2nd edn (London: Faber, 1961).
Engelberg, Edward, *The Vast Design: Patterns in W. B. Yeats's Aesthetic*, 2nd edn (Washington DC: The Catholic University of America Press, 1988).
Farr, Florence, 'The Rites of Astaroth', *The New Age*, 1 (1907).
Faulkner, Peter, *William Morris and W. B. Yeats* (Dublin: The Dolmen Press, 1962).
Fay, Frank J., *Towards a National Theatre: The Dramatic Criticism of Frank J. Fay*, ed. Robert Hogan (Dublin: Dolmen Press, 1970).
Fay, W. G. and Catherine Carswell, *The Fays of the Abbey Theatre: An Autobiographical Record* (London: Rich & Cowan, 1935).

Fehsenfeld, Martha Dow and Lois More Overbeck, eds., *The Letters of Samuel Beckett*, vol. I, *1929–1940* (Cambridge University Press, 2009).
Figgis, Darrell, 'Some Living Poets I – Mr. W. B. Yeats', *The New Age*, 7:14 (1910).
Finneran, Richard J., George Mills Harper and William M. Murphy, eds., *Letters to W. B. Yeats*, 2 vols. (London: Macmillan Press, 1977).
Flannery, James, *W. B. Yeats and the Idea of the Theatre* (London: Macmillan Press, 1976).
  'W. B. Yeats, Gordon Craig and the Visual Arts of the Theatre', *Yeats and the Theatre*, ed. Robert O'Driscoll and Lorna Reynolds (London: Macmillan, 1975).
Foster, John Burt, *Heirs to Dionysus* (Princeton University Press, 1981).
Foster, R. F., *W. B. Yeats, A Life: Apprentice Mage*, vol. I (Oxford University Press, 1998).
  W. B. Yeats, A Life: The Arch-Poet, vol. II (Oxford University Press, 2003).
Foucault, Michel, *Madness and Civilization: A History of Insanity in the Age of Reason*, trans. Richard Howard (London: Tavistock Press, 1967).
  'Space, Knowledge, and Power', interview with Michel Foucault by Paul Rainbow in Michel Foucault, *Power: Essential Works of Foucault 1954–1984*, vol. III, ed. James D. Faubion, trans. Robert Hurley *et al.* (London: Penguin Press, 2002).
  'The Subject and Power', *Power: Essential Works of Foucault 1954–1984*, vol. III, ed. James D. Faubion (London: Penguin Press, 2002).
Frayne, John P., ed., *Uncollected Prose by W. B. Yeats*, vol. I (London: Macmillan Press, 1970).
Frayne, John P. and Colton Johnson, eds., *Uncollected Prose by W. B. Yeats*, vol. II (London: Macmillan Press, 1975).
Frazer, Sir James, *The Golden Bough* (London: Wordsworth Editions, 1993).
  Totemism and Exogamy, vol. I, 2nd edn (London: Macmillan Press, 1910).
  Totemism and Exogamy, vol. IV (London: Macmillan Press, 1910).
Frazier, Adrian, *Behind the Scenes: Yeats, Horniman, and the Struggle for the Abbey Theatre* (Berkeley, CA: University of California Press, 1990).
Freud, Sigmund, *The Interpretation of Dreams*, trans. A. A. Brill (New York: Random House, 1996).
  Totem and Taboo, trans. James Strachey (London: Norton, 1950).
Friedman, Barton R. *Adventures in the Deeps of the Mind: The 'Cuchulain Cycle' of W. B. Yeats* (Guildford: Princeton University Press, 1977).
  'Yeatsian (Meta)physics: The Resurrection and the Irrational', *Yeats: An Annual of Critical and Textual Studies*, 8 (1990).
Garrigan Mattar, Sinéad, 'Frazer, Yeats and the Reconsecration of Folklore', *Sir James Frazer and the Literary Imagination*, ed. Robert Fraser (London: Palgrave-Macmillan, 1991).
  Primitivism, Science, and the Irish Revival (Oxford: Clarendon Press, 2004).
Genet, Jacqueline, 'Yeats's *Deirdre* as a Chess-game and a Poet's Game', *Multiple Worlds, Multiple Words: Essays in Honour of Irene Simon*, ed. Hena Maes-Jelinek, Pierre Michel, Paulette Michel-Michot (University of Liège, 1988).

Gifford, Dona and Robert J. Seidman, *Ulysses Annotated*, 2nd edn (Berkeley, CA: University of California Press, 1988).
Gould, Warwick, John Kelly and Deirdre Twoomey, eds., *The Collected Letters of W. B. Yeats*, vol. II, *1896–1900* (Oxford: Clarendon, 1997).
Gramsci, Antonio, *Selections from the Prison Notebooks of Antonio Gramsci*, ed. and trans. Quintin Hoare and Geoffrey Nowell Smith (London: Lawrence and Wishart, 1971).
Greene, Catherine, 'The Cuchulain Legend in the Plays of W. B. Yeats', unpublished MA thesis, Liverpool University) (1973).
Gregory, Lady Augusta, *Cuchulain of Muirthemne* (London: John Murray, 1903).
Gods and Fighting Men (London: John Murray, 1904).
Our Irish Theatre: A Chapter of Autobiography, 3rd edn (Gerrards Cross: Colin Smythe, 1972).
Grgas, Stipe, 'Tragic Affirmation in Yeats and Nietzsche', *Orbis Litterarum*, 46 (1991).
Grierson, Francis, 'Materialism and Crime', *The New Age*, 17:15 (1910).
Guha, Naresha, *W. B. Yeats: An Indian Approach* (Calcutta: Jadavpur University, 1968).
Gutierrez, Donald, 'Ghosts Benefic and Malign: The Influence of the Noh Theatre on the Three Dance Plays of Yeats', *Forum*, 9:2 (1971).
Gwynn, Stephen, 'The Beginnings of Irish Drama' (1902), *W. B. Yeats: Critical Assessments*, vol. I, ed. David Pierce (Mountfield: Helm Information, 2000).
Hagan, Edward A., 'The Aryan Myth: A Nineteenth-Century Anglo-Irish Will to Power', *Ideology and Ireland in the Nineteenth Century*, ed. Tadhg Foley and Sean Ryder (Dublin: Four Courts Press, 1998).
Haims, Lynn, 'Apocalyptic Vision in Three Late Plays by Yeats', *Southern Review*, 14 (1978).
Hallström, Per, Presentation Speech, 10 December 1923, *Nobel Lectures, Literature, 1901–1967*, ed. Horst Frenz (Amsterdam: Elsevier, 1969).
Hand, Derek, 'Breaking Boundaries, Creating Spaces: W. B. Yeats's *The Words upon the Window-Pane* as a Postcolonial Text', *W. B. Yeats and Postcolonialism*, ed. Deborah Fleming (West Cornwall, CT: Locust Hill Press, 2001).
Harris, Roy, *Language, Saussure and Wittgenstein: How to Play Games with Words* (London: Routledge Press, 1988).
Harris, Susan Canon, *Gender and Modern Irish Drama* (Bloomington IN: Indiana University Press, 2002).
Harvey, David, *The Condition of Postmodernity: An Enquiry into the Origins of Cultural Change* (Oxford: Blackwell Press, 1989).
Hassett, Joseph, *Yeats and the Poetics of Hate* (Dublin: Gill & Macmillan, 1986).
Hastings, Beatrice, 'The Image, Heart's Desire', *The New Age*, 7:22 (1910).
Hegel, G. W. F., *Phenomenology of Spirit*, trans. A. V. Miller (Oxford University Press, 1977).

Heidegger, Martin, 'The Origin of the Work of Art', *Basic Writings*, ed. David Farrell Krell (London: Routledge Press, 1993).
Helmling, Steven, 'Marxist Pleasure: Jameson and Eagleton', *Essays in Postmodern Culture*, ed. Eyal Amiram and John Unsworth (Oxford: Oxford University Press, 1993).
Henn, T. R., *The Lonely Tower: Studies in the Poetry of W. B. Yeats*, 2nd edn (London: Methuen, 1965).
Herford, C. H., 'The Scandanavian Dramatists', *Beltaine*, 1 (1899).
Hevesi, Alexander, 'A Tribute to Craig from Hungarian Theatre', *A Living Theatre: The Gordon Craig School: The Arena: Goldoni: The Mask* (Florence: Edward Gordon Craig, 1913).
Hirsch, Foster, 'The Hearth of the Journey: The Mingling of Orders in the Drama of Yeats and Eliot', *Arizona Quarterly*, 27 (1971).
Hoffman, Daniel, *Barbarous Knowledge* (London: Oxford University Press, 1967).
Hogan, Robert and Richard Burnham, *The Years of O'Casey, 1921–1926: A Documentary History*, Modern Irish Drama, vol. VI (Newark: University of Delaware, 1992).
Hogan, Robert and James Kilroy, eds., *The Irish Literary Theatre, 1899–1901* (Dublin: Dolmen, 1975).
Hogan, Robert and Michael J. O'Neill, *Joseph Holloway's Abbey Theatre: A Selection from His Unpublished Journal 'Impressions of a Dublin Playgoer'* (Dixon, CA: Proscenium Press, 1967).
Holroyd, Michael, *Bernard Shaw: The Search for Love*, vol. I, *1865–1898* (London: Chatto & Windus Press, 1988).
Hone, Joseph, *W. B. Yeats: 1865–1939*, 2nd edn (London: Pelican Press, 1971).
Howes, Marjorie, *Yeats's Nations: Gender, Class, and Irishness* (Cambridge University Press, 1996).
Humble, Malcolm, 'German Contacts and Influences in the Lives and Works of W. B. Yeats and D. H. Lawrence, with Special Reference to Friedrich Nietzsche', unpublished PhD thesis, Cambridge University (1969).
Hunt, Hugh, *The Abbey: Ireland's National Theatre, 1904–1978* (Dublin: Gill and Macmillan, 1979).
Hyman, Stanley Edgar, *The Tangled Bank: Darwin, Marx, Frazer and Freud as Imaginative Writers* (New York: Atheneum Press, 1962).
Ibsen, Henrik, *A Doll's House, Four Major Plays*, trans. James McFarlane and Jens Arup (Oxford University Press, 1981).
  The Collected Works of Henrik Ibsen, vol. VIII, ed. William Archer (London: William Heinemann, 1907).
Iwata, Miki, 'Between Art and Life: W. B. Yeats's Cultural Dilemma in *The King's Threshold*', *Shiron*, 37:6 (1998).
Jackson, Holbrook, 'Failure as a Fine Art', *To-Day*, ed. Holbrook Jackson, 10:55 (1923).
  'Men of To-Day and To-Morrow', *To-Day*, ed. Holbrook Jackson, 1:3 (1917).
  'The War For Reality', *To-Day*, ed. Holbrook Jackson, 9:54 (1923).

Jameson, Fredric, 'Beyond the Cave: Demystifying the Ideology of Modernism', *The Ideologies of Theory: Essays 1971–1986*, vol. II (London: Routledge Press, 1989).
  Late Marxism (London: Verso, 1990).
  Marxism and Form: Twentieth Century Dialectical Theories of Literature (Princeton University Press, 1971).
  Postmodernism, Or the Cultural Logic of Late Capitalism (London: Verso, 1991).
  The Political Unconscious: Narrative as a Socially Symbolic Act (London: Methuen, 1981).
Jarry, Alfred, 'De l'inutilité du théâtre au théâtre', *Mercure de France*, September (1896).
  The Ubu Plays, trans. Kenneth McLeish (London: Nick Hern Books, 1997).
Jeffares, A. Norman, *W. B. Yeats: Man and Poet*, 2nd edn (London: Routledge & Kegan Paul, 1962).
Jeffares, A. Norman and A. S. Knowland, *A Commentary on the Collected Plays of W. B. Yeats* (London: Macmillan Press, 1975).
Jenkins, Angela, 'W. B. Yeats and Irish Mythology', unpublished MA thesis, University of Kent at Canterbury (1980).
Jochum, K. P. S., 'W. B. Yeats's *At the Hawk's Well* and the Dialectic of Tragedy', *Visra-Bharati Quarterly*, 31:1 (1965–66).
Johnson, Josephine, 'Yeats: What Method? An Approach to the Performance of the Plays', *Quarterly Journal of Speech*, 57 (1971).
Joyce, James, *Ulysses*, Bodley Head edition (London: Penguin Press, 1992).
Kant, Immanuel, *Critique of Pure Reason*, 2nd edn, ed. Vasilis Politis (London: Everyman, 1993).
Keane, Patrick J., *Yeats's Interactions with Tradition* (Columbia: University of Missouri Press, 1987).
Keene, Donald, *Noh, the Classical Theatre of Japan* (Tokyo, 1966).
Kelly, John, *A W. B. Yeats Chronology* (London: Palgrave Macmillan, 2003).
Kelly, John and Eric Domville, eds., *The Collected Letters of W. B. Yeats*, vol. I, *1865–1895* (Oxford: Clarendon Press, 1986).
Kelly, John and Ronald Schuchard, eds., *The Collected Letters of W. B. Yeats*, vol. III, 1901–1904 (Oxford: Clarendon Press, 1994).
  The Collected Letters of W. B. Yeats, vol. IV, *1905–1907* (Oxford University Press, 2005).
Kenner, Hugh, *Samuel Beckett: A Critical Study* (Berkeley, CA: University of California Press, 1968).
Kermode, Frank, *Romantic Image* (London: Routledge & Kegan Paul, 1957).
Kiberd, Declan, *Inventing Ireland: The Literature of the Modern Irish Nation* (London: Vintage, 1996).
Kiely, Declan, *The King's Threshold: Manuscript Materials* (New York: Cornell University Press, 2003).
Kinross, Albert, 'The German Theatre', *The Dome*, 6 (1900).

Knapp, Bettina L., *Women, Myth and the Feminine Principle* (State University of New York Press, 1998).
Knowland, A. S., *W. B. Yeats: Dramatist of Vision* (Gerrards Cross: Colin Smythe, 1983).
Knowlson, James, *Damned to Fame: The Life of Samuel Beckett* (London: Bloomsbury, 1996).
Kohfeldt, Mary Lou, *Lady Gregory: The Woman Behind the Irish Renaissance* (London: Deutsche Press, 1985).
Kokoschka, Oskar, *Murderer, Hope of Woman*, *Oskar Kokoschka: Plays and Poems* trans. Michael Mitchell (Riverside, CA: Adriadne Press, 2001).
Komesu, Okifumi, 'At the Hawk's Well and Taka No Izumi in a "Creative Circle"', *Yeats Annual*, vol. v, ed. Warwick Gould (London: Macmillan Press, 1987).
The Double Perspective of Yeats's Aesthetic (Gerrards Cross: Colin Smythe, 1984).
Kopper, Edward A., *Lady Isabella Persse Gregory* (Boston: Twayne Publishers, 1976).
Lang, Andrew, *Custom and Myth*, 2nd edn (London: Longmans, Green & Co., 1893).
Laurvik, John Nilsen and Mary Morison, trans., *Letters of Henrik Ibsen*, (Honolulu: University Press of the Pacific, 2002).
Lavrin, Janko, 'Nietzsche Revisited. IV – "We Immoralists"', *The New Age*, 30:23 (1922).
Le Bon, Gustave, *The Crowd* (London: T. Fisher Unwin, 1896).
Leerrsen, Joep, 'The Theatre of William Butler Yeats', *The Cambridge Companion to W. B. Yeats* (Cambridge University Press, 2004).
Lees, D. Nevile, 'About "The Mask"', *A Living Theatre: The Gordon Craig School: The Arena: Goldoni: The Mask* (Florence: Edward Gordon Craig, 1913).
Lefebvre, Henri, *The Production of Space*, trans. Donald Nicholson-Smith (Oxford: Blackwell, 1991).
Levine, Herbert J., 'Yeats's Ruskinian Byzantium', *Yeats Annual*, vol. II, ed. Richard Finneran (London: Macmillan Press, 1983).
Levitas, Ben, *The Theatre of Nation: Irish Drama and Cultural Nationalism 1890–1910* (Oxford University Press, 2002).
Leydecker, Karl, 'Afterword', *Oskar Kokoschka: Plays and Poems*, trans. Michael Mitchell (Riverside, CA: Adriadne Press, 2001).
Longenbach, James, 'Modern Poetry', *The Cambridge Companion to Modernism*, ed. Michael Levenson (Cambridge University Press, 1999).
Longley, Edna, *The Living Stream: Literature and Revisionism in Ireland* (Newcastle-Upon-Tyne: Bloodaxe Press, 1994).
Lucas, F. L., *The Drama of Chekhov, Synge, Yeats and Pirandello* (London: Cassell & Co., 1963).
Lukács, György, *History and Class Consciousness*, trans. Rodney Livingstone (London: Merlin Press, 1971).
MacDonagh, Thomas, *When Dawn is Come, Four Irish Rebel Plays*, ed. James Moran (Dublin: Irish Academic Press, 2007).

Maeterlinck, Maurice, *Pelléas et Mélisande, Les Aveugles, L'Intérieur*, ed. Leighton Hodson (London: Bristol Classical Press, 1999).
   Pelléas and Mélisande, trans. Erving Winslow (1894) (Amsterdam: Fredonia Books, 2001).
   The Blind, Three Pre-Surrealist Plays, ed. Maya Slater (Oxford University Press, 1997).
   The Hour-Glass, trans. Bernard Miall (New York: Frederick A. Stokes, 1936).
   The Treasure of the Humble, trans. Alfred B. Sutro (1897) (Amsterdam: Fredonia Books, 2001).
Malone, Christopher T., 'Modernist Ethos in the Postcolonial Moment: Yeats's Theory of Masks', *W. B. Yeats and Postcolonialism*, ed. Deborah Fleming (West Cornwall, CT: Locust Hill Press).
Mann, Thomas, 'Freud and the Future', *Essays of Three Decades*, trans. H. T. Lowe-Porter (London: Secker & Warburg, 1947).
Manson, J. B., *The Life and Work of Edgar Degas*, ed. Geoffrey Holme (London: The Studio, 1917).
Marcus, Phillip, *Yeats and Artistic Power* (London: Macmillan, 1992).
Marker, Frederick J. and Lise-Lone Marker, *Ibsen's Lively Art: A Performance Study of the Major Plays* (Cambridge University Press, 2005).
Martin, Augustine, 'Kinesis, Stasis, Revolution in Yeatsean Drama', *Gaeliana*, 6 (1984).
Martyn, Edward, 'A Comparison between Irish and English Theatrical Audiences', *Beltaine*, 2 (1900).
Marx, Karl, *Capital*, vol. 1, trans. Ben Fowkes (London: Penguin Press, 1990).
   Grundrisse, trans. Martin Nicolaus (London: Penguin Press, 1973).
   Selected Writings, ed. David McLellan (Oxford University Press, 1977).
Marx, Karl and Friedrich Engels, *The Communist Manifesto* (London: George Allen & Unwin, 1948).
Mathews, P. J., *Revival: The Abbey Theatre, Sinn Féin, the Gaelic League and the Co-operative Movement* (Cork University Press in association with Field Day, 2003).
   'Stirring up Disloyalty: The Boer War, the Irish Literary Theatre and the Emergence of a New Separatism', *The Irish University Review*, 33:1 (2003).
Mays, Michael, 'Yeats and the Economics of "Excess"', *Colby Quarterly*, 33:4 (1997).
Mays, Milton A., 'Strindberg's *The Ghost Sonata*: Parodied Fairy Tale on Original Sin', reprinted in *Eight Modern Plays*, 2nd edn, ed. Anthony Caputi (London: Norton, 1991).
McAteer, Michael, '"Kindness in Your Unkindness": Lady Gregory and History', *Irish University Review: Special Issue: Lady Gregory*, 34:1 (2004).
McBride, Maud Gonne, 'A National Theatre', *The United Irishman*, 10:243 (1903).
McCormack, W. J., *Blood Kindred: W. B. Yeats the Life, the Death, the Politics* (London: Pimlico, 2005).
   From Burke to Beckett: Ascendancy, Tradition and Betrayal in Irish Literary History, 2nd edn (Cork University Press, 1994).

Meihuizen, Nicholas, *Yeats and the Drama of Sacred Space* (Amsterdam: Rodopi, 1998).
Mercier, Vivian, 'The Morals of *Deirdre*', *Yeats Annual*, vol. v, ed. Warwick Gould (London: Macmillan Press, 1987).
Merritt, Henry, 'Dead Many Times: *Cathleen ni Houlihan*, Yeats, Two Old Women and a Vampire', *Modern Language Review*, 96:3 (2001).
Metcalfe, Andrew and Lucinda Ferguson, 'Half-Opened Being', *Timespace: Geographies of Temporality*, ed. John May and Nigel Thrift (London: Routledge Press, 2001).
Miller, Liam, *The Noble Drama of W. B. Yeats* (Dublin: The Dolmen Press, 1977).
Mills Harper, George, *The Making of Yeats's A Vision: A Story of the Automatic Script*, vol. 1 (Carbondale: Southern Illinois University Press, 1987).
Mills Harper, George and Walter Kelly Hood, eds., *A Critical Edition of Yeats's A Vision (1925)* (London: Macmillan Press, 1978).
Mills Harper, George, *et al.*, eds., *Yeats's Vision Papers*, vol. 1 (London: Macmillan Press, 1992).
Mills Harper, Margaret, *Wisdom of Two: The Spiritual and Literary Collaboration of George and W. B. Yeats* (Oxford University Press, 2006).
Moore, George, *Hail and Farewell*, ed. Richard Allen Cave (Gerrards Cross: Colin Smythe, 1976).
Moore, John Rees, *Masks of Love and Death: Yeats as Dramatist* (Ithaca: Cornell University Press, 1971).
Moran, D. P., *The Philosophy of Irish Ireland* (Dublin: Gill & Murphy, 1905).
Moran, James, *Staging the Easter Rising: 1916 as Theatre* (Cork University Press, 2005).
Morash, Christopher, *A History of Irish Theatre, 1601–2000* (Cambridge University Press, 2002).
Morretti, Franco, 'The Long Goodbye: *Ulysses* and the End of Liberal Capitalism', *Signs Taken for Wonders: Essays in the Sociology of Literary Forms*, trans. Susan Fischer, David Forgacs and David Miller (London: Verso, 1983).
Morris, William, *Political Writings of William Morris*, ed. A. L. Morton (London: Lawrence and Wishart, 1973).
Murphy, Daniel J., 'Lady Gregory, Co-Author and Sometimes Author of the Plays of W. B. Yeats', *Modern Irish Literature: Essays in Honor of William York Tindall*, ed. Raymond J. Porter and James D. Brophy (New York: Iona College Press, 1972).
Murray, Christopher, *Seán O'Casey: Writer at Work, A Biography* (Dublin: Gill & Macmillan, 2004).
Nägele, Rainer, 'The Eyes of the Skull: Walter Benjamin's Aesthetics', *The Aesthetics of the Critical Theorists*, ed. Ronald Roblin (New York: Edwin Mellen Press, 1990).
Nathan, Leonard F., *The Tragic Drama of W. B. Yeats: Figures in a Dance* (New York: Columbia University Press, 1965).

Negri, Antonio, *Marx Beyond Marx: Lessons on the Grundrisse* (London: Pluto Press, 1991).
Nevo, Ruth, 'Yeats and Schopenhauer', *Yeats Annual*, vol. III, ed. Warwick Gould (London: Macmillan Press, 1985).
'Yeats's Passage to India', *Yeats Annual*, vol. IV, ed. Warwick Gould (London: Macmillan Press, 1986).
'Yeats, Shakespeare and Ireland', *Literature and Nationalism*, ed. Vincent Newey and Ann Thompson (Liverpool University Press, 1991).
Nicholls, Peter, *Modernisms: A Literary Guide* (London: Macmillan Press, 1995).
Nichols, Roger and Richard Langham Smith, *Claude Debussy: Pelléas et Mélisande* (Cambridge Opera Handbooks, Cambridge University Press, 1989).
Nietzsche, Friedrich, *Beyond Good and Evil: Prelude to a Philosophy of the Future*, trans. R. J. Hollingdale (London: Penguin, 1973).
'On the Uses and Disadvantages of History for Life', *Untimely Meditations*, ed. Daniel Breazeale, trans., R. J. Hollingdale (Cambridge University Press, 1997).
'Richard Wagner in Bayreuth', *Untimely Meditations*, ed. Daniel Breazeale, trans. R. J. Hollingdale (Cambridge University Press, 1997).
The Anti-Christ (1888), Twilight of the Idols and The Anti-Christ, 2nd edn, trans. R. J. Hollingdale (London: Penguin Press, 1990).
The Birth of Tragedy out of the Spirit of Music, ed. Michael Tanner, trans. Shaun Whiteside (London: Penguin Press, 2003).
The Will to Power (London: Weidenfeld & Nicolson, 1968).
Thus Spake Zarathustra in *The Complete Works of Friedrich Nietzsche*, vol. IV, ed. Oscar Levy, trans. Thomas Common (London: T. N. Foulis, 1909).
Nordau, Max, 'Philosophy and Morals of War', *North American Review*, 169:6 (1899).
O'Brien, Conor Cruise, 'Passion and Cunning: An Essay on the Politics of W. B. Yeats', *Yeats's Political Identities*, ed. Jonathan Allison (Ann Arbor: University of Michigan Press, 1996).
Passion and Cunning and other Essays (London: Weidenfeld and Nicolson, 1988).
The Great Melody: A Thematic Biography and Commented Anthology of Edmund Burke (London: Sinclair-Stevenson, 1992).
The Suspecting Glance (London: Faber, 1972).
O'Donnell, Frank Hugh, 'Celtic Drama in Dublin', *Freeman's Journal*, 1 (1899).
Souls for Gold: A Pseudo-Celtic Drama in Dublin (London: Nassau Press, 1899).
O'Donoghue, Bernard, 'Yeats and the Drama', *The Cambridge Companion to W. B. Yeats*, ed. Marjorie Howes and John Kelly (Cambridge University Press, 2006).
O'Grady, Standish, *History of Ireland: Critical and Philosophical*, vol. 1 (London: E. Ponsonby & Co., 1881).
The Story of Ireland (London: Methuen, 1894).
Toryism and the Tory Democracy (London: Chapman & Hall, 1886).

Oppel, Frances Nesbitt, *Mask and Tragedy: Yeats and Nietzsche, 1902–10* (Charlottesville: Virginia University Press, 1987).
 'Yeats's *Purgatory* and Nietzsche's Eternal Return', *Journal of Australian Language and Literature Association*, 82 (1994).
Orr, John, *Tragic Drama and Modern Society* (London: Palgrave-Macmillan, 1981).
Owen, Alex, 'The "Religious Sense" in a Post-War Secular Age', *Past and Present*, 1, Supplement 1 (2006).
Oxon, M. B., *Cosmic Anatomy and the Structure of the Ego* (London: John Watkins, 1921).
Parkin, Andrew, *The Dramatic Imagination of W. B. Yeats* (Dublin: Gill & Macmillan, 1978).
Patanjali, Bhagavan Shri, *Aphorisms of Yoga* (London: Faber and Faber, 1938).
Patterson, Gertrude, 'W.B. Yeats in the Theatre: The Challenge of the Poetic Play', *Yeats Eliot Review*, 6:2 (1979).
Paulin, Tom, 'Yeats's Hunger-Strike Poem', *Minotaur: Poetry and the Nation State* (London: Faber, 1992).
Pethica, James, '"Our Kathleen": Yeats's Collaboration with Lady Gregory in the Writing of *Cathleen ni Houlihan*', *Yeats Annual*, vol. VI, ed. Warwick Gould (London: Macmillan Press, 1988).
Piaget, Jean, *The Child's Conception of the World*, trans. J. and A. Tomlinson (Frogmore: Paladin Press, 1973).
Pilkington, Lionel, *Theatre and State in Twentieth-Century Ireland: Cultivating the People* (London: Routledge Press, 2001).
Pirandello, Luigi, *Collected Plays*, vol. I, trans. Frederick May (London: John Calder, 1987).
 Collected Plays, vol. II (London: John Calder, 1987).
Ravindran, Sankaran, *W. B. Yeats and Indian Tradition* (Delhi: Konark Publishers, 1990).
Reiss, Timothy, 'The Golden Cradle and the Beggar-Man: Problems of Yeats's Poetics', *Canadian Review of Comparative Literature*, 3:1 (1976).
Roche, Anthony, *Contemporary Irish Drama: From Beckett to McGuinness* (Dublin: Gill & Macmillan, 1994).
Rohan, Virginia, 'Yeats and *Deirdre*: from Story to Fable', *Yeats Annual*, vol. VI, ed. Warwick Gould (1988).
Roston, Murray, *Biblical Drama in England: From the Middle Ages to the Present Day* (Evanston: Northwestern University Press, 1968).
Ruskin, John, *Fors Clavigera: Letters to the Workmen and Labourers of Great Britain*, vol. VI (London: George Allen, 1876).
Ryan, Frederick, 'Political and Intellectual Freedom', *Dana*, 1 (1904).
Saddlemeyer, Ann, *Becoming George: The Life of Mrs W. B. Yeats* (Oxford University Press, 2002).
Said, Edward, 'Yeats and Decolonization', *Culture and Imperialism* (London: Vintage, 1994).

Sands, Bobby, 'The Crime of Castlereagh', *Skylark Sing Your Lonely Song: An Anthology of the Writings of Bobby Sands* (Dublin: Mercier Press, 1982).
Sartre, Jean-Paul, *Being and Nothingness*, trans. Hazel E. Barnes (London: Methuen Press, 1969).
Critique of Dialectical Reason, trans. Alan Sheridan-Smith (London: New Left Books, 1976).
Schopenhauer, Arthur, *The World as Will and Representation*, trans. E.F.J. Payne, 2nd edn, vol. 1 (New York: Dover Publications, 1969).
Schuchard, Ronald, '*The Countess Cathleen* and the Revival of the Bardic Arts', *The South Carolina Review*, 32:1 (1999).
The Last Minstrels: Yeats and the Revival of the Bardic Arts (Oxford University Press, 2008).
'The Minstrel in the Theatre: Arnold, Chaucer, and Yeats's New Spiritual Democracy', *Yeats Annual*, vol. II, ed. Richard Finneran (London: Macmillan Press, 1983).
Schürer, Ernst, ed. and trans., *German Expressionist Plays* (New York: The Continuum Publishing Company, 2003).
Segel, Harold B., *Pinocchio's Progeny: Puppets, Marionettes, Automatons and Robots in Modernist Avant-garde Drama* (Baltimore, MD: The Johns Hopkins University Press, 1995).
Sekine, Masaru, 'Noh, Fenollosa, Pound and Yeats – Have East and West Met?' *Yeats Annual*, vol. XIII, ed. Warwick Gould (London: Macmillan Press, 1998).
Shaw, George Bernard, *John Bull's Other Island*, 2nd edn (London: Penguin, 1984).
Shiach, Morag, *Modernism, Labour and Selfhood in British Literature and Culture, 1890–1930* (Cambridge University Press, 2004).
Sidnell, Michael J., 'Manuscript Versions of Yeats's *The Countess Cathleen*', *Papers of the Bibliographical Society of America*, 56 (1962).
Sidnell, Michael J. and Wayne K. Chapman, eds., *The Countess Cathleen: Manuscript Materials* (Ithaca: Cornell University Press, 1999).
Skene, Reg, *The Cuchulain Plays of W.B. Yeats: A Study* (London: Macmillan Press, 1974).
Slater, Maya, ed., *Three Pre-Surrealist Plays* (Oxford University Press, 1997).
Smith, Stan, *The Origins of Modernism: Eliot, Pound, Yeats and the Rhetorics of Renewal* (London: Harvester Wheatsheaf, 1994).
Spengler, Oswald, *The Decline of the West: Form and Actuality*, 2nd edn, trans. Charles Atkinson (London: George Allen & Unwin, 1948).
Spenser, Edmund, *A View of the State of Ireland*, ed. Andrew Hadfield and Willy Maley (Oxford: Blackwell Press, 1997).
Stanfield, Paul Scott, *Yeats and Politics of the 1930s* (London: Macmillan Press, 1988).
Steiner, George, *The Death of Tragedy* (London: Faber, 1961).
Strindberg, August, *Strindberg: Plays One*, 2nd edn, trans. Michael Meyer (London: Methuen, 1976).
Suess, Barbara A., *Progress and Identity in the Plays of W.B. Yeats, 1892–1907* (London: Routledge Press, 2003).

Surette, Leon, *The Birth of Modernism: Ezra Pound, T.S. Eliot, W.B. Yeats, and the Occult* (Montreal: McGill-Queen's University Press, 1994).
Swami, Shree Purohit and W.B. Yeats, *The Ten Principal Upanishads* (London: Faber & Faber, 1938).
Swift, Jonathan, *A Modest Proposal for Preventing the Children of Poor People from being a Burthen to their Parents or the Country, And for making them Beneficial to the Publick*, 3rd edn (London: Weaver Bickerton, 1730).
Symons, Arthur, 'Ballet, Pantomime, and Poetic Drama', *The Dome*, 1 (1898).
 'Bayreuth: Notes on Wagner', *The Dome*, 4 (1899).
 'Nietzsche on Tragedy', *The Academy and Literature*, London, 30 August (1902).
 'The Ideas of Richard Wagner', *The Quarterly Review*, 203:404 (1905).
 'The New Bayreuth', *The Academy and Literature*, London, 27 September (1902).
Synge, J.M. *The Complete Plays* (London: Methuen, 1981).
Syrett, Netta, 'Thy Heart's Desire', *The Yellow Book* (July) (London: Elkin Mathews & John Lane, 1894).
Taylor, Richard, *A Reader's Guide to the Plays of W.B. Yeats* (London: Macmillan Press, 1984).
 The Drama of W.B. Yeats: Irish Myth and the Japanese No (Yale University Press: London, 1976).
Tedesco Hadwell, Janis, *Pressed Against Divinity* (DeKalb, IL: Northern Ilinois University Press, 1997).
Thompson, E.P., *William Morris: Romantic to Revolutionary* (London: Lawrence & Wishart, 1955).
Thompson, Spurgeon, 'Yeats and Eugenicism: The Garrison Mentality in a Decolonizing Ireland', *W.B. Yeats and Postcolonialism*, ed. Deborah Fleming (West Cornwall, CT: Locust Hill Press, 2001).
Toller, Ernst, *Plays One*, ed. and trans. Alan Raphael Pearlman (London: Oberon Books, 2000).
 Seven Plays (London: John Lane the Bodley Head, 1935).
Torchiana, Donald T., *W.B. Yeats and Georgian Ireland*, 2nd edn (Washington: Catholic University of America Press, 1992).
 'Yeats and Croce', *Yeats Annual*, vol. IV, ed. Warwick Gould (London: Macmillan Press, 1986).
Torres Ribelles, Francisco Javier, 'Predetermination and Nihilism in W.B. Yeats's Theatre', *Revista Alicantina de Estudios Ingleses*, v (1992).
Tymoczko, Maria, 'Amateur Political Theatricals, Tableaux Vivants, and *Cathleen ni Houlihan*', *Yeats Annual*, vol. x, ed. Warwick Gould (London: Macmillan, 1993).
Ure, Peter, *Yeats the Playwright: A Commentary on Character and Design in the Major Plays* (London: Routledge and Kegan Paul, 1963).
Vanderwerken, David L., '*Purgatory*: Yeats's Modern Tragedy,' *Colby Library Quarterly*, 10:5 (1974).
Vendler, Helen, *Our Secret Discipline: Yeats and Lyric Form* (Oxford University Press, 2007).
 Yeats's Vision and the Later Plays (London: Oxford University Press, 1963).

Villiers de l' Isle Adam, Philippe-Auguste, *Axël*, trans. Marilyn Gaddis Rose (Dublin: Dolmen Press, 1970).
Wade, Allan, ed., *The Letters of W. B. Yeats* (London: Rupert Hart-Davis, 1954).
Ward, David, 'Yeats's Conflicts with his Audience, 1897–1917', *ELH*, 49 (1982).
Ward, Margaret, *Unmanageable Revolutionaries: Women and Irish Nationalism* (London: Pluto Press, 1995).
Wedekind, Frank, *Spring Awakening*, trans. Edward Bond (London: Methuen, 1980).
Welch, Robert, 'Lady Gregory: A Language for Healing', *Lady Gregory, Fifty Years After*, ed. Ann Saddlemyer and Colin Smythe (Gerrards Cross: Colin Smythe, 1987).
The Abbey Theatre, 1899–1999: Form and Pressure (Oxford University Press, 1999).
Wellesley, Dorothy, ed., *Letters on Poetry from W. B. Yeats to Dorothy Wellesley* (London: Oxford University Press, 1940).
Wilde, Oscar, *Salomé, The Complete Plays* (London: Methuen, 1988).
'The Soul of Man under Socialism', *The Complete Works of Oscar Wilde*, vol. IV, ed. Josephine M. Guy (Oxford University Press, 2007).
Williams, Raymond, *Modern Tragedy*, rpt. 1966 (London: Hogarth Press, 1992).
Wills, Clair, *That Neutral Island: A Cultural History of Ireland During the Second World War* (London: Faber, 2007).
Wilson, F. A. C., *W. B. Yeats and Tradition* (London: Victor Gollancz, 1958).
Wittgenstein, Ludwig, *Philosophical Investigations*, 3rd edn, trans. G.E.M. Anscombe (Oxford: Blackwell Press, 1958).
Worth, Katharine, *The Irish Drama of Europe from Yeats to Beckett* (London: The Athlone Press, 1978).
'*The Words upon the Window-pane*: A Female Tragedy', *Yeats Annual*, vol. XI, ed. Warwick Gould (London: Macmillan Press, 1993).
Yeats, W. B., 'A People's Theatre: A Letter to Lady Gregory' (1919), *Explorations* (London: Macmillan Press, 1962).
'A Symbolic Artist and the Coming of Symbolic Art', *The Dome*, 1 (1898).
A Vision, 2nd edn (London: Macmillan Press, 1937).
'An Exhibition at William Morris's', *Providence Sunday Journal (1890), Uncollected Prose by W. B. Yeats*, vol. I, ed. John P. Frayne (London: Macmillan Press, 1970).
'An Irish National Theatre', *The United Irishman*, 10:241 (1903).
'Certain Noble Plays of Japan', *Essays and Introductions* (London: Macmillan Press, 1961).
Collected Poems (London: Macmillan Press, 1950).
'Dust Hath Closed Helen's Eye', *The Dome*, 4 (1899).
'Edmund Spenser', *Essays and Introductions* (London: Macmillan Press, 1961).
'First Principles', *Plays and Controversies* (London: Macmillan, 1923).
Four Plays for Dancers (London: Macmillan Press, 1921).
'Genealogical Tree of Revolution', *W. B. Yeats: Man and Poet*, 2nd edn, ed. Norman Jeffares (London: Routledge & Kegan Paul, 1962).
Ideas of Good and Evil, 2nd edn (Dublin: Maunsel, 1905).

'If I were Four and Twenty', *Explorations* (London: Macmillan Press, 1962).
'Instead of a Theatre', *To-Day*, 1:3 (1917).
'Interview,' *The United Irishman*, 7:162 (1902), 5.
'Interview,' *The United Irishman*, 7:163 (1902), 5.
'J. M. Synge and the Ireland of His Time', *Essays and Introductions* (London: Macmillan Press, 1961).
Letters to the New Island, ed. George Bornstein and Hugh Witemeyer (New York: Macmillan Press, 1989).
'Note on *Calvary*', *Four Plays for Dancers* (London: Macmillan Press, 1921).
'Note on *The Dreaming of the Bones*', *Four Plays for Dancers* (London: Macmillan Press, 1921).
'Note to "Deirdre"', *Plays for an Irish Theatre* (London: A. H. Bullen, 1911).
On the Boiler (Dublin: The Cuala Press, 1938).
Pages from a Diary Written in Nineteen Hundred and Thirty (Dublin: Cuala Press, 1944).
'Per Amica Silentia Lunae', *W. B. Yeats, Later Essays*, ed. William H. O'Donnell, *Collected Works of W. B. Yeats*, vol v (New York: Charles Scribner's Sons, 1994).
Purgatory: Manuscript Materials including the Author's Final Text, ed. Sandra F. Siegel (New York: Cornell University Press, 1986).
'Speaking to the Psaltery', *Essays and Introductions* (London : Macmillan, 1961).
The Death of Cuchulain: Manuscript Materials including the Author's Final Text, ed. Phillip Marcus (Ithaca: Cornell University Press, 1982).
'The Dramatic Movement', *Plays and Controversies* (London: Macmillan Press, 1923).
'*The Dreaming of the Bones*' and '*Calvary*': *Manuscript Materials*, ed. Wayne Chapman (Ithaca: Cornell University Press, 2003).
The Herne's Egg: Manuscript Materials, ed. Alison Armstrong (New York: Cornell University Press, 1993).
'The Holy Mountain', *Essays and Introductions* (London: Macmillan, 1961).
'The Irish Dramatic Movement', *Plays and Controversies* (London: Macmillan Press, 1923).
'The Irish Literary Movement', Radio Eireann Broadcast, 12 October 1935. *Collected Works of W. B. Yeats*, vol. x, ed. Colton Johnson (New York: Scribner, 2000).
'The Irish Literary Theatre, 1900', *The Dome*, 5 (1899–1900).
'The Irish National Theatre and Three Sorts of Ignorance', *The United Irishman*, 10:243 (1903).
'The Irish National Theatre and Three Sorts of Ignorance', *Uncollected Prose by W. B. Yeats*, vol. ii, ed. John P. Frayne (London: Macmillan, 1975).
The Land of Heart's Desire: Manuscript Materials, ed. Jared Curtis (Ithaca: Cornell University Press, 2002).
'The Literary Movement in Ireland', *North American Review*, 169:6 (1899).
'The Need for Audacity of Thought', *The Dial* (1926) in *Collected Works of W. B. Yeats*, vol. x, ed. Colton Johnson (New York: Scribner, 2000).

'The Philosophy of Shelley's Poetry', *The Dome*, 7 (1900).
'The Play, the Player, and the Scene', *Plays and Controversies* (London: Macmillan Press, 1923).
'The Poetry of Samuel Ferguson', *The Dublin University Review*, April (1886).
'The Reform of the Theatre', *Plays and Controversies* (London: Macmillan Press, 1923).
'The Symbolism of Poetry', *The Dome*, 6 (1900).
'The Theatre', *Beltaine*, 1 (1899).
'The Theatre', *The Dome*, 3 (1899).
'The Theatre, the Pulpit, and the Newspapers', *The United Irishman*, 10:242 (1903).
'The Tragic Generation', *Autobiographies* (London: Macmillan Press, 1955).
The Variorum Edition of the Plays of W. B. Yeats, ed. Russell K. Alspach (London: Macmillan Press, 1966).
The Variorum Edition of the Poems of W. B. Yeats, ed. Peter Allt and Russell K. Alspach (London: Macmillan Press, 1957).
'The Well at the World's End', [review] *Uncollected Prose by W. B. Yeats*, vol. 1, ed. John P. Frayne (London: Macmillan Press, 1970).
Wheels and Butterflies (London: Macmillan Press, 1934).
Where There Is Nothing / The Unicorn from the Stars, ed. Katharine Worth (Washington DC: The Catholic University of America Press, 1987).
Writings on Irish Folklore, Legend and Myth, ed. Robert Welch (London: Penguin Press, 1993).
W. B. Yeats: Prefaces and Introductions, ed. William H. O'Donnell (London: Macmillan, 1988).

Index

Abbey Theatre 43, 46, 49–50, 65–6, 72, 74–5, 78, 81, 111–2, 124, 127n, 128, 145, 156, 172, 176–7, 188
Adorno, Theodor 7, 76, 85–6, 90, 100–3, 107, 127, 134
Albright, Daniel 49n, 96–7, 99, 107, 111n
Allgood, Sarah 49, 134
Anderson, Perry 67, 73
Antheil, George 107, 171
Antoine, André 75
Archer, William 45
Arliss, George 75
Armstrong, Alison 167
Aveling, Eleanor Marx 45

Bachelard, Gaston 53
Badiou, Alain 126n
Bakhtin, Mikhail 77, 84
Barta, Szilvia 116n, 125
Baudrillard, Jean 27n, 36
Beckett, Samuel 3, 9, 90, 110, 124, 181
   A Piece of Monologue 189
   '… but the clouds …' 176–7
   Endgame 34, 176
   Footfalls 176
   Malone Dies 48, 143
   Play 178
   Waiting for Godot 10, 91, 178, 191
Beerbohm, Max 43
Benjamin, Walter 7, 100, 103, 126n
Bentley, Eric 3
Bergson, Henri 196
Berkeley, George 180–1
Berman, Marshall 194
Bernhardt, Sarah 33
Besant, Annie 5, 23
Binyon, Laurence 56–7
Bjersby, Birgit 65n, 95n
Blake, William 5, 27, 51n, 94, 145–6
Blavatsky, Helena Petrovna 169

Blin, Roger 10, 178
Block, Haskell M. 74n
Blueshirts 196–7
Bonafous-Murat, Carle 1
Boyce, D. George 140–1
Bradley, Anthony 71n, 189n
Brandes, George 45, 83n
Brearton, Fran 99
Brecht, Bertolt 90, 114–16, 126, 128, 172–4
Brook, Peter 82
Brown, Terence 46n
Buchelt, Lisabeth 170
Bull, Ole 18
Burke, Edmund 85
Bushrui, Suheil 42n, 60n

Caldwell, Helen 97
Campbell, Mrs Patrick 24, 25, 33, 50
Canon Harris, Susan 172
Cattell, Raymond 182
Cave, Richard 46n, 54, 121–2, 172
Chatterjee, Mohini 169
Chaucer, Geoffrey 82, 84–5
Chesterton, G.K. 76, 91n
Clark, Rosalind E. 100
Clarke, Austin 114
Clarke, Brenna Katz 2
Clinton, Alan Ramon 103n, 121n
Cocteau, Jean 153
Commedia dell'arte 107–8, 111–2, 143, 161
Connolly, James 8, 31, 67, 125–6, 146, 151
Cornillier, Pierre Emile 163n
Craig, Edward Gordon 7, 9, 42, 53–6, 88–9, 91–2, 132, 153, 171
Croce, Benedetto 146–7
Crohn Schmitt, Natali 92n, 139–40
Cubism 171
Cullingford, Elizabeth 156, 196n
Cunard, Lady Emerald 87, 93

Cunard, Nancy 147
Curtis, Jared 21

D'Ambrosio, John 188
Darragh, Florence 50
Daruwala, Maneck 42n, 49n
De Man, Paul 85
De Valois, Ninette 97, 135, 171
Debussy, Claude 24
Degas, Edgar 117, 125
Deleuze, Gilles 30n
Derrida, Jacques 99n, 127
DeValera, Eamonn 196–7
Dolmetsch, Arnold 71–2, 133
Domville, Eric 19
Donoghue, Denis 60
Doody, Noreen 124n, 139
Doone, Rupert 155
Dorn, Karen 3, 53n, 74n
Dublin Drama League 2, 34, 138, 153–4, 163, 177
Dukes, Ashley 94, 155
Dulac, Edmund 8, 74, 92, 131–5, 196
Duse, Eleonara 90

Eagleton, Terry 61, 67n, 195
Eaves, Gregory N. 99n, 104, 108
Ede, H.S. 196
Edwards, Phillip 43n, 65n
Einstein, Albert 137, 179–81, 192
Eliot, T.S. 3, 78, 84, 111–12, 144, 152–3
Ellmann, Richard 42n
Ellis, Sylvia 97
Ervine, St John 72
Expressionism 2, 7–10, 88, 94, 97–8, 155–8, 172

Farr, Florence 16–7, 41, 45, 71, 120, 133–4
Fauré, Gabriel 24
Fay, Frank 17n, 18, 49, 70–1, 75, 134
Fay, William 47n, 72n
Fenollosa, Ernest 90, 99n, 132
Ferguson, Samuel 21
Ferrar, Harold 2
Flannery, James 3, 46n, 53n, 54, 78
Foster, R.F. 1, 43n, 47, 61n, 91n, 99, 126n, 138n, 147, 163, 196
Foucault, Michel 54–5
Fraser, Winifred 17
Frazer, Sir James 30–1, 34n, 168
Frazier, Adrian 13, 18, 81
Freud, Sigmund 6, 14, 30, 33, 40, 104, 106, 160, 197
Friedman, Barton 113n, 161, 181

Garrigan Mattar, Sinéad 30–1, 70
Genet, Jacqueline 52

George, Lloyd 197
Goethe, Johann Wolfgang von 81, 167
Gonne, Maud 15, 31, 43, 61n, 67, 70, 98, 101, 105, 139
Gosse, Edmund 45
Gramsci, Antonio 146–7
Gregory, Lady Augusta 13, 41, 46–7, 50, 53, 65, 69, 82, 89, 137, 147
Grierson, Francis 143–4
Griffith, Arthur 31, 44, 47
Guattari, Félix 30n
Guha, Naresha 136n, 169n
Gutierrez, Donald 117

Hadwell, Janis 100–1n
Hagan, Edward 32
Haims, Lynn 122n, 176
Hallström, Per 1
Hand, Derek 162n
Harris, Frank 51, 180
Hastings, Beatrice 16n
Hegel, G.W.F. 86
Heidegger, Martin 61
Herford, C.H. 45–6
Hevesi, Alexander 88
Hirsch, Foster 28n
Hoffman, Daniel 65n
Holloway, Joseph 25, 33, 81, 83
Hone, Joseph 16, 93
Horkheimer, Max 85–6
Horniman, Annie 29n, 50, 134, 147
Howes, Marjorie 79, 81, 185, 192
Humble, Malcolm 51n
Hunt, Hugh 2
Hyde, Douglas 80
Hyde-Lees, George 8, 99–100, 132, 139

Ibsen, Henrik 2, 4, 15, 40–1, 43, 67–8, 75, 82, 88, 155, 197
  A Doll's House 5, 16–9, 35, 36, 68
  An Enemy of the People 6, 44–6, 48, 58, 60, 68, 95
  Ghosts 44–5
  The Vikings at Helgeland 46, 68
  The Wild Duck 17
Ito, Michio 93, 97
Iwata, Miki 43

Jackson, Holbrook 16n, 76, 88
Jameson, Fredric 29, 194
Jaques-Dalcroze, Émile 97
Jarry, Alfred 89, 198
  Ubu Roi 7, 49, 78–9, 82–4
Jeffares, Norman 91
Jenkins, Angela 70

Jochum, Klaus Peter 1, 93n
Jogand-Pages, Gabriel 168
Joyce, James
  Ulysses 111–12, 141, 167–8

Kant, Immanuel 42n
Keane, Patrick 82, 85, 145, 190–1
Kelly, John 19
Kenner, Hugh 176
Kermode, Frank 110, 114
Kiberd, Declan 21, 36
Kiely, Declan 22n
Kinross, Albert 18
Knapp, Bettina 53n
Knowland, A.S. 91, 110, 113n, 120n, 121n, 126, 164
Kokoschka, Oskar 198
  Murderer, Hope of Women 7, 88, 93–8, 172
Komesu, Ofikumi 90, 91n
Krop, Hildo van 171
Kropotkin, Prince Peter 5, 23, 67, 144, 199

Lang, Andrew 30
Lavrin, Janko 141–2
Lawrence, W.J. 47n, 75
Le Bon, Gustave 7, 79–81
Leblanc, Georgette 73
Leerssen, Joep 3
Lefebvre, Henri 53
Levitas, Ben 13, 18n
Lewis, Wyndham 111, 196
Loizeaux, Elizabeth Bergmann 132n, 171
Longenbach, James 193
Lucas, F.L. 110, 111
Lugné-Poe, Aurélien 15, 20
Lukács, György 39

MacDonagh, Thomas 126n, 145
MacSwiney, Terence 47, 48
Maeterlinck, Maurice 4–6, 14, 18, 21, 71, 75, 88, 97, 167, 197
  Pelléas et Mélisande 19, 24–5, 33, 53, 91–2
  The Blind 5, 19–20, 28, 91–2
  The Hour-Glass 42, 123
  The Interior 43
  The Intruder 19, 20–1, 32–3, 40, 52, 91, 119
  The Treasure of the Humble 16, 33, 42, 50
Maloney, Joseph 196
Mann, Thomas 160
Mannin, Ethel 147, 155–7, 183, 189, 196–7
Mansfield, Katharine 136n
Manson, J.B. 117n
Marcus, Phillip 47–8, 161n
Martin, Augustine 118, 120
Martyn, Edward 13, 66

Marx, Karl 5, 14–5, 27–9, 35, 37–8, 40, 148, 166, 198–9
Mathers, MacGregor 41, 167
Mathews, P.J. 31n
Mays, Michael 48, 147
McCormack, W.J. 100n, 156, 177, 183, 187, 196
Merritt, Henry 29n
Mills Harper, George 101
Mills Harper, Margaret 104–5, 132
Monck, Nugent 111
Moore, George 41, 60–1n, 80, 117
Moran, D.P. 22, 44
Moran, James 135
Morash, Christopher 25n, 61n
Moretti Franco 194
Morris, William 4, 5, 9–10, 14, 22–4, 27n, 28, 37–8, 40, 51–2, 61, 66, 80, 84, 112, 117, 131, 146–8, 177, 192, 197, 199
Moses, William Stanton 136n
Müller, Max 30n

Naturalism 5, 6, 15–6
Nevile Lees, D. 89
Nevo, Ruth 65n, 74n, 159–60, 186n
Nietzsche, Friedrich 7, 41, 71, 85–6, 141–2, 159, 164, 191
  The Birth of Tragedy out of the Spirit of Music 51
  The Will to Power 60, 82

O'Brien, Conor Cruise 79, 85, 196n
O'Brien, William 23
O'Casey, Sean 47, 161
O'Connor, Ulick 47n
O'Donnell, Frank Hugh 13, 31
O'Donoghue, Bernard 2–4
O'Grady, Standish 65, 95n
O'Higgins, Kevin 194
O'Casey, Sean
  The Silver Tassie 9, 94, 153, 156
Oppel, Francis 77–8, 164, 191
Orage, T.A. 136
Ossietzky, Carl von 156

Paget, Dorothy 16
Parnell, Charles Stuart 81
Partch, Harry 74
Paulin, Tom 139n, 150
Pearse, Patrick 8, 18, 125–6, 128, 151
Pilkington, Lionel 13, 14
Pirandello, Luigi 7, 9, 86, 90, 110–14, 131, 142, 146, 155, 174, 197
  Henry IV 111–13
  Lazarus 110, 143
  Six Characters in Search of an Author 111–12, 138, 141, 161–2

Pound, Ezra 90, 111
Price, Nancy 155

Quinn, John 20, 51, 133, 147, 150

Read, Herbert 133
Rees Moore, John 75, 78, 137n, 166
Reiss, Timothy 60
Ribelles, Franciso 113n, 118, 174, 189
Robinson, Lennox 1, 34, 112
Rolleston, T.W. 41, 65
Ruskin, John, 10, 58, 177, 179–80, 183–5, 187–8, 192
Russell, Bertrand 10, 137, 179–81, 192
Russell, George (A.E.) 73, 80, 137, 144, 169
Ryan, Frederick 67, 147

Saddlemeyer, Ann 98, 99, 132n, 139
Said, Edward 42
Sands, Bobby 47
Sartre, Jean-Paul 28, 29n
Savonarola, Fra. Girolamo 145
Schoenberg, Arnold 73–4, 134
Schopenhauer, Arthur 8, 94–5, 159–61, 185–6
Schrödinger, Erwin 181
Schuchard, Ronald 72–3, 146n
Segel, Harold B. 49n, 71
Sekine, Masaru 90n, 132
Shakespear, Olivia 19, 112, 155, 171, 196
Shakespeare, William 6, 46, 77, 82
Sharp, William 27
Shaw, G.B. 5, 23, 72, 136, 197
    Arms and the Man 17, 36
    John Bull's Other Island 36, 41, 146
Shelley, Percy Bysshe 146
Sheppard, Oliver 8, 125–6
Shiach, Morag 38n, 104
Skene, Reg 65n, 70, 79, 101n
Spengler, Oswald 144–5
Spenser, Edmund 157
Stanislavski, Constantin 97
Stepniak, Serge 67
Strindberg, August 1, 2, 198
    The Ghost Sonata 9, 10, 34, 35, 91, 163, 177–9
    There are Crimes and there are Crimes 1
Sturge Moore, Thomas 10, 159, 179–81, 196
Suess, Barbara 39
Surette, Leon 78
Surrealism 2, 7, 78–9, 82–3, 100, 108, 121, 153
Swami, Shree Purohit 136n, 160, 169, 171, 186
Swedenborg, Immanuel 27, 34, 193
Swinburne, Algernon Charles 24
Swift, Jonathan 9, 116, 162–5, 180, 182–4
Symbolism 5, 6, 14–16, 88
Symons, Arthur 49, 51, 56, 98, 167

Synge, J.M. 2, 47, 50
    In the Shadow of the Glen 43, 44, 57, 66–7
    The Playboy of the Western World 7, 77, 79, 84–5, 86, 127n, 137
    The Well of the Saints 59, 92
Syrett, Netta 16n

Tagore, Rabindranath 127n, 128
Taylor, Richard 3, 90, 93, 110, 122n, 132, 164, 172, 177
Tertullian, Quintus Septimius Florens 178
Thompson, E.P. 23
Thompson, Spurgeon 41, 81
Toller, Ernst 8, 122, 153, 157, 165, 174, 198
    Masses and Man 9, 158–9, 186
    Mrs Eddy 155–6
Tree, Beerbohm 20, 45
Tymoczko, Maria 13n

Ure, Peter 46n, 121, 161n

Vanderwerken, David 188
Vendler, Helen 2, 95n, 136
Villiers de l'Isle Adam, Philippe Auguste 14, 15, 16, 22, 24, 32, 167, 197
    Axël 5, 26, 33, 36, 53

Wagner, Richard 7, 60, 75, 77–8
Wallace, Richard 8, 136, 140, 181
Ward, David 127
Wedekind, Frank 36
Welch, Robert 2, 47n
Wellesley, Dorothy 140, 154–5, 159, 183, 186
Wilde, Oscar, 61, 139–40
    Salomé 6, 50, 84
    'The Soul of Man Under Socialism' 6, 51–2, 144
Wille, Bruno 68
Wills, Clair 156n
Wilson, F.A.C. 101, 120, 169–71
Winslow, Erving 24
Wordsworth, William 168
Worth, Katharine 3, 78, 113, 114n, 125, 137n, 145, 161n, 177

Yeats, W.B.
    A Vision 91, 99, 104, 111–12, 128, 136, 141, 145
    Autobiographies 1, 2, 15–6, 19
    And Automatic Writing 99–106, 127, 197
    And First World War 93, 95, 97, 99–100
    And 1916 Rising 125–8, 135, 138–9, 147, 149–51
    And relation to socialism 144–9
    'Genealogical Tree of Revolution' 148–9, 184–5

Ideas of Good and Evil 51n
'If I were Four and Twenty' 144, 148, 186
'Ireland after Parnell' 1, 186
'Irish Fairies' 16
'Irish Fairies, Ghosts, Witches' 16
Nobel Prize 1
'Notes for a Celtic Order of Mysteries' 26–7, 52–3, 77
On the Boiler 10, 146, 180, 182–7, 189, 192, 195–8
Pages from a Diary Written in Nineteen Hundred and Thirty 42n, 156n, 166, 168
'Per Amica Silentia Lunae' 2, 108, 157
Plays
  A Full Moon in March 124–5, 140, 168
  At the Hawk's Well 7, 25, 76, 86–8, 90–8, 115, 124, 132, 135, 150, 165, 190
  Calvary 8, 110, 131–2, 135–7, 140–3, 149–52, 164, 173, 190, 193
  Cathleen ni Houlihan 13–18, 22, 28, 33–5, 38, 47, 80, 89, 103, 139, 171, 188–9, 198
  Deirdre 6, 37, 39, 40, 42–4, 48, 49–53, 66, 68, 190
  Fighting the Waves 107, 171, 175
  Four Plays For Dancers 131–2, 135–6, 141–2, 161
  On Baile's Strand 6–7, 10, 48, 65–78, 81, 87, 96, 173, 188–9
  Purgatory 9, 10, 46, 96, 140–1, 163–4, 170, 175–93, 198–9
  The Cat and the Moon 125, 170
  The Countess Cathleen 3, 13–19, 22, 24–32, 34, 37–9, 49, 67, 77, 198
  The Death of Cuchulain 8, 65, 108, 110–28, 173, 180, 187, 189, 191
  The Dreaming of the Bones 8, 131–3, 135–41, 150–2, 163, 190
  The Green Helmet 6–7, 69, 78–86, 105, 125, 193
  The Herne's Egg 2, 9, 46, 152, 154, 157–9, 167–9, 171–6
  The King of the Great Clock Tower 124, 171
  The King's Threshold 1, 26, 40, 42–9, 52–61, 66–7, 77, 108, 114–15, 198
  The Land of Heart's Desire 1, 5, 13–21, 28–31, 33–9, 76, 78, 103, 163, 177, 186, 188
  The Only Jealousy of Emer 7, 86–8, 99–109, 111, 117–20, 124–5, 132, 193
  The Player Queen 2–3, 9, 94, 152–8, 166–8, 173–5
  The Resurrection 73, 148, 168, 180
  The Shadowy Waters 3
  The Unicorn from the Stars 84n, 163
  The Words upon the Window-pane 9, 111, 152, 161–6, 171, 173–5, 177, 179, 182–3, 192
  Where There Is Nothing, There Is God 34, 48, 80–2, 89, 103, 112
Plays and Controversies 21n, 68
Poems
  'Easter 1916' 47, 138–9
  'Leda and the Swan' 170
  'The Double Vision of Michael Robartes' 160
  'The Man and the Echo' 4
  'Upon a House Shaken by the Land Agitation' 85
Psaltery experiment 71–4
'The Bounty of Sweden' 1
The Celtic Twilight 21
'The Holy Mountain' 185–6
'The Need for Audacity of Thought'
'The Theatre' 19, 20n
'The Tragic Generation' 15n, 16, 49n, 140
'The Trembling of the Veil' 2
Wheels and Butterflies 73

Ze-Ami, Motokiyo 90

Lightning Source UK Ltd.
Milton Keynes UK
UKHW022147130120
356902UK00008B/141/P